New Ways of Organizing Work

Routledge Studies in Human Resource Development

EDITED BY MONICA LEE, *Lancaster University, UK*

HRD theory is changing rapidly. Recent advances in theory and practice, how we conceive of organisations and of the world of knowledge, have led to the need to reinterpret the field. This series aims to reflect and foster the development of HRD as an emergent discipline.

Encompassing a range of different international, organisational, methodological and theoretical perspectives, the series promotes theoretical controversy and reflective practice.

New Ways of Organizing Work

Developments, Perspectives
and Experiences

**Edited by Clare Kelliher
and Julia Richardson**

Routledge
Taylor & Francis Group
NEW YORK   LONDON

First published 2012
by Routledge
711 Third Avenue, New York, NY 10017

Simultaneously published in the UK
by Routledge
2 Park Square, Milton Park, Abingdon, Oxon OX14 4RN

*Routledge is an imprint of the Taylor & Francis Group,
an informa business*

Typeset in Sabon by IBT Global.

Library of Congress Cataloging-in-Publication Data
    New ways of organizing work : developments, perspectives and
experiences / edited by Clare Kelliher and Julia Richardson.
        p. cm. — (Routledge studies in human resource development ; 19)
    Includes bibliographical references and index.
    1. Flexible work arrangements. 2. Work environment. 3. Personnel
management. I. Kelliher, Clare, 1962– II. Richardson, Julia, 1964–
    HD5109.N49 2011
    331.25′72—dc23
    2011017799

ISBN: 978-0-415-88815-8 (hbk)
ISBN: 978-0-203-35735-4 (ebk)

Contents

Figures and Tables

TABLES

FIGURES

Preface

Work plays a dominant role in the lives of many people throughout the world. The way work is defined and organized has implications for the individuals who carry it out, the managers who manage it and the organizations that initiate it. Recent years have witnessed significant changes being made to the nature and organization of work, driven, at least in part, by increased competitive pressures, growing global integration and developments in information and communication technology (ICT). These changes and the way in which they are experienced are the subject of this book. The book is primarily aimed at scholars with an interest both in the field of change and the organization of work. The findings reported in each of the chapters will also be of value to those concerned with the development of employment policy and to managers and human resource (HR) professionals facing the challenge of designing and implementing new ways of organizing work.

Earlier versions of many of the chapters in this book were presented at the European Group for Organisation Studies (EGOS) conference in Barcelona in 2009, in a subtheme entitled "New Ways to Work: Organizing Work and Working Practices". As the discussions in the subtheme evolved over the course of the conference, it became apparent that although the papers addressed different themes and working contexts (nature of work, types of worker, geographical location, etc.), there was also a high degree of connectivity between them. The discussion that developed also drew our attention to the paucity of literature on the respective themes and, in particular, the lack of theoretical substance in this area. Therefore, in an attempt to move the field forward, the editors and the contributors came to the conclusion that an edited volume, bringing together a collection of papers, would make a valuable contribution to the field. This book represents their work and respective thinking.

The publication of this book would not have been possible without the co-operation and efforts of many people. First, we would like to extend our sincere thanks to all the scholars who contributed to the book for providing well-written and well-constructed chapters based on rigorous research. We are also grateful to them for making our lives easier by meeting deadlines and for prompt responses to our comments and queries. Second, we would like to pay tribute to Jayne Ashley for her assistance throughout the project and for her help in compiling the final manuscript. Third, we would like to thank Laura Stearns at Routledge for her enthusiasm and support for our proposal and advice throughout the process and also to Stacy Noto for her help during the production process. In addition, we would like to thank the organizers of the EGOS conference in Barcelona in 2009 for accepting our proposal for the subtheme, which brought this group of scholars together and where our conversations about new ways of organizing work were initiated. Finally, we would like to thank our families and friends who supported us throughout this project and tolerated our own new ways of working, adopted in order to complete the project.

Clare Kelliher
Julia Richardson
March 2011

1 Recent Developments in New Ways of Organizing Work

Clare Kelliher and Julia Richardson

INTRODUCTION

Changes to how work is done, where it is done and by whom has been a persistent theme in many economies in recent years. The pace and diversity of change to the nature and conduct of work and the impact of such changes, both on individuals and on organizations, is the subject of growing interest (Donkin, 2009; Moynagh & Worsley, 2005). These changes have been stimulated by both organizational needs and the needs and desires of individuals. Organizations have changed the way in which work is conducted in response to factors such as increased competitive pressure and need for greater efficiency, the demands of the global business environment and advances in Information and Communication Technology (ICT). For example, some organizations have used labor in more flexible ways, including greater use of temporary workers, in response to competitive pressures and the need to achieve greater efficiency (Olsen & Kalleberg, 2004). Globalization has also been a major driver of changes in the organization of work, not only as a result of increased competitive pressure, but also because of expanding operations across geographical boundaries and time zones (Gibson & Gibbs, 2006; Jarvenpaa & Leidner, 1999). Advances in information and communication technology have also been the stimulus for much change: the advent of the Internet has brought increasing opportunities for employees to work remotely; wireless technology has enabled employees to be 'ever available' and work to be carried out almost anywhere (Castells, Fernandez-Ardevol, Qui & Sey, 2007). In a context where social changes have influenced how work is organized, employees have also sought changes to the way in which work is carried out in order to allow them to achieve a more satisfactory relationship between their work and nonwork activities (Hooker, Neathey, Casebourne, & Munro, 2007; Korabik, Lero, & Whitehead, 2008, European Foundation for the Improvement of Living and Working Conditions, 2010a). New entrants to the workforce, the so-called Generation Y, have brought different aspirations and expectations to the workplace, seeking to engage with work in different ways, at different times and from different locations (Cates &

Rahimi, 2001). In addition, environmental concerns have become important associated considerations in how work is organized. Indeed, attempts to reduce their carbon footprint by re-examining the need for travel to and from and for work have stimulated exploration of alternative ways of organizing work (Harrison, Wheeler & Whitehead, 2004). Taken together, changes of this nature have potentially far-reaching implications for organizations, managers and employees. The aim of this book, therefore, is to consider these changes and their implications for relevant stakeholders.

Each chapter in this book is concerned with examining contemporary and emerging changes to how work is organized. The book also considers the implementation of these changes and how they are experienced by individuals. It brings together contributions from an international team of established scholars in the field and provides empirical evidence from Europe, North America, Asia and Australia. It is, therefore, likely to be of interest to the academic, professional and policy-making communities.

The new forms of organizing work examined in the book include those stimulated by cost reduction and flexibility in the public and private sectors (use of temporary workers, changes to service provision); the use of technology (remote/teleworking, mobile technology) and globalization (geographically distributed teams). Many of the contributions are concerned with examining the lived experiences and responses of employees subject to such changes (e.g., emotional outcomes, resistance, identity construction, (re) construction of work–non-work boundaries). The book explores the nature and implications of these new approaches for organizations, managers and individuals. While embracing practitioner concerns, the discussion in each chapter utilizes a range of theoretical frameworks and, as such, enhances the contribution to scholarly debate and policy development. This approach also provides for a more theoretically composite understanding of changing working arrangements and their impact on individual experiences, employment relationships and organizational performance.

The purpose of this introductory chapter is to set out and present a brief background to the main themes of the book and to provide some context for the empirical studies discussed in the subsequent chapters. It first explores contemporary developments in how work is organized and begins with a brief overview of the extant literature in the field. It also signals gaps in this literature, with a particular focus on questions relating to the implications for organizations, managers and employees. The chapter also connects current and future trends in the organization of work to broader societal, political and economic trends.

STRUCTURAL CHANGES

Changes in the nature and organization of work have been the subject of continued enquiry and debate among public policy makers, practitioners and scholars (Bloom, & Van Reenen, 2006; European Foundation for the Improvement of Living and Working Conditions, 2007a; Lero, Richardson & Korabik, 2009; Messenger & Ghosheh 2010). These changes can be connected with a number of more general economic and social shifts, which have impacted organizations and encouraged them to reassess the way in which they operate. These shifts include the interrelated factors of increasing global integration; more intense competitive pressures and the need to increase efficiency; developments in technology and changes in social attitudes and orientations to work. Below we will consider each of these themes and the implications for the organization of work.

Globalization

The implications of globalization in the business world have been the subject of much debate. Globalization is a complex process and may involve a variety of cross-border activities (Matlay, 2000). It is seen to go beyond international activities concerned with exporting and investing in manufacturing operations overseas, to include activities such as off-shoring (manufacturing, provision of services or administration); cross-border sourcing; joint ventures and merger and acquisition activity (Lawrence, 2002). Thus, a globalized organization moves from being a self-contained business unit situated in different countries, to a single company that views the world as one territory (Sedgley & White, 2002). Much of the debate has focused on the strategies that organizations might adopt in order to manage and respond to the demands of globalization (see, for example, Almond, Edwards & Clark, 2003; Berger, 2006; Harzing, 2004), but less attention has been given to the impact on people within organizations. Practitioners and scholars of human resource management (HRM) have also tended to focus on strategic approaches to managing people across international borders with a focus on how HRM is, or should be, managed in multinational organizations (see, for example, Von Glinow, 2002; Brewster, Wood & Brookes, 2008; Almond, 2011). What does globalization mean for those people who work for organizations responding to such pressures? To date, relatively little attention has been given to the impact of globalization at the micro level. However, Giddens (2002) argues, many of the changes associated with globalization are of a social, cultural and political nature. Indeed, Amoore (2002, 7) argues that,

> globalisation (sic) is experienced, given meaning, reinforced and/or challenged in the everyday social practice of individuals and groups at multiple levels, from state societies, and MNCs through to routine practices of the workplace.

Furthermore, Lawrence (2002) argues that the restructuring and growth of cross-border activities associated with globalization are likely to have implications for employees and managers in these organizations and that outsourcing and off-shoring in these companies may blur the focus and the identity of such organizations, becoming 'placeless and spaceless' operations. In practice, this is likely to mean that people from different parts of the organization, operating in different geographical and time zones, will be required to collaborate. Increasingly, teams are drawn from people who are not located in the same workplace, but who are distributed across the globe (Gibson & Gibbs, 2006) and their members may also be part of multiple virtual teams. This raises a range of questions such as how these teams function, how they co-operate and communicate, what are the implications for team effectiveness and how do individuals experience membership of these teams?

Increased Competitive Pressure and the Need to Increase Efficiency

Increased global integration and the more recent Global Financial Crisis (GFC) have led to pressure on organizations to be more competitive and to increase efficiency of operations. Competition in the developed world from lower-cost producers in the developing world has also prompted employers to re-examine how work is organized. In some instances this has resulted in the off-shoring and outsourcing of activities to lower-cost economies. It has also resulted in employers looking for ways in which to use labor more efficiently. For example, labor may be used in more flexible ways, including the increased use of temporary staff, such as agency workers, in order to achieve a closer match between the supply and demand for labor. OECD figures show that in 2007, 5–15% of the workforce in most member countries was engaged in some form of temporary employment, with figures in excess of 20% in countries including Spain, Poland and Portugal and among female workers in Japan and Slovenia (OECD, 2009). In addition to enhancing workforce flexibility, employers have also sought ways to increase the value added from labor by using human resource management practices designed to deliver higher performance (Macky & Boxall, 2007). Many countries have also experienced increased pressures for efficiency in the public sector, as a result of the spread of the New Public Management (NPM) ideology and the focus on a performance-driven approach (Hood, 2005, Mathiasen, 2005). More recently, pressure in the public sector has been further exacerbated as a result of austerity measures adopted in response to the GFC (The Economist, 2011).

Information and Communication Technology

The development of information and communications technology has enabled work to be carried out at a location remote from the workplace. In many countries there has been considerable growth in people working away from the workplace for some, or all, of their working time. For example, in Europe in 2005 it was estimated that 7% of employees were teleworkers

(European Foundation for the Improvement of Living and Working Conditions, 2007b), with significant variations between countries, ranging from Poland (15%) to Malta (0%). In the U.S. it was estimated that in 2008 just over 11% of employees were teleworkers (WorldatWork, 2011). Remote working, or teleworking as it is often termed, can take a number of forms (Moynagh & Worsley, 2005; Tietze, Musson & Scurry, 2009). This includes both those who are permanently based away from the workplace, often at home, and those who work away from the workplace for some of their working time, which may include a 'hot-desking' arrangement at the workplace. In this second, and generally more prevalent group, we may find those who work remotely on a regular basis (e.g., working from home on two set days a week) and those who work remotely on an ad hoc and informal basis. These types of arrangements may enable employers to reduce costs by reducing the amount of work space required, reduce their carbon footprint and enable higher levels of employee performance, where some types of work can be done more effectively away from the distractions of the workplace. For employees these types of working arrangements may reduce stress by avoiding what may be long commutes to work. It may also enable better integration of work and non-work commitments. Given these different forms and motivations, it is likely that employees will respond in different ways, depending on their personal and professional circumstances and expectations and how their work and well-being will be impacted.

Significant research has been undertaken to examine the implications and outcomes for individuals and for organizations of remote working (for overviews, see Bailey & Kurland, 2002; Gajendran & Harrison, 2007; Tietze et al., 2009). One stream of work, for example, has been concerned with examining how work changes when it is carried out away from the workplace and with the lived experiences of remote workers (Felstead & Jewson, 2000; Hyman, Scholarios & Baldrey, 2005; Kelliher & Anderson, 2010; Tietze & Musson, 2002, 2005). The contributions on remote working in this volume engage with this emerging theme.

The development of wireless technology has had further implications for how, when and where work is done (Castells et al., 2007), creating a context where employee availability need not be tied to a set location and time period (Kolb, 2008; Middleton, 2008). Taking a more critical view, some scholars have argued that such developments have resulted in an intensification of work, thus blurring putative boundaries between work and nonwork (Tietze and Musson, 2002; Brannen, 2005; Kelliher & Anderson, 2010). Others, however, have seen these developments in a more positive light, suggesting that they allow employees to combine and integrate their work and nonwork lives, thereby allowing them to be more productive overall (Cousins & Robey, 2005). To date, however, comparatively little research has been conducted in this field given the relatively short time that these technologies have been available and the different ways in which they have been adopted (Besseyre des Horts, 2008).

Societal Change

Changes in societal expectations and values, such as increasing demands for work–life balance (Korabik et al., 2008), have given rise to a situation where an increasing number of employees are seeking alternative ways of working. A growing body of empirical research suggests that achieving a more satisfactory relationship between work and nonwork activities is an important concern for an increasing number of employees (Hall & Atkinson, 2006; Kelliher & Anderson, 2008, Yanadori & Kato, 2009) and that organizations might use opportunities for flexible working arrangements as a recruitment tool (Richardson, 2010). Government agencies and policy makers are also important stakeholders in these trends and, in some countries, governments have provided legislative support for employees to request changes to their working arrangements and have developed supporting policy frameworks (e.g., the UK, Denmark). The European Union, for example, has sought to promote better jobs, which include the ability to more effectively combine work and nonwork activities (European Foundation for the Improvement of Living and Working Conditions, 2010b).

As growing account is taken of corporate social responsibility (CSR), there is a need for the consequences of different forms of work organization to be understood and, in particular, how they impact on the lives of those subject to them, both from the point of view of how they do their work, but also of how those changes may more generally impact their lives and well-being. Understanding how different forms of work and work organization impact the lives of those subject to them is important, particularly given calls for measures of performance to go beyond financial outcomes and to take into consideration broader aspects, such as sustainability and happiness (Blanchflower & Oswald, 2011).

Alongside the growing scholarly research and practitioner interest in changing working arrangements, public interest in the field also continues to grow. Challenges and competitions seeking to find 'the best place to work' have grown in popularity in many countries, including Canada, UK, U.S. and New Zealand. A frequent criterion for such awards is the willingness to provide flexible working arrangements. Other, alternative forms of working have also been the subject of increasing interest in the mainstream media with entrepreneurship gaining much attention. Thus, for example, 'The Dragon's Den' or 'Shark's Tank'—television programs aired in the UK or U.S.—pitted would-be entrepreneurs against potential investors. The film industry, particularly Hollywood, has also shown a growing interest in entrepreneurship with productions, such as The Social Network depicting the emergence of Facebook. In this respect, the message presented by the media is clear—opportunities to craft our work experiences and achievements outside traditional organizational contexts are available—it is simply a matter of taking our destinies in our own hands.

Many of the contributions in this book are concerned with some form of remote working. This includes examples of where employees work away from the workplace (e.g., designated office or factory) for some or all of their working time, frequently assisted by some form of technology. These chapters also explore the experiences of employees who are based in a workplace, but are working remotely from their team members, who are distributed across the globe and in different time zones.

Perhaps, not surprisingly, as knowledge work has increased, it has brought with it new ways of organizing work. Thus, many of the contributions are also concerned with knowledge workers. These chapters suggest that, because of the nature of their work, roles and responsibilities, many knowledge workers are not restricted to the traditional workplace of a designated office. This opens up further possibilities for knowledge work to be defined, designed and organized in different ways. While addressing the experiences of knowledge workers is important, the book will also address the experiences of service sector workers (hotels, health and social care), where the possibilities for remote working may be more restricted. In this regard, the book offers an insight into different and emerging work forms across different industries and professional and non-professional fields.

THE RESEARCH GAP

While some new forms of working, notably flexible working practices, have been the subject of much debate among research and practitioner communities, the focus of the debate has been relatively narrow. Thus, for example, much attention has focused on the business case for flexible working, investigating potential links with various measures of organizational performance, or with other employee outcomes as an indirect influence on performance (for overviews, see Beauregard & Henry, 2009; De Menezes & Kelliher, 2011; Kelly et al., 2008; Lero et al., 2009). Where the employee experience has been the subject of investigation, there has been a strong bias toward examining the implications for work–life balance and work–life integration (e.g., Kelliher & Anderson, 2008; Korabik et al., 2008; Bloom & Van Reenen, 2006). By comparison, less attention has been paid to the lived experiences of employees who adopt these new working arrangements, or to the experiences of managers managing them (Richardson, 2010). Moreover, albeit with some exceptions, few studies have attempted to examine the wider implications for issues such as employee identity (Grote & Raeder, 2009), or for the work itself, for example, in relation to issues such as creativity and employee well-being (Halpern, 2005). However, as the use of different work arrangements becomes more widespread and more embedded in organizations, there is a need to adopt a broader investigative approach to facilitate a deeper and more robust understanding of their consequences.

STRUCTURE

The purpose of this book is to offer a broad, yet robust, understanding of changes in contemporary work practices and the implications for relevant stakeholders. It brings together contributions from an established group of international scholars to examine the nature and consequences of new ways of organizing work. Drawing on studies of a variety of new forms of work, involving a diverse range of employees and work experiences, the book extends what we know about contemporary work arrangements and their implications for relevant stakeholders. In doing so and by presenting an analysis of the issues raised in the introductory and concluding chapters, the material presented contributes to knowledge and understanding in this field. It will be a valuable resource for scholars, practitioners and policy makers concerned with the management and organization of work.

The book is divided into three main empirical sections. The first section focuses on different forms of work and/or working arrangements. The contributions in this section go beyond examining ways of working that have been current for some time, such as various forms of flexible working and includes other working arrangements, stimulated by the development of enhanced technologies, the use of temporary agency labor and media depiction of work opportunities for women, which have received only limited attention. In contrast to much of the extant literature in the field, a strong theme of this book is the 'emic' perspective focusing on individuals' experiences of new ways of working. The second empirical section examines these experiences and related employee responses. It focuses, in particular, on forms of resistance and coping mechanisms; outcomes for employees and wider implications for employee identity and well-being. The third section examines the implications of changing working arrangements for teams and team members, as well as those concerned with managing distributed teams. The connections between changing team dynamics and emerging working practices is discussed, alongside the implications for managers and organizational decision-makers.

The book takes a broader perspective on new ways to work than many other texts in the field. It addresses contexts where changes to working arrangements have emerged, both as a result of employee choice and where changes have been imposed by employers. It also includes the experiences of a variety of workers in different industries, ranging from managers and professional workers, to those in service occupations, such as care workers and hotel housekeeping staff. Below we present a more detailed outline of the content with a brief overview of each chapter.

CONTENT

The first empirical section deals with new and emerging forms of work. In Chapter 2, Besseyre des Horts, Dery and MacCormick examine how work and the way it is organized has been changed by the advent and development of wireless, mobile technologies. Located within a social constructionist paradigm, this chapter connects innovation in Information and Communication Technologies (ICT) with how work is organized and where it can be done. Drawing on data from 19 interviews with employees of a financial institution in Australia and France, the chapter emphasizes mobility and flexibility. Using Johnson and Hall's (1988) Job Demand–Control–Support model, the findings demonstrate a paradoxical effect, whereby enhanced contactability both creates new demands and increased stress and increases control and autonomy associated with increased mobility which reduces stress.

In Chapter 3, Knox examines temporary work in Australia, where although the use of temporary labor is comparatively common, little research has been conducted into its character and implications for employees. Drawing on a study of hotel housekeeping staff, the chapter examines both employers' strategies and the concomitant experiences of temporary workers. The study shows that although the use of temporary staff is widespread, employers use different strategies according to the nature of their respective markets. In essence, the use of temporary workers is driven by the desire to reduce costs by matching the supply and demand for labor more closely, avoidance of recruitment and training costs (these are borne by the Temporary Work Agency [TWA]) and by avoiding paying overtime to permanent staff. The reported strategies varied both in relation to the ratio of permanent to temporary staff and whether temporary staff are directly employed casuals or employed via a TWA. Cost savings were achieved in spite of higher levels of labor turnover and a fairly widespread view that temporary staff were less committed and less motivated. The chapter documents the experience of temporary staff, often overseas students and more highly educated than their permanent counterparts, who reported inferior terms and conditions of employment, lack of training and development opportunities and less favorable and/or inequitable treatment by other hotel staff.

In Chapter 4, Eikhof and Summers take a different, critical perspective on new ways of working by exploring how media images shape perceptions of what is acceptable and desirable work. In particular, the chapter explores how acceptable and desirable work for women is presented in the media, by drawing on a content analysis of articles featured in a UK women's magazine, where 'new' entrepreneurial opportunities for women are presented as an alternative to 'regular', 'office-based' work. The focus on entrepreneurship, or women 'doing their own thing' portrays this form of work as providing freedom, flexibility, personal and professional fulfillment. The authors suggest that this social construction of desirable work for women promotes a neo-traditional picture of women's work based on 'feminine' skills, domestic work and constrained independence. The chapter provides a more critical perspective exploring themes relating to the 'manufacture', 'social construction' and presentation of new ways of working and their connections to editorial decision-making.

The second empirical section of the book explores employees' experiences of new ways of working/new ways of organizing work. Chapter 5 by Linehan explores the impact of changing work organization and work practices on employee identity. Drawing on contemporary ideas about identifications, it explores the dynamic, subjective and multiple identity possibilities that emerge from changing work practices. Echoing the work of Sveningsson and Alvesson (2003), an in-depth case study is presented based on the account of a manager in the Irish Health Service with responsibility for the provision of home-based services to the elderly. The study explores the evolving identity of a middle manager in the context of public sector change. It focuses on the dilemmas faced in constructing what it means to be a manager in a setting characterized by competing discourses (quality service versus budgetary pressures) and upward and downward pressures. The chapter also explores contradiction, tension and paradox in emergent identities and uses Bakhtin's (1993) concepts of self and subjectivity to add to the dialog on the potential impact of new work practices.

Wilkinson and Jarvis also deal with the implications of new forms of work organization for employee identity in Chapter 6. Drawing on an empirical study carried out in the UK, this chapter explores the emotional experience of remote working and examines the interplay between identity and perceptions of agency (whether and when to work remotely) and the ensuing emotions. Located within an interpretivist paradigm, the chapter considers how the removed physical state of remote workers and their perceptions of agency affect how and/or the extent to which they identify with their employer. The authors propose how remote workers undertake identity work is influenced by the emotions they experience and that this influence is mediated by their perceptions of agency.

Continuing with the theme of examining the experiences of remote workers, Chapter 7 by Richardson presents findings from interviews with 76 employees in a Canadian subsidiary of an MNC. Drawing on Gergen's concepts of 'saturation of the self' and 'dis-ease', the chapter considers the extent to which bringing work into the home environment results in pressures from the close proximity of the 'home self' and the 'work self' and their respective role demands. It also examines how employees cope with this proximity and the implications for individual well-being. The findings suggest that remote workers are challenged by the close proximity, but that over time they adopt coping mechanisms to avoid 'dis-ease' and 'saturation of the self'. Coping mechanisms involved redrawing the work–home boundaries according to their own individual circumstances. For some employees it also involved order and separation of the work and home self, whereas for others it allowed them to construct their lives in a more holistic way.

In Chapter 8, Wade-Clarke examines resistance to new ways of organizing work. This chapter presents findings from an ethnographic study of the relocation of a small business in Scotland. The implications of relocation for the organization of work are explored and the case is made for a place-sensitive approach to understanding changing work practices. The chapter goes beyond existing studies, which have recognized resistance to new ways of working, in that it examines the 'doing' and 'meaning' of resistance to remote working. The findings explore the themes of place, aspiration and identity as sources of resistance. In this respect, the chapter extends our understanding of changing work organization toward an appreciation of work as a physical locale and the implications for how work as a 'space' is experienced.

Continuing with the focus on remote working, in Chapter 9 Peters and Wildenbeest contribute to the debate about how teleworking is experienced. Drawing on findings from a study of telecommuters in Holland in both public and private sector organizations, they examine the employee experiences of 'flow' and exhaustion and the extent to which they are influenced by working conditions. 'Flow' is a situation where employees are so intensely involved in their work that nothing else seems to matter and that because the experience is enjoyable, they will do it for the sheer sake of doing it (Csikszentmihalyi, 1992). Exhaustion, by contrast, implies extreme fatigue, which may lead to burnout (Schaufeli & Bakker, 2004). The chapter explores how a number of conditions, based on the job demands and resources model (Demerouti et al., 2001), influence flow and exhaustion among teleworkers. Although job resources were found to support flow, not all job demands have a negative influence. Only two of the job demands examined were shown to contribute to exhaustion and only one job resource (autonomy) contributed to reducing exhaustion.

In the third empirical section the contributions continue with the theme of remoteness, but examine the work of employees who are remote from each other working in distributed teams. Consideration is also given to the implications of these arrangements for managers who are part of the respective teams. Collins and Kolb (Chapter 10) start from the premise that while creativity requires connection, it also requires periods of contemplation and reflection. Based on a study of geographically distributed teams, they examine how teams manage connectivity, both in terms of the kind and amount of team connectivity. The findings show that the right kind and amount of connectivity is important for innovation and that how team members connect is more important than when they connect. Importantly, this relationship is found to be moderated by human agency and that where connectivity is high, the benefits of choice are high, but that conversely where connectivity is low, high choice has negative implications for innovation.

In Chapter 11, Bosch-Sijtema, Fruchter, Vartiainen and Ruohomäki are also concerned with teams that are geographically distributed. Drawing on two case studies in the high-tech industry, one in the U.S. and one in Europe, they examine the challenges that global middle managers face when working with distributed teams and where they may also be members of multiple teams. The findings show that workload, increased complexity and resource allocation were found to be particularly challenging for managers, in addition to maintaining visibility and awareness and taking account of time and cultural differences. The authors also examine impediments to global collaborative working, such as workplace policies and IT infrastructures, which are not aligned to the new ways of working.

Finally, in Chapter 12, Kelliher and Richardson make a number of observations and draw some conclusions based on the evidence about new ways of organizing work presented in the preceding chapters. The specific aim of this chapter is to connect, but also to distinguish between, emerging themes and theories in order to move toward a more composite understanding of the field. Consideration is given to the significance of the different contexts of worker, workplace, industry and country. The chapter will also consider the themes that have emerged in light of contemporary social policy and the implications for how work arrangements might continue to evolve.

REFERENCES

Almond, P., Edwards, T. & Clark, I. 2003. Multinationals and changing national business systems in Europe: Towards the 'shareholder value' model? *Industrial Relations Journal* 34(5), 430–445.

Amoore, L. 2002. *An international political economy of work*. Manchester: University Press.

Bailey, D. & Kurland, N. 2002. A review of telework research: Findings, new directions and lessons for the study of modern work. *Journal of Organizational Behaviour* 23(4), 383–400.

Bakhtin, M.M. 1993. Toward a philosophy of the act, Eds. Liapunov, V. (Tr.), Lianpunov, V. and Holquist, M. Austin: University of Texas Press.

Beauregard, T. A. and Henry, L. C. 2009. Making the link between work-life practices and organizational performance, *Human Resource Management Review* 19(1), 9–22.

Berger, S. (Ed.) 2006. *Who's afraid of globalization? How we compete. What companies around the world are doing to make it in today's global economy.*New York: Currency/Doubleday, 3–28.

Besseyre, des Horts, C.H. 2008. *L'entreprise mobile, comprendre l'impact des nouvelles technologies*. Paris: Pearson Education.

Blanchflower, D.G. & Oswald, A.J. 2011. International happiness: A new view on the measure of performance. *Academy of Management Perspectives* 25(1), 6–22.

Bloom, N. & Van Reenen, J. 2006. Management practices, work-life balance and productivity: A review of some recent evidence. *Oxford Review of Economic Policy* 22(4), 457–482.

Brannen, J. 2005. Time and negotiation of work-family boundaries. *Time and Society* 14(1), 113–131.

Brewster, C., Wood, G. &Brookes, M. 2008. Similarity, isomorphism and duality: recent survey evidence on the HRM policies of MNCs. *British Journal of Management* 19(4), 320–342.

Castells, M., Fernandez-Ardevol, M., Qui, J. & Sey, A. 2007. *Mobile communication and society*. Cambridge MA: MIT Press.

Cates, K. & Rahimi, K. 2001. Algebra lessons for older workers. Mastering People Management. *Financial Times*, 19 November.

Cousins, K. & Robey, D. 2005. Human agency in a wireless world: Patterns of technology use in nomadic computing environments. *Information and Organization* 15, 151–180.

Csikszentmihalyi, M. 1992. *Flow. The psychology of happiness*. London: Rider.

De Menezes, L.M & Kelliher, C. 2011. Flexible working and performance: A systematic review of the evidence for a business case. *Journal of International Management Reviews*, forthcoming.

Demerouti, E., Bakker, A.B., Nachreiner, F. & Schaufeli, W.B. 2001. The Job Demands-Resources model of burnout. *Journal of Applied Psychology* 86(3), 499–512.

Donkin, R. (2009). *The future of work*. Basingstoke: Palgrave Macmillan.

European Foundation for the Improvement of Living and Working Conditions. 2007a. *ERM report 2007: Restructuring and employment in the EU: The impact of globalisation*. Luxembourg: Office for official publications of the European Communities.

European Foundation for the Improvement of Living and Working Conditions. 2007b. *Fourth European working conditions survey*. Luxembourg: Office for official publications of the European Communities.

European Foundation for the Improvement of Living and Working Conditions. 2010a. *European company survey 2009—Overview*. Luxembourg: Office for official publications of the European Communities.

European Foundation for the Improvement of Living and Working Conditions. 2010b. Annual review of working conditions 2009–2010. Luxembourg: Office for official publications of the European Communities.

Felstead, A. & Jewson, N. 2000. *In work at home. Towards an understanding of homeworking*. Routledge: London.

Gajendran, R.S. & Harrison, D.A. 2007. The good, the bad, and the unknown about telecommuting: Meta-analysis of psychological mediators and individual consequences. *Journal of Applied Psychology* 92(6), 1524–1541.

Gibson, C.B. & Gibbs, J.L. 2006. Unpacking the concept of virtuality: The effects of geographical dispersion, electronic dependence, dynamic structure and national diversity on team innovation. *Administrative Science Quarterly* 51(3), 451–495.

Giddens, A. 2002. *Runaway world: How globalization is reshaping our lives*. London: Profile Books.

Grote, G. & Raeder, S. 2009. Careers and identity in flexible working: Do flexible identities fare better? *Human Relations* 62(2), 219–244.

Hall, L. & Atkinson, C. 2006. Improving working lives: Flexible working and the role of employee control. *Employee Relations* 28(4), 374–386.

Halpern, D. 2005. How time-flexible work practices can reduce stress, improve health and save money. *Stress and Health* 21, 157–168.

Harrison, A.,Wheeler, P. & Whitehead, C. 2004. *The distributed workplace: Sustainable work environments*. London: Routledge.

Harzing, A-W. (2004). Strategy and structure of multinational companies. In *International human resource management*. Eds. A-W. Harzing and J. Van Ruysseveldt 2nd ed. London: Sage Publications. 33–64

Hood, C. 2005. Public management: The word, the movement, the science. In *The Oxford handbook of public management*, Eds. Ferlie, E., Lynn, L. & Pollitt, C. Oxford: Oxford University Press.

Hooker, H., Neathey, F., Casebourne, J. & Munro, M. 2007. *The third work-life balance employee survey: Main findings*. Institute for Employment Studies.

Hyman, J., Scholarios, D. & Baldrey, C. 2005. Getting on or getting by? Employee flexibility and coping strategies for home and work. *Work Employment and Society* 19(4), 705–725.

Jarvenpaa, S.L. & Leidner, D.E. 1999. Communication and trust in global virtual teams. *Organization Science* 10(6), 791–815.

Johnson, J.V. & Hall, E.M. 1998. Job strain, workplace social support, and cardiovascular disease: A cross-country race-sectional study of a random sample of the Swedish working population. *American Journal of Public Health* 78(10), 1336–1342.

Kelliher, C. & Anderson, D. 2008. For better or for worse? An analysis of how flexible work practices influence employees' perceptions of job quality. *International Journal of Human Resource Management* 19(3), 419–431.

Kelliher, C. & Anderson, D. 2010. Doing more with less? Flexible working practices and the intensification of work. *Human Relations* 63(1), 83–106.

Kelly, E.L., Kossek, E.E., Hammer, L.B., Durham, M., Bray, J., Chermack, K. Murphy, L.A. & Kaskubar, D. 2008. Getting there from here: Research on the effects of work-family initiatives on work-family conflict and business outcomes. *Academy of Management Annals* 2(1), 305–349.

Kolb, D. 2008. Exploring the connectivity of metaphor: Attributes, dimensions and duality. *Organization Studies* 29(1), 127–144.

Korabik, K., Lero, D.S. & Whitehead, D.L. (Eds.). 2008. *The handbook of work-family integration: Research, theory and best practices.* San Diego: Elsevier.

Lawrence, P. 2002. *The change game: How today's global trends are shaping tomorrow's companies.* London: Kogan Page.

Lero, D.S., Richardson, J. & Korabik, K. 2009. *Cost-benefit review of work-life balance practices—2009.* Canadian Association of Administrators of Labour Legislation.

Macky, K. & Boxall, P. 2007. The relationship between 'high-performance work practices' and employee attitudes: An investigation and interaction effects. *International Journal of Human Resource Management* 18(4), 537–567.

Mathiasen, D. 2005. International public management. In *The Oxford handbook of public management.* Eds. Ferlie, E., Lynn, L. & Pollitt, C. Oxford: Oxford University Press.

Matlay, H. 2000. Globalization, employment and employee relations in the small business sector of the British economy. *Management Research News* 23(2–4), 20–22.

Messenger, J.C. & Ghosheh, N. 2010. *Offshoring and working conditions in remote work.* Basingstoke: Palgrave MacMillan.

Middleton, C.A. 2008. Do mobile technologies enable work-life balance? Dual perspectives on BlackBerry usage for supplemental work. In *Mobility and technology in the workplace.* Ed. D. Hislop. London: Routledge, 209–255.

Moynagh, M. & Worsley, R. 2005. *Working in the twenty first century.* Swindon: Economic and Social Research Council.

OECD. 2009. *OECD Reviews of labour market and social policies: Slovenia.* Paris: OECD.

Olsen, K. & Kalleberg, A. 2004. Nonstandard work in two different employment regimes: the United States and Norway. *Work, Employment and Society* 18(2), 321–348.

Richardson, J. 2010. Managing flexworks: Holding on and letting go. *Journal of Management Development* 29(2), 137–147.

Schaufeli, W.B. & Bakker, A.B. 2004. Job demands, job resources, and their relationship with burnout and engagement: A multi-sample study. *Journal of Organizational Behavior* 25(3), 293–315.

Sedgeley, M. & White, W. 2002. *Globalization and the knowledge society.* London: Management Consultancies Association.

Sveningsson, S. & Alvesson, M. 2003. Managing managerial identities: organizational fragmentation, discourse and identity struggle. *Human Relations* 56(10), 1163–1193.

Tietze, S. & Musson, G. 2002. When "work" meets "home" temporal flexibility as lived experience. *Time and Society* 11(2/3), 315–334.

Tietze, S. & Musson, G. 2005. Recasting the home-work relationship: A case of mutual adjustment. *Organization Studies* 26(9), 1331–1352.

Tietze, S., Musson, G. & Scurry, T. 2009. Homebased work: A review of research into themes, directions and implications. *Personnel Review* 38(6), 585–604.

The Economist. 2011. *Austerity's winner. Outsourcing firms reckon on fixing Britain's public finances.* March 10th.

Von Glinow, M. 2002. Best practice in IHRM: Lessons learned from a ten country/regional analysis. *Human Resource Management* 41(1), 3–4.

WorldatWork. 2011. *Survey of workplace fclexibility.* Scotsdale, AZ: World at Work.

Yanadori, Y. & Kato, T. 2009. Work and family practices in Japanese firms: Their scope, nature and impact on employee turnover. *The International Journal of Human Resource Management* 20(2), 439–456.

2 Paradoxical Consequences of the Use of Blackberrys

An Application of the Job Demand–Control–Support Model[1]

Charles-Henri Besseyre des Horts,
Kristine Dery and Judith MacCormick

INTRODUCTION

Information and Communication Technologies (ICT) have transformed organizational structures and processes in the past decade. The exponential growth of the use of Internet both at work and outside work has resulted in new organizational challenges associated with both the management and use of the technology (Basole, 2008). The use of mobile communication tools, such as smartphones, deeply modifies how we view time and space, and thus understand the boundaries between work and nonwork (Chen & Nath, 2008). Mobile technologies give individuals the potential for ubiquity, enabling them to engage in their work and nonwork activities anytime, anywhere, embracing remote work and telecommuting (Hoang et al., 2008). The oft-cited benefits of this ubiquity include improved communication capacities, coordination and collaboration, reduced time and space constraints, increased access to decision makers, better reactivity and greater autonomy in decision-making (e.g., Basole, 2008). Equally, disadvantages are also associated with their use, such as erosion of boundaries between work and nonwork, veneration of urgency, diminution of thinking in decision-making processes, excess information and overinvolvement in activities (Besseyre des Horts, 2008; Jarvenpaa & Lang, 2005).

The goal of this chapter is to theoretically and empirically examine the paradoxical consequences of the use of smartphones in the work context. We examine the activities of managers in a leading investment bank and their use of BlackBerrys. Drawing on Johnson and Hall's (1988) "Job Demand–Control–Support" model that recognizes the requirements for greater consideration to be given to the social context of work, we use a social constructivist approach to understand the role of this technology in shaping work and to provide insights into its apparent contradictions in use. These findings suggest new challenges for managers to realize the benefits of mobile connectivity without the downsides of increased stress.

SPECIFIC CHARACTERISTICS OF MOBILE TECHNOLOGIES

The smartphone has enjoyed an exponential growth over the last few years largely because of its ease of receiving and sending emails. Gartner (2010) reported a 56.7% increase in smartphone sales from 2009 to 2010. This capacity has led observers to predict that there will soon be a smartphone in "every pocket" (Communication News, 2007). What differentiates smartphones from other mobile devices is their size, weight, ease of transport and integrated functionality. Within the smartphone category, the BlackBerry is a major player and, as such, is the focus of this study.

PARADOXICAL CONSEQUENCES OF MOBILE TECHNOLOGIES

As underlined by Varshney (2003), smartphones enable new forms of flexibility in space and time and offer promises of, for example, reduced coordination costs, improved communication, better access to information and improved decision-making (Gebauer, 2008). Conversely, while the technology can be empowering it can also create an "extended present" in which people are forever on call (Brannen, 2005). This capacity of the BlackBerry to connect an individual to work at all times raises concerns. While mobile email usage can allow users to be efficient and flexible, usage of the devices may be dangerous, distracting, antisocial and can infringe on work–life boundaries (Middleton & Cukier, 2006).

Central to understanding the implications of BlackBerry use is recognizing that these devices are not objective, external tools that have a deterministic impact. Although there is no doubt that technology does have an impact on human behavior (Kallinikos, 2005), users interact with the technology to shape the way in which it is used in particular contexts (Schwartz & Whittaker, 1999) to reconstruct, reestablish, strengthen and renegotiate organizational boundaries. Thus, while the BlackBerry can for some be "a curse" and for others "an invaluable tool", for many it is a combination of both as they describe their "love–hate relationship" with the device (MacCormick & Dery, 2008). To analyze and understand this apparent paradox, we recognize the recent debates about technology and the organization that highlight the importance of social context and develop frameworks which acknowledge both the material and social character of technologies (Orlikowski & Barley, 2001). This social constructivist perspective provides a valuable lens for this study recognizing that technologies, such as BlackBerrys, cannot be evaluated and analyzed without having an explicit understanding of the context of individuals and groups, which consequently comprehend, interpret, use and engage with the technology (Pinch & Bijker, 1984).

Consequently, in this study, we draw on the social construction of technology and technology-in-practice literatures. The social construction of the technology approach challenges the idea that technologies themselves have the capacity to determine behavioral outcomes. Rather, the meaning and impact of the technology is constructed through the use and actions of various relevant social groups who articulate and promote particular interpretations of it (Orlikowski, 2000). This meaning, over time, tends to become accepted and embedded in behavioral outcomes. The technology-in-practice approach similarly recognizes the inability to separate the technology from its social context (Orlikowski, 2000).

The important implication of these theoretical perspectives for this research is that it is only when individuals use BlackBerrys that the associated social practices frame and determine the value they attribute to it. Hence, as the users interact with 'facilities' (such as the capabilities of the BlackBerry), 'norms' (such as the accepted use of the BlackBerry), and 'interpretative schemes' (such as the expectations of availability of the user) (Dery, Hall & Wailes, 2006) they form patterns of use. Therefore, the opinions of respondents can only be understood in the context of individuals and groups comprehending, interpreting, using and engaging with the technologies (Karasek, 1979).

To better understand the dynamics of the impact of BlackBerrys on the conduct and consequence of work, we introduce the dimensions of job demand, job control and job support. The original *"Job Demand–Control"* framework developed by Karasek (1979) proposed that a psychological work environment can be characterized by a combination of the demands of the work situation and the amount of control (for example, discretion, authority or decision latitude) employees have to cope with these demands. This creates four types of jobs: passive, active, low strain and high strain—having decision latitude over work processes will reduce a worker's stress and, when combined with high demands, learning will increase. However, high demands with low control lead to high strain. To minimize stress, job demand should be matched to job control, such that when job demands are high, job control should be correspondingly high. High job control allows workers to adapt to demands by developing appropriate behavioral response patterns. Workers in demanding jobs who are able to proactively manage how their work is done can channel their energy in constructive ways, thus reducing the stress brought on by job demands. In the BlackBerry context, while users may experience higher job demands, they can also perceive their mobile devices as allowing them to better organize their work-time, communicate with others and access crucial information, thereby facilitating higher job control. This positive perception of BlackBerry usage is consistent with the active learning hypothesis (Karasek, 1979). Conversely, users may perceive BlackBerrys as intrusive tools reducing their autonomy in and outside work, that is, lower job control—resulting in increased strain.

JOB DEMAND–CONTROL–SUPPORT MODEL

Johnson & Hall (1988) enhanced this model by acknowledging the role of social context with the addition of the "social support" dimension. Social support refers to a work environment (culture, group norms, interpersonal relationships) that is favorable or unfavorable for the individual in a work situation. In work situations where job demands are high, job control is low, and social support is nonexistent, the negative consequences for both physical and psychological health are greatest (Van Yperen & Hagedoorn, 2003). However, Johnson and Hall (1988) have shown that social support can significantly impact the relationship between job demand and job control. High levels of social support can reduce signs of stress or job strain when demand is high and control is compromised.

By applying the Job Demand–Control–Support model in the context of executives and their use of BlackBerrys, we believe we can begin to untangle the paradox of mobile technology. The rhetoric surrounding this technology supports the view that increased connectivity increases job demands and can both increase and decrease perceived control depending on the level of social support present both at work and outside of work. With little known about the applicability of this model in the context of executives or mobile technology, this approach makes a significant contribution to both the theoretical and empirical literature.

We present three propositions as follows:

Proposition 1: *The increased connectivity made possible by the use of BlackBerrys is likely to increase job demands*

Proposition 2: *The use of BlackBerrys is likely to reconstruct the meaning of job control as users gain increased availability, mobility and flexibility*

Proposition 3: *The level of support, from both work and outside work, for BlackBerry use will moderate the effect of perceived control and demand resulting in either strain or learning.*

METHODOLOGY

The study presented here is part of a broader research project on mobile technologies. Given the relative paucity of research on the organizational and human dimensions in the field, (Dery, Grant, Harley and Wright, 2006), an exploratory approach was selected, adopting a qualitative methodology of semistructured interviews.

To maintain the focus on the behavioral outcomes, the research design attempts to hold key variables constant. All interviewees were selected from a single financial institution, headquartered in France. This 160,000-employee organization operates in 85 countries and represents a major global player in the financial sector. The technology was held constant by interviewing only BlackBerry users (the BlackBerry is the standard mobile technology deployed across the company worldwide[2]). We were thus able to create a series of literal replications (Yin, 2003) to gain insights into a range of behaviors within the same context and using the same technology.

Respondents were selected using the "key informant" approach and the snowball sample method. Each informant nominated other potential respondents likely to correspond to the definition of an "ideal" sample: policy makers and users of BlackBerry at various hierarchical levels (managers, department heads, line officers). A total of 19 semistructured interviews were conducted in both France (14) and Australia (5). Each interview lasted approximately 1 hr, and was recorded and transcribed (and translated from French to English as required). To facilitate comparison of responses across the two countries, a loosely constructed set of interview questions was used. However, interviewees were encouraged to explore issues and deviate from the structure enabling interviewers to gather more contextual material to enhance understanding.

The transcripts were then coded using both NVivo coding trees and manual methods where all three researchers combined to cross-reference the allocation of codes. In this way, translations from French to English were checked for meaning and the researchers were able to cross-reference their decisions and develop and allocate new coding as required. The standard codes were devised based on the Job Demand–Control–Support model with user responses coded based on how their responses aligned with each component of the framework. Interviewees were not asked questions based on the framework so they were not encouraged to group their responses in this way. The Job Demand–Control–Support framework was applied after the transcripts revealed that interviewees' responses were grouping in these categories, e.g., demand was talked about in terms of user expectations and temporal/spatial discussions. Researchers gained insights into user behavior in context and observed similarities and differences across transcripts.

Additional contextual material was gathered from publically available websites, news clippings and other published material, together with site observations during interviews, which were conducted at the organization's office.

FINDINGS AND ANALYSIS

Blackberrys-In-Use Perceived to Increase Job Demands

Respondents consistently attributed a perceived increase in external environmental pressures to the widespread adoption and use of BlackBerrys in the financial sector. As illustrated in the following quotations[3], use of this mobile device cannot be avoided, particularly in investment banking where high pressure and high demand is an institutionalized norm (DiMaggio & Powell, 1983). Table 2.1 provides examples of responses indicating an

Table 2.1   Changing Expectations

Users' expectations of themselves	*With a BlackBerry I feel compelled to carry it all day long, to look at it at least once an hour, to react if I have been reached. There are no more complete breaks.*
Users' expectations of others	*Indeed, the Investment Banking division insisted on the fact that the business bankers needed it, especially for certain businesses, such as projects' financing, where it was a standard. . . .*

increase in job demands resulting from increased expectations that users had of themselves and from others. While there was little evidence that the job itself had changed, increased levels of connectivity meant BlackBerry users reconstructed their expectations around availability and responsiveness, thereby increasing their perceived level of job demand.

Respondents also perceived increasing internal job requirements were making the use of BlackBerrys compulsory, even though the organization's official policy was that uptake was voluntary. Most respondents emphasized that the use of these devices was now a part of their job with a clear expectation to answer the requests of their stakeholders anytime, anywhere. In addition, they talked about job demands increasing as they worked longer hours and with greater job intensity. Longer hours were reflected both in the use of the BlackBerry to engage with work during commuting time and in nonwork contexts as work hours extended into the evenings, weekends and leave time. Job intensity was also amplified as users made increased use of microtime—using the BlackBerry to respond to emails in taxis, airports and other traditional downtimes. Table 2.2 illustrates increased demands to spend more time working as users reconstructed their use of work and nonwork time to further engage in work.

Overall, most respondents recognized that the impact of these mobile devices on their perceived work experience increased job demands because of the permanent connectivity enabled by BlackBerrys. Users perceived that email volume had increased dramatically resulting from increased connectivity and ease of sending emails, and the expectations to respond quickly meant a significant increase in job demands.

Table 2.2   Longer Hours and Job Intensity

Increased job duration	*. . . it extends [my working day] a lot. I will work to around 9pm . . . but keep flicking back and forth until midnight when I switch the lights off.*
Increased job intensity	*It's a godsend to be able to catch up on emails in trains, in cabs, waiting in queues.*

Blackberrys-In-Use Reinforce Active Learning by Increasing Job Control

When examining the mobile technology literature on the human and organizational impact, advantages largely exceed disadvantages (Besseyre des Horts, 2008). The most quoted advantages for individuals were: improved communication capacities, coordination and collaboration; reduced time and space constraints; easier access to key decision makers, better reactivity and greater decision autonomy (Davis, 2002). Based on Johnson and Hall's (1988) Job Demand–Control–Support theoretical framework, the advantages enabled by the BlackBerry are likely to reinforce individuals' learning capacities in work situations. In other words, the BlackBerry is likely to help the user transition from a passive work situation to an active one. While job demand may have increased with users being contactable anytime, anywhere, the BlackBerry simultaneously allows them to better control their job, facilitating access to critical people and information, better responsiveness to stakeholders and new possibilities to reorganize their working day. Table 2.3 highlights the increased sense of control BlackBerry users expressed as they constructed meaning through task, space, time and accessibility.

These perceptions of positive consequences of BlackBerry use may be understood as a the validation of the "learning hypothesis" of the initial Job

Table 2.3   Increased Control Over Work Activities, Work Relationships and Workplace

Better control over work activities	*It helps executives' mobility, they access their data any time anywhere, including attachments, presentations, even(sic) it is not very practical. It is an extremely powerful tool. It contributes to reach the employee any time, and it gives the manager the possibility to reach his team, his own manager and send them information.*
Improved control over work relationships	*So fantastic in terms of staying in touch. It's completely seamless to clients, prospects, whether I'm in the office or not, pretty much. I don't have my BlackBerry set up so that it says, you know, this is coming to you from Black-Berry, or whatever.*
Increased control over where work takes place	*It is clear (from thinking about) the time which I spend physically behind my desk. I realize that without this tool, things would go much slower. I would be obliged to answer emails at the end of the day, I shall probably be obliged to stay much later in the office in the evening to handle all which arrived during the day. Thus this tool allows (me) to optimize working time and handling emails as they arrive, between two meetings or in the train or by waiting for a plane.*

Demand–Control model (Karasek, 1979): increased job demands because of the anytime, anywhere work combined with higher job control resulting from the new capabilities offered by this mobile device enabled users to reconstruct their functional, spatial and temporal work boundaries and, therefore, develop learning capabilities.

Blackberrys-In-Use Generating Strain by Diminishing Job Control

While some interviewees suggested that the impact of increased job demands were mitigated by significant increases in job control, others found the BlackBerry reduced their ability to manage connectivity. While acknowledging that the organization did not require them to be connected 24/7 it was often simply the existence of the possibility that they may be required to connect with the workplace that resulted in the feeling of diminished control (Dery & MacCormick, 2008). Table 2.4 provides evidence of users feeling that they lost control over their work boundaries and felt conscious of the need to be connected.

Most users felt that they could not work without their BlackBerry or that life would certainly be more difficult if they had to give it up. The increased job demands as a result of mobile-enabled connectivity meant

Table 2.4 Lack of Control Over the Requirement to Be Connected with Work

Inability to disconnect and, thereby, control availability	*. . . you have kind of got this obligation if you want to be, you know, dedicated to your role . . . it would be easy to say [that] you've got the control [over the BlackBerry] because you can turn it off. But there is always a major [issue] . . . a client about to leave, a massive client joining . . . so if you are like me and have a no-regrets-type person-ality then you know (that) if I turn that thing off, I am conscious that I could have a regret because I could've actually done something. Whereas if I didn't have a BlackBerry, I wouldn't have had that . . . to be honest, though, it would be hard to do my job without it*
Inability to control work boundaries and lack of choice over the level of work connectivity expected	*. . . , again, there is an expectation internally that even if you're on holidays that you are able, because it is true, you are able to see emails. So you know, there's this sort of thing about, you know, if someone puts on Please Read, Urgent that enables you to quickly, while on holidays, navigate and work out what you really have to look at. (During my recent holiday) I was pretty much on it every day . . . look it's like any interaction with work when you are on holiday, you don't feel like you have had a holiday, you know?*

that the BlackBerry had become an invaluable device. However, whereas they valued the flexibility it gave them to spend more time on nonwork activities, they expressed the stress and conflict of being constantly connected to the work place.

Use of BlackBerrys reinforces active learning or job strain depending upon the level of social support. Despite the commitment of the HR department to email management and support for work–life balance boundaries, in practice there appeared little support for the protocols they sponsored (i.e., web-based guidelines were not accessed by users). The espoused support was not reflected in the enacted culture. Users reported continuing increases in email volume and expectations of constant connectivity. In terms of organizational culture, there was support for connectivity everywhere, every time, particularly for those in positions that involved a direct client relationship or a significant global responsibility.

At the same time, there was evidence of lack of support for connectivity for some users in the nonwork context. For those who kept their BlackBerrys turned on in nonwork contexts, whether through formal or informal requirements, the BlackBerry was often seen as a significant intrusion by partners and children. Table 2.5 summarizes the evidence of users as they reflect on perceived levels of support in work and nonwork environments:

Table 2.5   Support, and Its Absence, from Work and Nonwork Environments

Lack of support for use of the BlackBerry in nonwork environment	*My wife and son absolutely hate it . . . I find myself upstairs secretly looking at the BlackBerry and putting it away before anyone finds me.*
Lack of organizational support	*For the holidays, I find a real difference. I realized that, when we only had a professional cell phone, I was reachable but I could listen to my messages when I wanted. With a BlackBerry, I feel compelled to carry it all day long, to look at it at least once a day, to react if I have been reached, there are no more complete breaks. It is a sort of permanent connection that did not exist before. . . .*
Organizational support reflecting new ways of work enabled by the BlackBerry	*My manager did not influence the way I used the BlackBerry. We had agreed from the beginning that I had family constraints, it was clear that I had to deal with them. It may have happened once in the eighth months that I received an email I was asked to answer the same evening. Otherwise, he pays attention, is respectful. . . .*
Support from the nonwork environment	*I extend my working hours all the way till home . . . but it's not intrusive, I don't go and sit in front of the computer while the family is having dinner, I use my BlackBerry. It means I can be at home, but monitor how things are working through.*

The understanding of support for acceptable BlackBerry behavior was, at times, conflicting and views on what was acceptable for the collective were often contradicted by their own behavior. For example, there were numerous references to other people who used BlackBerrys in meetings, often 'surreptitiously' under the table. While condemned as inappropriate and distracting by others, the individual valued such behavior as an efficient way to quickly action ideas or requests from the meeting.

Although some expressed the need to engage in surreptitious use of the BlackBerry to avoid the wrath of family and friends, others used the Black-Berry to effectively integrate their work and nonwork sphere and, in doing so, their connectivity was positively supported by others in their nonwork sphere. The latter behavior appeared to result in less strain and, in turn, was reciprocated with more support for such connectivity from the non-work sphere as the user took advantage of the mobility of the technology to physically attend personal events and still meet work obligations.

The antecedents of organizational support for high levels of connectivity appeared to include a competitive industry (such as finance), the internal competitive processes (rewards based on personal performance), behavior of their manager (role modeling always on, anywhere connectivity and proac-tive interaction with subordinates in nonwork time), geographical location (distance from other offices, such as a head office in Europe). These factors supported working longer hours and with greater intensity. Whether the use of the BlackBerry was interpreted by the user as enhancing the ability to balance the needs of work and personal spheres, or whether it was per-ceived to construct a sense of conflict between the two seemed to depend on the user's ability to generate their own boundaries at individually pre-scribed levels or their willingness to integrate work and nonwork spheres.

DISCUSSION

The *Job Demand-Control-Support* model provides a valuable framework for unraveling the paradoxes associated with the use of handheld mobile computing devices as exemplified by the BlackBerry. Furthermore, by examining the use of BlackBerrys through a social constructivist lens, we uncovered evidence about how users of the same technology constructed meaning through the use of the BlackBerry resulting in different out-comes. Either strain or learning was experienced depending on whether the technology-in-use enabled the user to perceive increased or dimin-ished control in managing increased work demands, and this relationship, in turn, was impacted by support from the work and nonwork spheres. These findings make a significant contribution to theory and practice as little has been previously written about the applicability of this model in the context of executives or mobile technology. Furthermore, impor-tantly, this approach demonstrates the value of bringing together both psychological and sociological perspectives.

All users reported an increase in work demands produced by extended hours and intensity of work. These increased demands were further enhanced by the collective activity of BlackBerry users as they constructed new expectations of themselves and others around their availability and connectivity to work. New work practices were evidenced as BlackBerry users found ways to work in a more mobile environment, unconstrained by physical space and time. One manager summarized this relationship succinctly *"You can have the BlackBerry, but be cautioned, you will be expected to be much more available"*. Availability appeared to be redefining users' understanding of job demands as they struggled to make sense out of the resulting expectations.

The relationship between BlackBerrys and control is even more complex. Some executives perceived control to be generally enhanced through the use of the Blackberry and thus were able to reframe their work to more readily meet their individual lifestyle requirements (that is, a learning outcome rather than strain). These executives reported being able to more easily choose when and where they would work by using the technology to reconstruct their work/nonwork boundaries. They tended to emphasize the technological features of the artifact itself (such as the on/off button and alarm features) together with the increased autonomy to engage with the technology in ways that were more aligned to their personal and professional needs. These users considered the BlackBerry a tool that enabled them to filter the workload and make productive use of downtimes (such as waiting and traveling time), making them more efficient and better able to focus in both their work and nonwork spheres. Thus, through the use of the BlackBerry, executives were able to construct work practices that enabled them to have more control over increasing work demands.

Others, however, felt that their control over increasing work demands was inhibited by the constant levels of connectivity generated through the use of the technology. While recognizing the technological features of the BlackBerry facilitated control for other users, these users felt that the connectivity enabled by the device meant that the "pie of opportunities" was increased. For these users the potential offered by the BlackBerry to, for example, make more sales calls or respond more quickly and more often to customers, gave those added advantages that they valued. However, this very increase in opportunities reduced their capacity to control their time and place of work. Users reflected that they felt they had lost control over their availability for work-related activities as the collective use of Black-Berrys constructed a world where they were expected to be contactable 24/7, and even on annual leave.

While some users considered the option to deploy technological features of the BlackBerry to control their work demands was viable, for others it was not. Given that the technology was constant across all users interviewed, and most users were found to have similar levels of technological experience, then a social constructionist perspective is useful in explaining the wide variance in outcomes in this research. Just as this paradox of use occurs between users, so it is evident within the spectrum of experiences of a single user, i.e., some users expressed a love/hate relationship with the BlackBerry reflecting on their ability to exercise greater control over their work, on one hand, and an inability to meet increased work demands, on the other. Thus the role of social support enables us to have some insights into this apparent paradox.

Building on Johnson and Hall's (1988) definition of social support, this research highlights an important distinction between support from the work and nonwork environments (as recently pointed out by Cousins & Varshney, 2009). We found the relationship between support from the work and nonwork environments appeared to interact with perceived control, which, in turn, either buffered or fostered strain. In other words, expectations of connectivity from the workplace (for example, an organizational culture that encouraged work flexibility and work anywhere, anytime, and managers that expected and role modeled high levels of connectivity) could lead to strain or buffer the negative effect of high demands depending on whether the user perceived a level of support to construct their work boundaries according to their individual requirements (see Jarvenpaa & Lang, 2005). The potential for connectivity to result in strain or learning was further impacted by support from the nonwork environment. If support from family and friends was low, this effect could compound low perceived job control/high demand and result in additional strain. Conversely, if the user perceived social support from the nonwork environment for the requirement to be connected, this was more likely to result in positive outcomes through the buffering effect on strain. Thus social support appeared to enable the user to use the BlackBerry to engage in work practices that supported requirements for increased connectivity in ways that produced positive outcomes for the user.

CONCLUSION: MANAGERIAL IMPLICATIONS AND DIRECTIONS FOR FUTURE RESEARCH

These findings have significant implications for management of mobile connectivity, in particular, smartphones in the workplace. They indicate that without effective management practices the impact of connectivity can result in the negative consequences of job strain rather than the learning consequences of an increase in efficiency and effectiveness. Management practices that do not support individually constructed requirements to manage work/nonwork boundaries can result in BlackBerry users feeling a lack of control over increasingly demanding work processes and thus experiencing the negative effects of increased job strain. This effect was further compounded by the influence of geography and time zone differences, as well as reward systems that encouraged unrestrained use of the device. Thus there is a need to establish organizational expectations of employee availability and connectivity at mutually agreeable levels, to implement strategies to empower employees to exercise the liberating impact of the technology to manage their work/nonwork spaces with a focus on outcomes rather than availability (typifying high-performance work practices), and to make explicit "organizational permission" to manage connectivity in the nonwork context. This clearly requires a change in management perspectives surrounding the need to manage mobile connectivity.

Whereas this work highlights the applicability of the *Job Demand–Control–Support* model in the organizational context, it also brings into focus the requirement to understand more about the support construct in the context of mobile connectivity. It is recommended that further research is required to define this construct and understand more about the impact on job control in the increasingly mobile context of work.

NOTES

1. This research has been made possible, in part, thanks to a fund provided by Toshiba Systems France as a part of the endowment of the research chair HEC Paris-Toshiba "Mobility & Organization"
2. In late 2007 it was one of the most significant corporate users of BlackBerrys in Europe with more than 6,000 individual users within the organization.
3. Quotations have been minimized due to space restrictions

REFERENCES

Basole, R.C. 2008. Enterprise mobility: Researching a new paradigm. *Information Knowledge Systems Management* 7(1/2), 1–7.
Besseyre des Horts, C.H. 2008. *L'entreprise mobile, comprendre l'impact des nouvelles technologies*. Paris: Pearson Education.
Brannen, J. 2005. Time and negotiation of work-family boundaries. *Time and Society* 14, 113–131.
Chen, L. & Nath, R. 2008. A socio-technical perspective of mobile work. *Information Knowledge Systems Management* 7(1/2), 41–60.
Communication News 2007. A BlackBerry in every pocket 44, 11, 8.
Cousins, K.C. & Varshney, U. 2009. Designing ubiquitous computing environments to support work life balance. *Communications of the ACM* 52(5), 117–123
Dery, K., Grant, D., Harley, B. & Wright, C. 2006. Work, organisation and enterprise resource planning systems: An alternative research agenda. *New Technology, Work and Employment* 21(3), 199–214,
Dery, K., Hall, R. & Wailes, N. 2006. ERPs as 'technologies-in-practice': Social construction, materiality and the role of organisational factors. *New Technology, Work and Employment* 21(3), 229–241.
Dery, K. & MacCormick, J. 2008. "To be seen or not to be seen", a study of the BlackBerrys in the context of organisational surveillance. Paper presented at the *24th EGOS Colloquium*, Amsterdam.

DiMaggio, P.J. & Powell, W.W. 1983. The iron cage revisited: Institutional isomorphism and collective rationality in organizational fields. *American Sociological Review* 48(2), 147–160.

Gartner, International Data Corporation, Worldwide quarterly mobile phone tracker (2010). May 6.

Gebauer, J. 2008. User requirements of mobile technology: A summary of research results. *Information Knowledge Systems Management* 7(1/2), 101–119.

Hoang, A.T., Beckman, P. & Eng, J. 2008. Telecommuting and corporate culture: Implications for the mobile enterprise. *Information Knowledge Systems Management* 7(1/2), 77–97.

Jarvenpaa, S.L. & Lang, K.L. 2005. Managing the paradoxes of mobile technology. *Information Systems Management* Fall, 7–23.

Johnson, J.V. & Hall, E.M. 1988. Job strain, workplace social support, and cardiovascular disease: A cross-country race-sectional study of a random sample of the Swedish working population. *American Journal of Public Health* 78(10), 1336–1342.

Kallinikos, J. 2005. The order of technology: Complexity and control in a connected world. *Information and Organization* 15, 185–202.

Karasek, R.A. 1979. Job demands, mental job decision latitude, and strain: Implications for research design. *Administrative Quarterly Science* 24, 285–311.

MacCormick, J.S. & Dery, K. 2008. Too much of a good thing? BlackBerry use changing the terms of engagement. Paper presented at *22nd ANZAM Annual Conference*, Auckland, NZ.

Middleton, C.A. & Cukier, W. 2006. Is mobile e-mail functional or dysfunctional? Two perspectives on mobile email usage. *European Journal of Information Systems* 15, 252–260.

Orlikowski, W.J. 2000. Using technology and constituting structures: A practice lens for studying technology in organizations. *Organization Science* 11, 404–428.

Pinch, T.J. & Bijker, W.E. 1984. The social construction of facts and artefacts: Or how the sociology of science and the Sociology of technology might benefit each other. *Social Studies of Science* 14, 399–441.

Schwartz, H.B.N. & Whittaker, S. 1999. The hidden work in virtual work. *International conference on critical management studies*. Manchester: UK.

Van Yperen, N.R. & Hagedoorn, M. 2003. Does high job demand increase intrinsic motivation? The role of job control and social job support. *Academy of Management Review* 46, 339–348.

Varshney, U. 2003. Mobile and wireless information systems: Applications, networks, and research problems. *Communications of the Association for Systems Information* 12, 155–166.

Yin, R. 2003. *Case study research: Design and methods*, 3rd ed. Thousand Oaks: Sage.

3 Temporary Work and Temporary Work Agencies in Australia
Going from Bad to Worse?

Angela Knox

INTRODUCTION

In recent years, research examining the frequency, nature and implications of temporary work has grown. While much of this research has occurred in the UK (e.g. Druker & Stanworth, 2004; Forde & MacKenzie, 2007; Kirkpatrick & Hoque, 2006), far less exists in Australia. Temporary work, including agency-based work, is surprisingly underresearched in Australia, which is odd given its strong presence and growth (Campbell & Burgess, 2001; Curtain, 2004; Hall, 2000). Australia has one of the highest rates of temporary work, including temporary work agency employment, in the developed world and an analysis of this phenomenon will undoubtedly extend our understanding, particularly in relation to the factors that may have precipitated and maintained such high rates of temporary work and the implications of such employment for both employers and employees. Surprisingly, few studies have disaggregated the data on temporary work and explored its character or potential variations at the industry or workplace level. As such, our understanding of temporary work within specific sectors is limited, including its use within sectors that are heavily reliant on such forms of work, such as the hospitality industry, which includes the large and influential hotel sector.

The Australian hotel sector forms the focus of this chapter. In response to the scarce and patchy nature of research on temporary employment in Australia, this case study-based research provides new Australian data on temporary work by examining the character, patterns of use and implications of temporary employment in the Australian hotel industry. Around 70% of Australia's gross domestic products derive from the service sector (Bamber et al., 2004). Within this, the hospitality sector, including the hotel industry, is an expanding and influential segment. Data from the Australian Bureau of Statistics (ABS) indicates that licensed hotels are the most significant category of accommodation with respect to employment and financial takings (ABS, 2005, Cat. No. 8635.0). Thus, an analysis of hospitality/hotel industry-specific trends and variations, which have largely gone unexplored, will have important implications for workers, practitioners and policy makers. The chapter begins by examining the extant literature on temporary work in the UK and Australia. It then discusses the significance of the Australian hospitality/hotel industry and its reliance on temporary work. The methods and findings are then described. Finally, the findings are discussed and conclusions are drawn out.

TEMPORARY WORK IN THE UK

A temporary worker earns financial rewards from work established by the employer or contract for a limited duration. More specifically, temporary workers can be classified into subgroups: fixed-term contractors, casual, seasonal and agency workers (Biggs et al., 2006). Employers' use of temporary labor is widespread in both the UK and Australia (Campbell & Burgess, 2001; Forde & Slater, 2006; Hall, 2000; Organisation for Economic Cooperation and Development [OECD], 2002). Yet, temporary work has been studied more intensively in the UK than in Australia.

In the UK, research has focused on analyzing the proliferation of temporary work, reasons for its growth and subsequent implications (e.g, Forde & MacKenzie, 2007; Forde & Slater, 2006; Kirkpatrick & Hoque, 2006). Research findings typically highlight cost effectiveness (/minimization) and flexibility as factors driving growth, while the experience of temporary work tends to be less than ideal for the employees involved; it is associated with more insecure employment and wages, reduced protection and entitlements and an intensification of work (Beynon et al., 2002; Grimshaw & Rubery, 1998; Lapido & Wilkinson, 2002).

For example, an analysis of large-scale surveys in the UK reveals that employers' use of agency labor is largely driven by pressures related to labor costs, thought to reflect short-term considerations (Forde & Slater, 2006, 155). Agency workers indicate that they are significantly less able to exercise discretionary work effort, they express little loyalty to, or pride in, the organization they are working for and they are less likely to demonstrate a desire to remain in that firm (Forde & Slater, 2006). Thus,

> whilst the use of agency workers may provide short-term benefits for organizations, these considerations provide evidence of the longer-term costs associated with the use of this form of labor (Forde & Slater, 2006, 155).

Other studies have illustrated how some temporary workers gain very real benefits from their work because it enables them to escape the pressures and organizational demands associated with working on a permanent basis and often superior financial rewards (Alonzo & Simon, 2008; Kirkpatrick & Hoque, 2006; Tailby, 2005). According to Kirkpatrick and Hoque (2006, 659), organizational changes and the degradation of permanent employment have been so extensive that agency work has become an attractive alternative in spite of its costs; "the lesser of two evils" (Kirkpatrick & Hoque, 2006, 662).

Further, valuable findings revealed by Forde and MacKenzie (2007, 559) highlight employers' increasingly constrained choice to utilize temporary workers resulting from labor shortages and recruitment difficulties in the industry. In turn, such "choices" contribute to skill shortages in the industry as training offered to contracted workers is more limited in scope. Their findings are consistent with other research that has noted some deleterious effects of using temporary workers as well as questioning the extent and depth of training received by temporary workers.

The extent and depth of the UK research has precipitated, at least in part, the development of new regulatory protection for temporary workers, namely the *Fixed-term Employees (Prevention of Less Favorable Treatment) Regulations* and *Conduct of Employment Agencies and Employment Businesses Regulations* [see Biggs et al., 2006]). Subsequently, an analysis of *Labor Force Surveys* at the aggregate level indicated that the utilization of temporary workers had declined following the introduction of the legislation. Among temporary workers, declines of around 24% occurred in real terms and agency workers declined by approximately 11%.

These declines corresponded with an increased take-up of permanent work by temporary workers, increasing from 22% prelegislation to 27% postlegislation (Biggs et al., 2006, 191). Significantly, directly equivalent legislation does not exist in Australia at this time. The regulations are more fragmented and primarily concerned with assigning worker responsibilities related to occupational health and safety (Burgess & Connell, 2004).

TEMPORARY WORK IN AUSTRALIA

In Australia, temporary work has also grown significantly over the past few decades, over one-half of which is accounted for by casual employment. Casual employees are typically defined as "employees who are not entitled to either annual leave or sick leave in their main job", whereas permanent employees are "employees who are entitled to annual leave or sick leave in their main job" (ABS 1996, cited in Campbell & Burgess, 2001, 176). The coexistence of high rates of growth and very high levels of temporary employment have been noted and Australia represents an "extreme case" relative to other countries (Campbell & Burgess, 2001). Illustrating this, through the 1990s, casual (temporary) employment accounted for approximately 71.4% of Australia's net growth in employment (Campbell & Burgess, 2001, 178). Similarly, temporary agency workers are estimated to have grown from around 84,300 in 1998 to 274,180 in 2002, representing between 2.5% and 3% of all employees in Australia (Hall, 2006, 159). This places Australia near the top of the OECD international table of agency work, with higher rates of agency work as a proportion of total employment higher only in the Netherlands and Luxembourg (Curtain, 2004). The reliance on agency workers in Australia is spread across every industry and occupation, although it is more common among lower skilled occupations (Freidin et al., 2002; Hall, 2006). Within the accommodation, café and restaurant industry, which includes hotels, approximately 3% of the labor force consists of agency workers; consistent with the national average (Freidin et al., 2002). Yet, there is a paucity of research examining temporary work in hospitality.

In general, the growth of temporary forms of work in Australia, including agency-based work, can be explained by similar factors to those identified in the UK. Temporary workers are often deployed in order to achieve the following: enhanced numerical flexibility; reduced costs; simplified recruitment and selection processes; greater access to specific skills; and/or to ease risk management and other administrative issues (e.g., Brennan et al., 2003; Hall, 2000; Houseman, 2001). Coinciding with these explanations, others have suggested that workers are willingly supplying their labor on a temporary basis because it affords certain benefits, namely, flexibility and variety with limited job security (RSCA, 2004).

Based on quantitative data from secondary sources, Hall (2006) reveals that the supply-based argument underpinning the growth of temporary agency workers is misguided. While agency work provides substantial flexibility for client firms, agency workers themselves report no greater level of satisfaction with their flexibility and ability to manage their external commitments, and they report high levels of job insecurity compared to directly employed workers (Hall, 2006). Agency workers are also reportedly less likely to be using their skills, learning new skills or doing work that is complex or difficult. Moreover, they perceive their pay as less fair and they are less likely to have a high degree of freedom in their job or to participate in determining how the workplace is managed (Hall, 2006). Importantly, Hall (2006, 171) concludes:

> While agency workers in Australia are a very diverse group, spanning all occupational levels across all industries, they do, on average, exhibit the characteristics of marginal, peripheral workers .

This chapter seeks to contribute to our patchy and scant understanding of temporary work in Australia, especially in hospitality, by presenting contemporary data examining employers' use of temporary work and individuals' experiences of such work in the hotel industry. The significance of the hotel industry is discussed next.

THE AUSTRALIAN HOTEL INDUSTRY

Around 70% of Australia's gross domestic product derives from the service sector. Within this, the hospitality sector, including hotels, is an expanding and influential segment. In 2004, the hospitality sector employed in excess of 345,000 workers across Australia (ABS, 2006). Approximately 21.3% of these hospitality workers were employed in accommodation, while the remainder was employed in cafes and restaurants (43.9%) and the club, pub, tavern and bar sector (34.8%) (ABS, 2006). Data from the Australian Bureau of Statistics (ABS) indicate that licensed hotels are the most significant category of accommodation with respect to employment and financial takings (ABS, 2005), and the larger businesses in the industry are responsible for employing the most significant proportion of the hotel workforce. Much of this employment is accounted for by large hotel chains (ABS, 2005).

Research in the hotel industry has highlighted distinctive characteristics, including its nonstandard and often continuous (24 hours per day, 7 days per week) hours of operation, which involve seasonal and unpredictable patterns of customer demand, and the existence of penalty rates, that have traditionally led employers to rely on cost minimization strategies and secondary labor (Barnes & Fieldes, 2000; Timo & Davidson, 2005). It is estimated that almost half of all employees working in the hospitality industry are employed on a nonpermanent basis (van Barneveld, 2006, 156). Moreover, hospitality is the lowest paid industry in Australia, paying just over one-half ($431.50) of the average weekly earnings that would be paid to an all-industries worker ($823.00) (ABS, 2006).

Hotel workers are typically temporary, young, female and of a non-English speaking background (Timo & Davidson, 2005). While these employees tend to possess low-level skills and relatively low pay compared to other industries, they are often multiskilled and functionally flexible in order to respond efficiently to fluctuations in customer demand across hotel departments (Knox & Nickson, 2007; Knox & Walsh, 2005; Timo & Davidson, 2005). It is perhaps unsurprising to find that the industry experiences high rates of absenteeism, turnover and grievance activity (Knox & Nickson, 2007; Knox & Walsh, 2005).

While the hospitality industry is generally characterized as weakly unionized (7.2% compared to the all-industries average of 22.4%) (ABS, 2006), rates are often considerably higher in large workplaces (up to 37%) (Knox & Walsh, 2005). Employment regulation in the industry has traditionally relied on the award system, supplemented by managerial prerogative (Timo & Davidson, 2005). The award system enshrines legally binding minimum wages and conditions at the industry-level, although it does not prohibit employers from paying discretionary overaward payments to employees. However, most hospitality employers do not pay overaward wages (ABS, 2005).

METHODOLOGY

The research design is case-study based, involving qualitative methods. In addition, quantitative, performance-related, data were collected from some hotels. All hotel sites are based in Sydney, Australia. Sites were selected on the basis of market segment, including upper-(four-/five-star) and middle-(three-star) market hotels in order to allow for comparison of high and middle quality product offerings and to determine (and control for) the effect that market segment may have upon employment strategy and labor utilization. Three of the sites were selected from the upper market and three from the middle market (see Table 3.1). The sites also include a mix of international and national chain hotels, catering for a range of guests and

Table 3.1   Case Study Hotel Characteristics

Hotel	1	2	3	4	5	6
Ownership	International chain	International chain	International chain	National chain	International chain	International chain
Market segment	Upper	Upper	Upper	Middle	Middle	Middle
Location	Sydney CBD	Sydney CBD	Sydney CBD	Sydney CBD	Sydney CBD	Sydney CBD
Number of rooms[a]	< 400	> 400	> 400	<100	< 100	< 100
Number of staff[a]	< 400	> 400	> 400	< 100	< 100	< 100
Housekeeping staff[a]	<100 Total 20% Full time 80% TWA staff	> 100 Total 70% Full time 30% TWA staff	< 100 Total 100% TWA staff	< 100 Total 50% Full time 50% Casual	< 100 Total 50% Casual 50% Full time	< 100 Total 50% Casual 100% Full time
Business segmentation	90% Business 10% Leisure	70% Business 30% Leisure	70% Business 20% Leisure 10% Aircrews	Budget travelers and school groups	60% Tour groups 40% Independent travelers	50% Leisure 50% Business
Employment regulation	Award only	Award only	Award only	Award and AWAs	Award only	Award only

[a] Categories have been used to protect the identities of the hotel sites.

accounting for a diversity of hotels within the industry, as well as different business strategies. While the larger hotels employed several hundred staff, the smallest hotel employed less than 100 staff (see Table 3.1).

In each hotel the general, human resource and housekeeping managers were interviewed, as well as housekeeping supervisors and room attendants. In addition, the director and a senior manager of the Temporary Work Agency (TWA) supplying staff to two of the upper-market hotels were interviewed. All interviews were semistructured and focused on examining the use of temporary employment within the hotels' housekeeping departments, as well as the employment characteristics of the hotel room cleaners; "room attendants". The research focused on housekeeping departments in order to allow comparisons between hotel sites while also providing the opportunity to increase depth (rather than breadth) of understanding regarding temporary employment in this segment of the industry.

Each interview lasted approximately 90 minutes. Semistructured interviews were most appropriate because they involve a line of questioning around particular themes while also allowing the parties to discuss additional issues that may arise. This enables the interviewer to elicit interviewees' viewpoints more effectively than a standardized interview (Flick, 1998). The main themes of questioning related to: the hotel's product market and business strategy; employment and labor utilization strategies; training and development; pay and benefits; and employee demographics. Quantitative data on hotel performance and employment figures were also collected from management, although this data was patchy, in some instances, because of a combination of commercial confidentiality and incomplete or out-of-date records. The data were content analyzed in order to identify common themes and to draw out trends across the sample of hotel sites.

CASE STUDY FINDINGS

Hotel Product Markets and Business Strategies

The hotels in the upper-market segment provided superior quality service with both an extensive and impressive range of facilities throughout the hotel and within rooms. Each of these hotels adhered to the brand standards of its chain and as four- to five-star properties in the upper tier of their respective chains, service standards are high and monitored regularly through key performance indicators, performance reviews and audits. Although business strategies and policies are initiated within the head offices of each chain, hotel managers indicated that there is some scope to tailor them to the needs of particular regions and individual properties. Hotel managers suggested that they are required to maintain a delicate balance between provision of service quality and cost minimization—an ongoing challenge. In comparison, the hotels in the middle-market segment provided more basic services and their facilities were quite limited. As expected, the business strategies of these hotels were less focused on high-quality service provision, rather, the emphasis lies with maintaining a basic standard of comfort at minimum cost. Labor costs represented a significant concern for all hotels. All of the hotels had annual occupancy rates above 75%, although there were variations throughout the year, in line with tourist seasons and special events.

EMPLOYMENT AND LABOR UTILIZATION STRATEGIES

Although full-time employment dominated all housekeeping departments, it frequently consisted of a combination of permanent and casual staff employed directly, while the upper-market hotels also deployed additional TWA staff (see Table 3.1). A combination of permanent, casual and/or TWA staff enabled managers to cost effectively adjust their staffing levels to the seasonal fluctuations in customer demand. Permanent full-time employees possess regular and guaranteed working hours, while casual employees' working hours can be more irregular and are not guaranteed. TWA staff often work up to 38 hrs/wk at a hotel, but their hours can change and fluctuate with demand patterns. In addition, managers would deploy TWA or casual staff to avoid overtime among full timers, although paid overtime was occasionally offered to full timers. Managers' reliance on TWA staff varied across the hotels. While none of the middle-segment hotels used TWA staff, they did utilize casual employees. In the upper-hotel market, TWA staff made up 80% and 30%, respectively, of housekeeping employment in two hotels (hotels 1 and 2); a third hotel completely outsourced its housekeeping operations to a TWA (hotel 3). These variations in housekeepers' reliance upon TWA employment tended to reflect their emphasis on cost minimization; a greater reliance upon TWA employment coincided with more proactive cost-minimization strategies (hotels 1 and 3) as opposed to prioritizing quality standards (hotel 2). However, all relied to some extent on TWA employment in order to manage unexpected fluctuations in demand, as well as staff absences and leave.

Overall, the proportion of permanent staff employed directly by the hotels (in-house staff) declined over recent years. TWA staff had become important among the upper market hotels for several reasons. First, TWA staff provided substantial numerical flexibility, thereby offering potential labor cost savings. While the cost savings were not as great as they had been in past years, as TWA costs had increased, some managers suggested that longer term cost savings were still possible, although others debated this. Second, the costs associated with recruitment and selection and training were not incurred if TWA staff were hired, as the TWA bears responsibility for such costs. Third, TWAs enabled hotel managers to avoid Worker's Compensation claims, usually related to back-strain injuries incurred by housekeepers, which were often litigious and expensive. This burden is shifted to the TWA itself when agency staff are employed. Finally, the ability to attach a finite cost to labor was enhanced through the use of TWAs and managers indicated that this is extremely beneficial as it simplifies their budgets.

While there were advantages associated with using TWAs, there were also disadvantages. Managers indicated that it was more difficult to maintain high-quality standards. Poor experience and/or inefficiency were associated with many TWA staff as a result of their inadequate training by the TWA and this compromised quality standards. In addition, both managers and staff highlighted that there were divisions between the hotel's in-house staff and the TWA staff and this affected morale and commitment. A room attendant contracted to work at hotel 3 by her TWA stated that: "the other staff working [directly] for the hotel treat you differently, you are singled out a bit. They look at you differently and there is a bit of a divide". The deputy housekeeper at hotel 1 also noted this issue, even though all efforts were being made to avoid such problems. This may contribute to the higher rates of turnover associated with TWA staff. At hotel 3, it was also noted by managers and some TWA staff that training and development opportunities were not provided to TWA staff. The executive housekeeper stated that:

> The downside [of outsourcing to a TWA] is that turnover is probably higher than it would be if we had our own in-house staff and we can't take advantage of training and developing the staff like we might like to. There are a few staff in particular that are very good and I would really like to develop them further, their skills are not being fully utilized. They could go a long way but I can't take advantage of that for obvious reasons (hotel 3).

Furthermore, these staff cannot access the self-development and leadership programs run by the hotel chain or attend its "University". Moreover, a TWA supervisor working at hotel 3 indicated that:

> My job is much more repetitive now than it ever has been before [working directly for a hotel], all I do is check rooms. I used to go into the office with other supervisors and the managers and do other things. Sometimes I would fill in for the assistant or executive housekeeper but that never happens now. There isn't any extra training either and there isn't anyone to organize things that can be used to motivate staff.

A room attendant at hotel 3 stated: "everyone is replaceable in an agency, I think, so if there is a problem they just replace the person rather than helping and developing them".

TRAINING AND DEVELOPMENT

At both the middle- and upper-market hotels, new room attendants are trained on-the-job and then partnered up with a "buddy" (an experienced worker) during their first week of work. New staff then work on their own, cleaning a reduced quota of rooms, with their room quota increasing incrementally until the the full quota is reached. Beyond this, training at middle-market hotels occurs on an "as needed" basis. In the upper-market hotels, there is additional training focusing on the "brand standards" (upgraded annually) of the hotel chain, as well as ad hoc training regarding quality customer service. Where TWA staff are used, they are trained by the TWA itself. The effectiveness of training provided by the TWA is questionable however, as discussed below.

Among full-time and casual staff employed directly, opportunities for career progression within housekeeping, and other hotel departments, are available, although they are more accessible in the upper-than middle-market hotels. The upper-market hotels tend to be larger, offering more job openings and formalized training programs and structured career paths. Despite this, the majority of room attendants indicated that they were not interested in advancement or transfers to other parts of the hotel. Most room attendants highlighted that all other areas of the hotel relied on rotating rosters, often involving evening work. Many room attendants have domestic responsibilities and childcare commitments that would be difficult to fulfill if their working time was more irregular or involved evening work. In addition, many room attendants indicated that they did not want extra responsibilities or work pressures and/or they lacked the confidence to progress.

Ironically, the room attendants who might best take advantage of career progression opportunities, as they tended to be younger, better educated and childless, were unable to do so because they were employed by a TWA and could not access the hotel's developmental opportunities/career structure. From the TWA's perspective, the sooner employees are able to clean rooms the better, as they are not productive unless they are providing an income stream for the TWA. Subsequently, training is minimized and there are few opportunities for career advancement within the TWAs.

PAY AND BENEFITS

The majority of room attendants received award-based rates of pay, in accordance with the federal hospitality award (The Hospitality Industry-Hotels, Accommodation, Resorts and Gaming Award 1998). The basic rate of pay is $14.18 per hour for permanent staff and $17.72 per hour for casual staff (including a 25% casual wage loading). These rates compare to a minimum wage set by the Australian Fair Pay Commission in July 2007 of $13.74 (Grade 1 full rate). According to managers, award-based rates of pay are received by permanent, casual and TWA staff at all of the hotels, with the exception of hotel 4 (discussed below). However, some staff indicated that the use of room quotas could impact pay rates. For instance, a TWA employee stated that:

> Staff working full time have a 7.6 hour shift per day but they are paid by the number of rooms that they complete so if they only clean 10 rooms in that time they only get paid for 10 rooms not their full 7.6 hour shift because the quota is 14 for a day. But if they get all their rooms done in 6 hours they will only get paid for 6 hours work, so they have to stay around for the extra 1.6 hours and do extra cleaning, say in public areas, to get their full day's money. It is not just the agency that does this, this is how it works in a lot of hotels even though they say it is not piece rates. This is how the hotels have a rort [deceptive practice that benefits the hotel] (Supervisor, hotel 3).

The director of the TWA supplying staff to hotels 2 and 3 confirmed that his employees are paid according to the number of rooms cleaned. At the international chain hotels, in-house employees are eligible for additional benefits including: social club membership, discounted accommodation, food/beverages, gym membership, parking and movie tickets. TWA employees are not eligible to receive these benefits, however, so they receive fewer benefit entitlements than in-house staff.

At hotel 4, individually bargained arrangements (known as Australian Workplace Agreements; AWAs) had been formed with the hotel's casual employees in mid-2007. These agreements provided a flat rate of pay, which bought out award-based penalty rates that otherwise apply when work is performed during nonstandard hours, and casual employees received approximately $19/hr, rather than $26.58, $31.01 and $35.50/hr on Saturdays, Sundays and public holidays, respectively. Their permanent colleagues remained within the award system. However, permanent employees indicated that their weekly take-home wages had declined as a result of these changes because their working hours during weekends and public holidays (attracting penalty rates) had declined. Casuals were being deployed on weekends and public holidays because their hourly wage rates were now lower. Permanent employees suggested that their fortnightly wages had declined from $1091 to $1045 but this also included a $46 tax break so in terms of real wages they were approximately $90 worse off per fortnight.

One of the room attendants stated: "it has affected me a lot, I am stressed and cannot sleep. It has put buying a house on hold and I can just buy what is needed, milk and bread and pay the rent and bills" (room attendant, hotel 4). Moreover, employees at hotel 4 did not receive any additional benefits, such as those provided by some of the international chain hotels and staff were said to be using their own wages to buy resources required to perform their work. Illustrating this:

> I don't like having to fight for resources, you know getting the things you need to do the job. Half the time we buy our own scourers and rubber gloves because we get sick of waiting for management to provide what we need (supervisor, hotel 4).

ROOM ATTENDANT DEMOGRAPHICS

Overall, room attendants originated from many countries including: China, Brazil, the Philippines, Vietnam, India, Russia and Thailand. In-house workers employed on a permanent basis were typically female and slightly older than their temporary colleagues. Most commonly, permanent employees are married women with children and their working hours suit them. The majority originate from non-English speaking backgrounds (NESBs) and possess few or no formal qualifications. In some instances, they possess professional qualifications from their home country that are not recognized in Australia. These workers are unable to upgrade their qualifications because of the time/money involved: "some of the women intend on upgrading their qualifications for Australia but they just get stuck in housekeeping, they get used to the job and never leave" (executive housekeeper, hotel 2). Although these employees are from NESBs, their English language skills are said to be very good, which is important in the upper-market hotels as attendants are encouraged to interact with guests.

In contrast, room attendants employed on a casual basis and those employed by TWAs are younger, often international students on working visas. Although predominantly female there are also males. In many instances, TWA and casual staff lack housekeeping experience and some have not ever worked previously. The assistant housekeeper at hotel 1 indicated that the TWAs:

> advertise at Uni.'s for students on six-month working visas. They are very highly educated but they have never cleaned before, many have their own cleaners and domestic staff when they are at home in China or Brazil and they struggle to clean adequately and meet their quotas.

All managers indicated that they faced constant challenges managing these staff as they are "less committed to the job and sometimes lack motivation" (executive housekeeper, hotel 1). In the upper-market hotels, these staff require more regular monitoring and training in order to meet the quality standards. Consequently, managers in the upper-market hotels expressed a preference for older, more experienced staff.

DISCUSSION AND CONCLUSIONS

The findings reveal that the majority of hotels rely, to some extent, on temporary workers. However, the type and number of temporary workers varies across the sector. In the upper-market hotels, both TWA and casual staff were utilized whereas the middle-market hotels did not make use of TWA staff. The absence of TWA staff in the middle market is largely because of their smaller size and more predictable occupancy patterns. Hotel 6 was the only hotel in which permanent full-time employees were exclusively deployed, which was possible because of the hotel's high and stable occupancy rates. Overall, these findings illustrate substantial variation in hotel employers' use of temporary workers, extending to each of the hotel market segments. Such evidence is consistent with UK research by Stanworth and Druker (2006) that revealed a diversity of labor use strategies in firms, and it highlights the heterogeneous mix of strategies within the Australian hotel sector.

Within the upper-market hotels, reliance on TWAs was said to have increased. Typically, managers' increased reliance on TWAs was associated with their need to enhance flexibility while reducing costs. To this extent, hotel managers are demonstrating imperatives that reflect those of their counterparts within other sectors in both the UK (e.g., Druker & Stanworth, 2004; Forde & MacKenzie, 2007; Forde & Slater, 2006) and Australia (e.g., Brennan et al., 2003; Hall, 2000; Houseman, 2001), rather than a different or unique set of imperatives.

Given this consistency, managerial efforts directed toward cost reduction are likely to produce longer term costs for the organizations. This counterproductive effect has been highlighted by Forde and Slater (2006) in their cross-sectional analysis of UK data, leading them to suggest that shortterm cost savings are not necessarily sustainable over the longer term, nor wholly beneficial for the organizations concerned. Similarly, while hotel managers may be yielding short-term cost savings, they compromise quality standards, and more intensive monitoring and supervision was necessary as a result of reliance on TWAs. TWA employees tended to be less experienced and inadequately trained compared to in-house staff and workforce camaraderie and morale was a problem. Moreover, managers suggested that employee commitment was lacking and turnover rates were elevated as a result of their TWA labor strategy. Maintaining such a strategy seems strangely at odds with the hotels' goal of delivering quality focused, luxury standards of service.

For employees, temporary work offers limited benefits, especially for those employed by a TWA. Although temporary (both casual and TWA) employees do *technically* have more temporal flexibility than their permanent full-time colleagues, because their contracts of employment are not ongoing, the *actual* nature of temporary employees' working time is frequently fixed and ongoing such that they have minimal flexibility. Casual

employees do at least have the option of applying for permanent employment within the hotel, whereas TWA employees are bound to their TWA
contractually and cannot apply directly for employment at the hotel(s).
While all of these temporary employees receive a salary loading (although
significantly reduced for casual employees at hotel 4) to compensate for
their insecure status, they are obviously denied substantive job security,
leave entitlements and financial stability. While we have been aware for
some time that these problems confront temporary workers in Australia
(e.g., Campbell & Burgess, 2001; Hall, 2006; Knox & Walsh, 2005), the
results of this research highlight that little appears to have changed. Perhaps more worrying, however, is evidence revealing the additional challenges faced by TWA employees.

Consistent with UK results (CITB, 2003; Forde & MacKenzie, 2007),
TWA employees examined here received less effective training and development than their directly employed counterparts. Inadequate training led
to excessive unpaid working hours and unnecessary physical strain likely
to lead to injuries. In addition, TWA employees have near non-existent
career progression and as previously mentioned are unable to transfer into
more secure employment at their place of work. Therefore, the likelihood
of being able to advance their opportunities is limited severely. Moreover,
TWA employees' work is reportedly more routine and monotonous (cf.
Hall, 2006), than would otherwise be the case, and they are maligned by
their directly employed colleagues. Overall, TWA employees seem substantially worse off than other temporary workers, namely, directly employed
casuals. In this context, you might say that TWAs are "the worst of the
worst", which is a stark contrast to Kirkpatrick and Hoque's (2006) assertion that TWAs may be "the lesser of two evils." This phenomenon seems
likely to continue unabated in Australia unless legislation is introduced in
order to regulate TWAs.

Policy development that focuses on protecting TWA labor is clearly
required in Australia. In order to be most effective, such policy is likely to
require a two-pronged approach. First, the findings presented here illustrate
that TWA workers are receiving inferior entitlements (including wages and
conditions) than their casual and permanent counterparts. This issue could
be addressed through the development of regulation similar to that adopted
in the UK [*Fixed-term Employees (Prevention of Less Favourable Treatment) Regulations*], which prevents this kind of less favorable treatment.
Second, the findings presented here also suggest that TWAs are engaging in
practices that are unfavorable at best, such as minimizing training provision, and illegal at worst, including the provision of piece-rate wages and
unpaid overtime. In order to redress such problems, TWA-based regulation
is necessary to ensure that minimum employment standards are established
and enshrined. It may also be necessary to monitor and/or audit the TWA
industry in order to ensure that these standards are being effectively upheld.
Policy responses of this type would clearly benefit workers and ultimately

they would also produce benefits at the firm- and industry-level as quality and safety standards would be improved and turnover could be reduced, thereby enhancing service provision.

REFERENCES

Australian Bureau of Statistics (ABS). 1998. *Tourist accommodation, Australia.* (No. 8635.0). Canberra: ABS.
Australian Bureau of Statistics (ABS). 2005. *Accommodation services- Australia, 2003–2004* (No. 8695.0). Canberra: ABS.
Australian Bureau of Statistics (ABS). 2006. *Labor force Australia- detailed, 2004–2005* (No. 6291.0.55.001). Canberra: ABS.
Alonzo, A. & Simon, A. 2008. Have stethoscope, will travel: Contingent employment among physician health care providers in the United States. *Work, Employment and Society* 22(4), 635–654.
Bamber, G., Lansbury R. & Wailes, N. (Eds.) 2004. *International and comparative employment relations.* Sydney: Allen and Unwin.
Barnes, A. & Fieldes, J. 2000. "Monday I've got Friday on my mind": Working time in the hospitality industry. *Journal of Industrial Relations* 42(4), 535–550.
Beynon, H., Grimshaw, D., Rubery, J. & Ward, K. (Eds.) 2002. *Managing employment change: The new realities of work.* Oxford: Oxford University Press.
Biggs, D., Burchell, B. & Millmore, M. 2006. The changing world of the temporary worker: The potential HR impact of legislation. *Personnel Review* 35(2), 191–206.
Brennan, L., Valos, M. & Hindle, K. 2003. On-hired workers in Australia: Motivations and outcomes. *RMIT Occasional Research Report.* Melbourne: School of Applied Communication, RMIT University.
Burgess, J. & Connell, J. 2004. International aspects of temporary agency employment: An overview. In *International perspectives on temporary agency work,* Eds. J. Burgess & J. Connell, London: Routledge, 54–75.
Campbell, I. & Burgess, J. 2001. Casual employment in Australia and temporary employment in Europe: Developing a cross-national comparison. *Work, Employment and Society* 15(1), 171–184.
Construction Industry Training Board (CITB). 2003. *The effect of employment status on investment in training.* CITB: Bircham Newton.
Curtain, R. 2004. *Affidavit of Dr Richard Curtain.* (No. IRC 4330 of 2003). Sydney: Industrial Relations Commission of New South Wales.
Druker, J. & Stanworth, C. 2004. Mutual expectations: A study of the three-way relationship between employment agencies, their client organizations and white collar agency temps. *Industrial Relations Journal* 35(1), 58–75.
Flick, U. 1998. *An introduction to qualitative research.* London: Sage.
Forde, C. & MacKenzie, R. 2007. Getting the mix right ? The use of labor contract alternatives in UK construction. *Personnel Review* 36(4), 549–563.
Forde, C. & Slater, G. 2006. The nature and experience of agency working in Britain: What are the challenges for human resource management? *Personnel Review* 35(2), 141–157.
Freidin, S., Watson, N. & Wooden, M. 2002. *Household, Income and Labor Dynamics in Australia (HILDA) Survey.* Melbourne: University of Melbourne.
Grimshaw, D. & Rubery, J. 1998. Integrating the internal and external labor markets. *Cambridge Journal of Economics* 22(1), 199–220.
Hall, R. 2000. Outsourcing, contracting-out and labor hire: Implications for human resource development in Australian organizations. *Asia Pacific Journal of Human Resource Management Journal* 38(2), 23–41.

Hall, R. 2006. Temporary agency work and HRM in Australia: Cooperation, specialization and satisfaction for the good of all? *Personnel Review* 35(2), 158–174.

Houseman, S. 2001. Why employers use flexible staffing arrangements: Evidence from an establishment survey. *Industrial and Labor Relations Review* 55(1), 149–170.

Kirkpatrick, I. & Hoque, K. 2006. A retreat from permanent employment?: Accounting for the rise of professional agency work in UK public services. *Work, Employment and Society* 20(4), 649–666.

Knox, A. & Nickson, D. 2007. Regulation in Australian hotels: Is there a lesson for the UK? *Employee Relations* 29(1), 50–67.

Knox, A. & Walsh, J. 2005. Organizational flexibility and HRM in the hotel industry: Evidence from Australia. *Human Resource Management Journal* 15(1), 57–75.

Lapido, D. & Wilkinson, F. 2002. More pressure, less protection. In *Job insecurity and work intensification*. Eds. B. Burchell, D. Lapido, & F. Wilkinson. London: Routledge.

Organisation for Economic Cooperation and Development 2002. Taking the measure of temporary employment. *Employment outlook*. Paris: Organisation for Economic Cooperation and Development.

RSCA 2004. And what do you do . . . ? Re-branding the recruitment industry. *Recruitment Journal*, 7(2), 10–14.

Stanworth, C. & Druker, J. 2006. Human resource solutions? Dimensions of employers' use of temporary agency labor in the UK. *Personnel Review* 35(2), 175–190.

Tailby, S. 2005. Agency and bank nursing in the UK National Health Service. *Work, Employment and Society* 19(2), 369–389.

Timo, N. & Davidson, M. 2005. Flexible labor and human resource practices in small- to medium-sized enterprises: The case of the hotel and tourism industry in Australia. In *HRM in tourism and hospitality: International perspective on small- to medium-sized enterprises*, Ed. D. Lee-Ross. London: Cassell, 28–45.

van Barneveld, K. 2006. Hospitality. In *Evolving employment relations: Industry case studies from Australia*. Eds. P. Waring, P. & M. Bray. . Sydney: McGraw Hill, 153–168.

4 Women Doing Their Own Thing
Our Picture of Modern Women at Work?

Doris Ruth Eikhof and Juliette Summers

INTRODUCTION

The 20th century has seen a steady increase in female workforce participation and in a general acceptance of women undertaking paid, independent work outside the home. Traditional gender roles in the public workplace have changed along with women's attitudes toward work (McRae, 2003). As Powell and Butterfield (2003, 89) point out, "women's occupational aspirations have become similar to those of men". The recognition of women's work outside the home, however, has also re-affirmed the low status of women's work in the home as undertaking unpaid or low-paid domestic tasks. In addition, gender discrimination in work still persists (Hibbert & Meager, 2003) and there is considerable debate over how much choice women can actually exercise over their work and careers (e.g., Crompton & Lyonette, 2005; Hakim 1991, 2004). Caring responsibilities still predominantly rest with women and consequently debates around work–life policies focus on how female workers can be enabled to balance work and family (Eikhof et al., 2007). Despite such progress on these issues, factors such as child rearing or caring for elderly parents still play an important role in women workers opting to 'off-ramp' (Hewlett, 2007) or 'opt-out' (Cabrera, 2007) and leave paid employment.

From the 1990s onward, the development of new ways to work beyond traditional 9- to -5 jobs with rigid working hours and places gave hope for improvements in women's work experiences and career outcomes. Working from home, or teleworking, either for an employer or in self-employment for some or all of one's job, was initially viewed as particularly conducive (Bøgh, Fangel & Aaløkke, 2007; Kylin & Karlsson, 2007). This way to work seemed to offer opportunities for better reconciling work and caring commitments, thereby improving both women's career prospects and recognition of their work achievements. However, with teleworking becoming widespread, critical aspects of such ways to work have come to the fore, especially around gendered roles associated with work in the home and their intersection with the nature and demands of working from home.

Teleworking has been revealed as a gendered practice (Sullivan & Lewis, 2001; Steward, 2000) infused with expectations that women working from home will undertake housework as well as paid work. Gendered domestic expectations also influence the use of space within the home. Female home workers are more likely to work in shared domestic spaces, while male home workers tend to have separate, dedicated work spaces (Sullivan, 2000). Although seemingly providing a solution to gendered challenges of reconciling career and caring responsibilities, relocating women's work into the home has thus proved to be a contested step toward gender equality in work—if one in that direction at all.

In combination with work–life balance policies, new ways to work, such as teleworking, have nevertheless opened up considerable choice for women on how to reorganize their work and employment. Importantly, such choices are influenced by what is perceived to be socially recognized as acceptable and desirable. In particular, and the focus of this chapter, media images play a crucial role in constructing such perceptions. Women's magazines have been found to be not only "mirroring current cultural concerns" (Holmes, 2008, 517), but also to actively influence women's perceptions and aspirations. These influences are most extensively documented for women's body images, where, for example, Park (2005, 594) found, "reading beauty and fashion magazines increased the drive for thinness". The lack of reality of some media images, such as the airbrushed celebrity image, has lead to the media being cited as a causal factor in eating disorders (Wykes & Gunter, 2005). The operation of media influence, especially on body image, may be achieved through individuals' potential to make comparisons (Festinger, 1954) with these images and to interpret what they read or view as realistic or attainable. Generally, comparisons between reader and media representations are the more influential the more the readers identify with the protagonists, for instance, because they are of the same age or share the feelings, experiences or aspirations described in the magazine. As with the airbrushed images, the presentation of image and content as realistic or factual is part of the editorial process. Such editorial decisions are decisive insofar as where media representations do not reflect reality, "repeated exposure to stereotypical images cultivates beliefs, assumptions, and common conceptions of societal facts or norms" (Robinson & Callister, 2008, 3). Similarly, Beetham (1996) has argued that with a widespread availability and considerable female readership, "the meaning of femininities . . . have been made in and through [women's] magazine[s]".

These powerful influences on societal expectations and perceptions also extend to women's careers, work and employment. Media studies have analyzed how work-related femininity and women's work have historically been represented in women's media and how these representations have shaped societal accepted views of women's work. Victorian and Edwardian magazines associated "true" femininity with the English middle-class woman" (Beetham, 1996, 8), whose life centered firmly on the domestic sphere. Not much had changed by the 1950s and 1960s, when women were represented as 'happy housewives' (Friedman, 1963). However, by the 1970s and 1980s, magazines started to treat women as individuals who increasingly worked outside the home and were expected to be treated as equals (Ferguson, 1983; Winship, 1987). Magazines, such as Bella and Best, had "weekly columns on paid work . . . but [that were] marginal in the context of the publication as a whole" (Ballaster et al., 1991, 153). Cosmopolitan's monthly column titled "Career Ahead" (ibid, 154) was more indicative of a shift to presenting women's work outside the home "as the way creativity, responsibility, and self-actualization can be achieved" (Bardwick, 1980, 40). At the same time, female identity had become firmly associated with consumption-led lifestyles, where shopping was "the ultimate form of self-expression" (Ballaster et al., 1991, 149). The discourse disclosed views of women as "individualistic and narcissistic" (ibid, 150), as aspirational and as engaged in paid employment "because they are looking for egocentric gratification" (Bardwick, 1980, 42). Into the 1990s, the normalized media image was one of women with the desire and rights to work outside the home on an equal basis and alongside of men. However, despite such changes in the representation of women's work in women's magazines, the media image of women remains stereotyped, consisting of "highly restricted (for which read patriarchal) versions of 'acceptable' femininity" (Byerly & Ross, 2006, 50). The images produced by women's magazines are thus far from benign and still form the basis of "baleful influences in the normative construction of gender and identity" (Holmes, 2008).

Against this backdrop of, first, women still face difficult choices about ways to work and, second, the influence of media images on such choices, this chapter analyzes media images of women finding new ways to work. The media in question is a women's magazine, eve, which features a monthly series "Women doing their own thing" (WDTOT). This series describes women who choose to escape the corporate world through self-employment and to reorganize their work according to their own preferences, typically and often not only initially, relocating work to the home. Although this relocation of work clearly overlaps with gendered domestic expectations on working at home, these reorganizations of work are presented as empowering and liberating. They echo the promotion of teleworking as enabling women to balance work and life, but also as providing an escape from the bureaucracy of the office (Tremblay, 2002). Using *eve's WDTOT* as an example and providing a content analysis of this series, the chapter offers, first, an in-depth exploration of contemporary representations of women's work. Second, and based on this analysis, the chapter discusses the implications such representations may have for women's choices in finding new ways to work in general—and therefore, for gender equality in work and employment more broadly.

EMPIRICAL STUDY

As a cultural product, women's magazines are created by their editors, advertisers and features writers and targeted at a particular female demographic—either a teenage market, for instance, Just Seventeen in the UK, or the more affluent, educated woman (Marie Claire, Vogue, Good Housekeeping, *eve*, Red), essentially with money to spend on the products advertised. The publication studied in this paper is a UK-based glossy women's monthly magazine, *eve*. At the time of study, *eve* claimed to have a readership of "294,000 readers per month within the UK", with an average reader age of 37 and average household income of £46,237 (www.evemagazine.co.uk/eveglobalmediainfo.pdf, accessed Jan 08). The magazine is aimed at "intelligent, independent and stylish women in their 30's", who are said to be

> key consumers for luxury global brands. They are well educated, aspirational and demanding of themselves, interested in personal development and an increasingly broad range of experiences. They are also individuals with time pressures and busy lifestyles for whom 'time for me' and 'treats for me' are essential rewards for their efforts and commitment. (www.evemagazine.co.uk/eveglobalmediainfo.pdf, accessed Jan 08).

Our analysis centers on the monthly feature, 'Women doing their own thing', which features a different female entrepreneur each month. Data analyzed was drawn from 17 editions of *eve* published consecutively between 2006 and 2008. WDTOT constitutes a major share of work-related content in each of these issues. The articles were analyzed using qualitative content analysis (see Bryman, 2004, 392–393; Mayring, 2002, 141–121), which seeks to unveil underlying themes, perceptions and meanings of texts by investigating what information is presented and how. According to Moeran (2003, 15), editors are relatively independent from advertisers in deciding about the content of magazine features. The editorial decision about the inclusion or omission of aspects from the available narratives can thus be understood as a purposeful shaping of texts. It was the aim of this analysis to describe and analyze the picture of women at work presented in WDTOT as a result of such editorial decisions. Such an approach is common in the qualitative analysis of mass media outputs (see Bryman, 2004, 388).

After a first sighting of the complete data, one-half of the WDTOT articles were analyzed more closely with respect to meaningful themes (see Bryman, 2004, 408–411). Based on these themes, a coding scheme was devised that was subsequently used to code all articles. The coding scheme contained codes relating to, for example, personal information about the protagonists (e.g., age, ethnicity, marital and family status), their previous occupations and qualifications, their new occupation/ business and various aspects of work. Work-related codes comprised, among others, hours, location, work attitudes, positive and negative work experiences. Further codes included lifestyle changes/changes in the perceived work–life balance, indicative language and undercurrents. For several of these codes, subcodes were used to identify the specific phrasing of the information presented. The coding scheme was revised and reapplied during the analysis, following the mostly inductive processes recommended for qualitative data analysis (see Bryman, 2004, 398–411; Flick, 1995, 164–166).

WOMEN DOING THEIR OWN THING: AN OVERVIEW

As a background to the analysis of the picture the WDTOT series paints of women at work, this section gives an overview of the protagonists and the businesses featured in the articles.

The 17 'Women doing their own thing' articles reported on 18 women starting their own business (one article featured 2 female friends starting the business together). The average age of the protagonists was 35 years, with the youngest being 32 and the oldest 46 years old. Thirteen of the 18 women were married, 2 were divorced and for 3 no information on their relationship was given. Ten women had children (2.2 on average) and all women were Caucasian.

Before setting up the businesses featured in the articles, these female entrepreneurs worked in predominantly new professions, including as a film producer's assistant, buyer for Disney, client manager in a bank, account director in advertising, hospitality manager, colorist, corporate lawyer, corporate interior designer and teacher. Most of these occupations will have required formal qualifications of some sort and will have offered access to decent pay and career progressions. Several articles mention that the protagonists earned substantial or high incomes in their former positions.

Leaving these careers behind, the women portrayed in WDTOT founded a range of new micro businesses including the development, production and wholesale of various products (handbags, organic shampoo, brie cheese and lavender crafts); a flower shop, a bakery and a cooking school cum take-away; trading French furniture and toys, as well as setting up a hotel in Switzerland and guided tours in Greece and India. Other protagonists worked as a property developer, a doula, a painter, and a wedding planner. Only 2 women were reported to be employers, albeit on a small scale, and 4 others were more vaguely described as working "with a team". Table 4.1 provides an overview of the sample. It includes the article titles, which will hereafter be used to refer to articles and protagonists.

Table 4.1   Businesses and Protagonists of the 'Women Doing Their Own Thing' Sample

Article title	Business featured	Protagonist's former occupation
Ma Vie en Rose	Flowershop "La maison des Roses"	Client manager in bank
My Very Own Property Boom	Hospitality business development	Hospitality manager
The French Mistress	Furniture import "The French Bedroom Company"	Worked in public relations
Let's Do Lunch	Cooking school cum take away "Soulsome Foods"	Worked in marketing
Special Delivery	Doula & hypnotherapist	Worked in conference industry
The Snow Queen	Activity hotel "Whitepod" in Switzerland	Corporate lawyer
My Life Is One Long Holiday	Guided tours in Greece, "Walking with Anna"	Office worker
A Slice of the Good Life	Bakery cum wholesale "Honeybuns"	Teacher
Purple Haze	Lavender crafts shop "Millcroft Lavender"	"High-flying business trouble troubleshooter"
Blessed Are the Cheese-makers	Cheese "Tunworth Soft Cheese"	Worked in conference industry
The Green Goddess	Organic shampoo range "Sacred Locks"	Colorist
From Bags to Riches	Handbag range "ZPM"	Worked in sales
Art House	Paintings	Corporate interior designer
Easy Rider	Motorbike tours in India "Blazingtrailstours"	Worked for travel insurance company
Toys Are Us	Kids & family products mail-order company "Hippychick"	Worked in marketing
The Wedding Guru	Boutique weddings in Italy "Love and Lord"	Account director advertising
The Bag Ladies	Handbag range "Wilbur & Gussie"	Brett: film producer's assistant; Lucy: buyer for Disney

WDTOT: A PICTURE OF MODERN WOMEN AT WORK?

Being published in a women's glossy magazine, WDTOT certainly seeks to entertain its readers with engagingly told stories of other women's dreams, trials, tribulations and successes. However, our inductive content analysis of WDTOT revealed that these stories share a number of common images and themes. Although the personalities, businesses, products and events differ from story to story, the type of content presented and the language used for this presentation are remarkably consistent and combine to form a very distinct picture of women's work presented to eve's readers. In the following, we will examine both WDTOT content and language in more detail.

The New Businesses

Analysis of the data coded as relating to the nature of the businesses, qualifications and start-up capital revealed a particular choice and presentation of start-up businesses. Although the 17 WDTOT businesses operate in various industries and differ with respect to processes, products and resources, they share several characteristics particularly relevant at the start of a new venture and which allowed the protagonists

- to start their new business from home or to turn their home into their business location,
- to work with external contract partners such as laboratories, factories or wholesalers rather than with employees,
- to produce to demand and
- to start their business by moonlighting.

As a consequence, none of the businesses had to be portrayed as causing significant costs for buying materials, renting offices or production facilities, or employing staff. The start-up budgets cited in the articles are low, with an average of £22,930 across all articles and at times downplayed to a mere £70 investment in a second-hand bicycle (A Slice of the Good Life). The only article that does not mention start-up costs is "The Snow Queen", whose protagonist must have incurred significant expenses for setting up a camp of pods and a chalet housing the kitchen, spa and office facilities. The protagonists claim to have sourced their start-up capital from low-threshold sources, such as savings, their husband or family, mortgages and overdrafts or combinations thereof. Only one woman, Sofia (The Snow Queen), is reported to have started her new business by writing a business plan. Overall, the way start-up costs and their sources are presented creates the impression that starting one's own business does not require any substantial financial capital. Similarly, only five WDTOT protagonists were reported to have undergone any type of training: a diploma in clinical hypnosis combined with a 3-day doula training, on the job-training as an adventure tour guide, a cookery course, floristry night classes and, notably, only in one case, a business skills workshop. None of this training required previous qualifications or substantial investments of time or money.

This specific choice of 'facts' on starting a business is complemented by a language that emphasizes the alleged feasibility of 'doing their own thing'. Protagonists are described as "armed with nothing but nous" and as having "not one single formal qualification in business" (My Very Own Property Boom). Assuring the readers that "you don't need an earth-shattering invention to start a new business" and that "ideas are right under your nose" (From Bags to Riches), WDTOT emphasizes the protagonists' individuality as their source for success "She had the creative flair—so what if she lacked the scientific expertise?" (The Green Goddess). Entrepreneurship is portrayed as not requiring business skills, but "personality" and "passion" (My Very Own Property Boom), "patience" (Easy Rider) or, in the worst case, "hard work" (My Very Own Property Boom). The transition into business ownership is represented as quick, easy and seamless: "She handed in her notice at work and spent every spare moment [. . .] experimenting with recipes until Tunworth [cheese] was born" (Blessed Are the Cheesemakers) or "I made a few phone calls and persuaded the makers to let me sell it. We called it the Hipseat, named the company Hippychick and that was that; I had my own business" (Toys Are Us).

Traditional Femininity as the Key to Business Success

With regard to the work featured in WDTOT, two aspects clearly emerged from our analysis. First, all work is undertaken in businesses centered on upscale markets and luxury lifestyle products and services. Second, this work either consists of producing and selling products traditionally associated with women (e.g., handbags, shampoo, food, crafts, flowers) or of providing services centered on activities traditionally perceived as female, such as nurturing, caring, entertaining and hosting (e.g., hospitality, wedding planning, doula service). With regard to the products, female traditions feature strongly as WDTOT entrepreneurs reportedly turn to their grandmothers for inspiration. A typical example is Emma (A Slice of the Good Life), who "tried out some of her grandmother's old recipes and soon [. . .] was selling cakes to friends". Traditional and grandmothers' recipes and designs are also revealed as the secret behind the successful production of handbags, cheese and lavender crafts. With respect to the service providers among the WDTOT entrepreneurs, 'caring for others' emerged as the dominating narrative. Jennie (Let's Do Lunch) sells food that "makes [her friends] feel happy, it's like a hug" and hospitality property developer Sue (My Very Own Property Boom) loves "thinking up little ways to surprise and delight my customers". Holiday organizers Sofia and Anna describe the highs of their work as focusing on their customers' well-being, stating: "I wanted to give people an experience they are totally immersed in" (The Snow Queen) and "The only thing you don't do for them is make love" (My Life Is One Long Holiday). The intensity with which these portrayals of women's work focus on traditionally female pursuits and skills, often harking back to housewifery and traditional gender roles, is compounded by statements such as "the most useful technique I learned was to go to offices at the highest levels and burst into tears" (Easy Rider) and recommendations to simply "trust female intuition" (A Slice of the Good Life).

Throughout the WDTOT features, production processes are not described as, for instance, sourcing materials or writing marketing strategies, but as shopping, browsing and chatting with friends, for instance as "jet[ting] off to Milan, Barcelona and New York" and "quietly strolling round bejeweled stores filled with swathes of shimmering fabric" (The Bag Ladies). Alluding to similar allegedly female interests, Georgia (The French Mistress) dubs her business "a celebration of pretty things". Moreover, although the WDTOT businesses could conceivably have been located outside the domestic sphere, the majority of WDTOT entrepreneurs work at home. Businesses are run from home, production is undertaken at home and homes are turned into business locations. These decisions to relocate economic activity into the domestic sphere are portrayed as conscious and attractive lifestyle choices, as a result of which "the hub of their working life is Lucy's big kitchen table [where] many of their beautiful handbag ideas are born, fuelled by tea and biscuits" (The Bag Ladies) and Emma (A slice of the good life) "spends her days in her steaming kitchen perfecting sweet treats". Work and home, business and private life are depicted as blending without any problems, most overtly in the case of Georgia (The French Mistress), who has turned her flat into a showroom and emphasizes that "if the phone goes on a Friday evening it's just as likely to be a client as a friend". Notably, in the case of several WDTOT protagonists, the relocation into the domestic sphere asserted them as primary careers. This traditionally female role is not described as problematic, however, but as a chance to better balance work and life (e.g., Toys Are Us, From Bags to Riches) and as fulfilling personal preferences: "working from home means I'm always around for the family. It's brought me back to my roots" (Blessed Are the Cheesemakers).

Work Experiences

With regard to the typical descriptions of work experiences in the WDTOT's new businesses, a key theme is that of work as an enjoyable, pleasant activity. 'Doing their own thing' has enabled the women to undertake work that is not experienced as hardship and effort. Across the articles, protagonists stress that "my job doesn't feel like work" (Art House) and "it doesn't feel like work, despite the long hours" (Let's Do Lunch). Moreover, work is depicted as chiming with the women's personality, as for instance Emma (A Slice of the Good Life) emphasizes that "baking did come naturally". Emphasizing the notion of capitalizing on the women's personal strengths, work is offered as a route to personal fulfillment, for example with Louise (The Green Goddess) feeling "100% fulfilled" and Julie (Blessed Are the Cheesemakers) relishing the opportunity to work from home because her "heart was always at home at our old farmhouse in the Hampshire countryside". WDTOT explicitly portrays work as the practice of earning a living from doing something the WDTOT entrepreneurs enjoy as an (integral) part of a desirable lifestyle befitting their personality and human nature. We term this kind of work 'soft work'.

In contrast, work in the WDTOT entrepreneurs' previous careers is depicted as taking place in "grey, corporate offices" (The Bag Ladies) and as leaving the women "well and truly in the rat race" (Purple Haze). Various protagonists describe their former working experiences as leaving them feeling "guilty", "frustrated", "bored" and "stagnant". Alluding more directly to an alienation from their creative selves, work is reported to leave them feeling "jaded", "soulless . . . starved and stifled" and as "zapping my natural get-up-and-go" (My Life Is One Long Holiday). Against this backdrop, the starting of their own business and with it often the relocation into the domestic sphere is lauded as liberating and energizing, for instance, stating that "Anna rediscovered her joi de vivre" (My Life Is One Long Holiday) or quoting Sofia (The Snow Queen) as saying "I have constant sparks of energy and I'm much more creative".

In sum, our analysis showed that WDTOT clearly juxtapositions, on the one hand, soft work that centers on traditional femininity and is located in the domestic sphere, where private life and business seem to amalgamate seamlessly. On the other hand, hard work in the public sphere is presented as a pathologized female identity, one that denies these women self-expression, and leads to an alienation of the women's true identities. The transition from hard to soft work is presented as highly feasible and as, more than anything, a lifestyle choice.

DISCUSSION

Obviously, eve is neither an academic publication nor an outlet for serious investigative journalism, but a lifestyle magazine. That *eve* presents work as a lifestyle issue is therefore logical rather than surprising. However, and as we have outlined above, evidence from media studies has conclusively shown how such media images shape individual and collective perceptions, in general (e.g. Robinson & Callister, 2008), and, in the case of women's magazines, of gender and 'acceptable' feminine identity at work (Byerly & Ross, 2006, 50; Beetham, 1996; Holmes, 2008). Although ostensibly addressing lifestyle issues, women's magazines can thus both sanction and perpetuate particular images of women's work and careers (Ballaster et al., 1991; Bardwick, 1980). WDTOT, indeed, openly emphasizes, and thus reproduces, images that are considered to be socially acceptable and desirable, for instance with 12 out of 17 articles starting with a variation of the following:

> Why can't your life be more like that—a bit less Changing Rooms, a bit more like Chocolate? (The French Mistress)

> Picture a job where finding the right dark chocolate is crucial to the company's share price. (A Slice of the Good Life)

> How do you make an eco-friendly fortune while living in one of the most beautiful places on earth? (The Snow Queen)

Such appeals clearly signal to the reader that the described scenarios are recognized as desirable and that the readers are expected to share this view. However, while WDTOT presents the women's lifestyles almost as dream sequences, they are not represented as fantasies. First, this is because, and as we have shown above, WDTOT features occupations in low-cost, ease-of-entry sectors that women can readily and independently access and find success in via their supposed innate female skills. Second, the WDTOT main articles are supplemented by features with step-by-step advice and encouragement on setting up a business (Eikhof & Summers, 2008). Continuing the facilitative theme, WDTOT is notably silent on business skills, objective measures of business success or enterprise viability, focusing instead on how the women run their enterprises through chatting over a cup of coffee at the kitchen table. Similarly, career prospects in protagonists' new line of work are a non-issue, as are the risks of quitting an established career and foregoing returns on previous, career-specific investments in education and training or in social capital, which will disintegrate without continuous reinvestment. The promise of lifestyle change, through a different and differently organized way to work, is held out tantalizingly and with it a shift to a work identity that is packaged as more appropriate and desirable for women.

The picture of women's work presented in WDTOT is one of pursuits and activities traditionally stereotyped as female, undertaken at home and appealing to allegedly innate female skills and qualities—intuition at best, tearful despair at worst. While such occupations are traditionally regarded as low-status work, as leisure activities they are associated with the Victorian 'cult of domesticity' and middle class homemaking skills. In WDTOT such traditional locations and skills of women's work are presented as high-status choices because they enable the women to pursue personal fulfillment and work at home (presenting a reactionary treatment of female locations and qualities), while at the same time earning an independent income. Nevertheless, WDTOT's focus is squarely on achieving a lifestyle, and not on career or business success. In light of the women's feelings about their corporate work experiences, the significance of opting to work at and from home suggests home as a refuge that "can also provide a sense of place and belonging in an increasingly alienating world" (Mallett, 2004, 66).

However, while such a picture of work may whitewash the achievements of the feminists of the 1960s and 1970s, it does not represent a complete return to traditional gendered work roles. WDTOT draws on an established narrative of female withdrawal from the public sphere, but presents it as a search for a feminized self-actualization through self-employment. WDTOT creates a neo-traditional image of work in which women may constrain themselves to domestic spaces and pursuits, but, unlike their grandmothers' generation, expect to make an independent income from predominantly home-based work. Unlike 'off-rampers' (Hewlett, 2007) these women continue to earn a living through their work that supports their avowedly middle class lifestyles. Neither have they opted out of a wider social existence because they sell and market their businesses through their social networks and contacts. Last, but not least, the series title, "Women Doing Their Own Thing", emphasizes empowerment and independence. The articles thus attempt to reconcile the low status of traditional female work and skills with the aspirations and perceptions of the professional, independent women who make up the *eve* readership.

The articles' picture of empowerment and independence is, however, challenged by several more hidden aspects suggesting underlying tensions in WDTOT's portrayal of women's work. First, most WDTOT articles feature a 'silent male', either as a formal business partner, who may have also undergone a lifestyle shift or as crucial financial or emotional support. The women's partners contribute financial resources and labor power to the running of the businesses and make lifestyle compromises and alterations, such as downsizing, in terms of property or taking on a longer commute. These contributions are only alluded to in passing, for instance, when Georgia (The French Mistress) mentions that the home she shares with her fiancé is also the showroom where "even their bed is part of the collection". The rhetoric of independent female entrepreneurial achievement is thus subtly contradicted by revelations concerning the women's reliance on the informal and financial support from their partners. Maintaining a low but continuous profile in the articles, this picture of continued dependence on the women's partners' support contributes to the neotraditional tone of WDTOT's portrayal of women's work. Consequently, the potential constraints that 'doing their own thing' can have as women's professional achievements become more reliant on the support of family and friends (and thus not truly independent or autonomous) are underplayed in favor of representations of self-expression and independent and empowering female entrepreneurial work.

Second, and as outlined in our analysis, the majority of WDTOT's female entrepreneurs relocate their economic activity to the domestic sphere. This relocation leads to a substantial blurring of the boundary between work and life with respect to place, time, financial resources and partners in interaction (Eikhof et al., 2007; Warhurst et al., 2007). Not only are homes transformed into businesses and houses and cars sold to finance their start-up (My Very Own Property Boom, The Green Goddess), but friends become clients (Let's Do Lunch) and clients and business contacts become friends or even husbands (The Green Goddess). In one of the most extensive examples of blurred work–life boundaries (Toys Are Us) wife and husband are business partners, the children are taken to trade fairs to promote the products and function as product testers and even the family bathroom is used as a product storeroom. Notably, such blurring of work–life boundaries is presented as positive or nonproblematic. Current research contradicts such views and reveals more contentious consequences of domestic relocation, in particular, around overcoming the stigma of women's work within the home not being 'real' or 'serious' work. Women's choice to work at home is often met with expectations that they will undertake housework as well (Sullivan, 2000), which diverts time and energy from the women's professional achievements. Having to be available for both work and life concerns in the same space frequently leaves workers feeling guilty toward their family for restricting access to their person although in the home while still not 'getting the job done' (Bøgh, Fangel & Aaløkke, 2007). Home-based workers generally report struggling to make family and friends as well as colleagues understand that they are working, although they are at home (Kylin & Karlsson, 2007). Moreover, women working at home often have to make do with shared rather than dedicated domestic working spaces, which, as Sullivan (2000) argues, also evidences the devaluation of women's economic activity. Such gendered use of space features strongly in WDTOT as well, for instance, when the women entrepreneurs are portrayed as working from the kitchen table. The gendered image of work locations in WDTOT is further compounded by the fact that investigating the domestic spaces presented in the features we mostly do not see the garage or shed, but the kitchen, bedroom or living space—traditionally female-controlled areas. The picture WDTOT presents of women is, therefore, imbricated with the expectations and constraints built into the gendered location of home spaces (see Cassidy, 2001). Despite the rhetoric of liberation and empowerment, WDTOT thus portrays a particular type of self-employment and an independence that is likely to be heavily constrained by problematic and undervaluing perceptions of work at home, in general, and of women's work at home, in particular.

In the light of such critical analysis, WDTOT's portrayal of women's choices to not only relocate their economic activity into the domestic sphere, but to focus on work that "doesn't feel like work" (Art House, Let's Do Lunch), does not require specific training and does not offer career progression are unlikely to help overcome gendered perceptions of women's work as less serious or valuable work.

CONCLUDING COMMENTS

The emergence of new ways to work in combination with work–life balance policies has opened up considerable choice for women on how to re-organize their work and employment. As far as home-based work is concerned, these choices often lead to work practices that are still notably gendered. From a gender equality point of view, such new ways to work, therefore, have to be viewed critically. When analyzing women's choices on how to reorganize work, perceptions of what is societally recognized as acceptable and desirable come into play. As such perceptions are influenced by media, this chapter has presented a content analysis of a women's magazine feature, WDTOT, that centers on the idea of women shaping their work and employment according to their individual ideals, career aspirations and work–life preferences. The analysis has revealed that the picture painted by the WDTOT articles presents the protagonists' happiness and fulfillment as the result of a neotraditional form of women's work. This neotraditional way to work eulogizes a dependent form of entrepreneurship and presents the restrictions of domestically confined work as empowering and liberating for women. Given the above outlined findings from critical studies, WDTOT's image of this neotraditional form of women's work is, therefore, doubly problematic. First, it propagates a way to work that is likely to re-inforce the notion of 'separate spheres', reinvigorate old gender divides and underpin inequalities in the workplace. Second, this image of a desirable work situation is presented as a realistic aim to those women who, given their education and access to financial capital, are most likely to contribute to an overcoming of old gender divides in the workplace: professional women. In so doing, it links to a wider contemporary debate about women who, as Stone (2007) describes, 'opt out' of professional careers in favor of domestic and predominantly unpaid roles. At present it may still be too early to say whether 'opting out' and women relocating from the public into the domestic sphere to undertake soft work will permanently change the gender balance in professional work. However, and if gender equality remains a societal aim, what is needed are critical discussions of the relationship of media images, such as those produced by WDTOT to women's actual work and career choices. This chapter is a contribution to kick-starting those discussions.

REFERENCES

Ballaster, R., Beetham, M., Frazer, E. & Hebron, S. 1991. *Women's worlds: Ideology, femininity and women's magazines*, London: Macmillan.
Bardwick, J.M. 1980. *Women in transition: How feminism, sexual liberation and the search for self-fulfillment have altered our lives*, Brighton: Harvester Press.
Beetham, M. 1996. *A magazine of her own? Domesticity and desire in the women's magazine, 1800–1914*, London: Routledge.

Bøgh, Fangel, A. & Aaløkke, S. 2007. Getting the job done: The impact of employees' conception of work on work-life balance. In *Work less, life more? Critical analysis of the work-life boundary*. Eds. C. Warhurst, D.R. Eikhof, & A. Haunschild. Basingstoke: Palgrave MacMillan.

Bryman, A. 2004. *Social research methods*, 2ⁿᵈ ed. Oxford: Oxford University Press.

Byerly, C.M. & Ross, K. 2006. *Women & media: A critical introduction*, Oxford: Blackwell Publishing.

Cassidy, M.F. 2001. Cyberspace meets domestic space: Personal computers, women's work, and the gendered territories of the family home. *Critical Studies in Media Communication* 18(1), 44–65

Crompton, R. & Lyonette, C. 2005. The new gender essentialism—domestic and family 'choices' and their relation to attitudes. *British Journal of Sociology* 56(4), 601–620.

Eikhof, D.R. & Summers, J. 2008. '"Women doing their own thing": Our picture of modern women at work?', paper presented at the 26th Annual *International Labour Process Conference*, Dublin.

Ferguson, M. 1983. *Forever feminine: Women's magazines and the cult of femininity*, London: Heinemann.

Festinger, L. 1954. A theory of social comparison processes. *Human Relations* 7(2), 117–40.

Flick, U. 1996. Stationen des qualitativen Forschungsprozesses. In *Handbuch qualitative sozialforschung*. Eds. U. Flick, E. von Kardoff, H. Keupp, L. von Rosenstiel & S. Wolff, München: BeltzPVU.

Friedman, B. 1963. *The feminine mystique*, New York: Dell.

Hakim, C. 1991. Grateful slaves and self-made women: Fact and fantasy in women's work orientations. *European Sociological Review* 7(2), 101–121.

Hakim, C. 2004. *Key issues in women's work: Female diversity and the polarisation of women's employment*, 2ⁿᵈ ed., London: Glasshouse Press.

Holmes, T. 2007. Mapping the magazine. *Journalism Studies* 8(4), 510–521.

Kylin, C. & Karlsson, J. Chr. 2007. Re-establishing boundaries in home-based telework. In *Work less, life more? Critical analysis of the work-life boundary*. Eds. C. Warhurst, D.R. Eikhof, & A. Haunschild , , Basingstoke: Palgrave MacMillan.

Mallett, S. 2004. Understanding home: A critical review of the literature. *The Sociological Review* 52(1), 62–89

Mayring, P. 2002. *Einführung in die qualitative sozialforschung*, 5th ed. Weinheim und Basel: Beltz.

McRae, S. 2003. Constraints and choices in mothers' employment careers: a consideration of Hakim's preference theory. *British Journal of Sociology* 54(3), 317–338.

Moeran, B. 2003. International Fashion Magazines, paper presented to the 6ᵗʰ *ESA Conference*, Murcia, 2003.

Neuman, W.L. 2000. *Social research methods. Qualitative and quantitative Approaches*, 4ᵗʰ ed. Needham Heights: Allyn & Bacon.

Park, S. 2005. The influence of presumed media influence on women's desire to be thin. *Communication Research* 32(5), 594–614.

Patterson, N. & Mavin, S. 2009. Women entrepreneurs: Jumping the corporate ship and gaining new wings. *International Small Business Journal* 27(2), 173–192

Powell, G.N. & Butterfield, D.A. 2003. Gender, gender identity, and aspiration to top management. *Women in Management Review* 18(1/2), 88–96

Robinson, T. & Callister, M. 2008. Body image of older adults in magazine advertisements: a content analysis of their body shape and portrayal. *Journal of Magazine and New Media Research* 10(1), 1–16.

Steward, B. 2000. Changing times: The meaning, measurement and use of time in teleworking. *Time and Society* 9(1), 57–74.

Stone, P. 2007. *Opting out? Why women really quit careers and head home*, Berkeley: University of California Press.

Sullivan, C. 2000. Space and the intersection of work and family in homeworking households. *Community, Work & Family* 3(2), 185–204.

Sullivan, C. & Lewis, S. 2001. Home-based telework, gender, and the synchronisation of work and family: perspectives of teleworkers and their co-residents. *Gender, Work and Organization* 8, 123–145.

Tremblay, D.G. 2002. Balancing work and family with telework? Organizational issues and challenges for women and managers', *Women in Management* 17(3/4), 157–170.

Warhurst, C., Eikhof, D.R. & Haunschild, A. (2008). Out of balance or just out of bounds? Mapping the relationship between work and life. In *Work less, Life More? Critical Analysis of the Work-life Boundary*. Eds. C. Warhurst, D.R. Eikhof, & A. Haunschild , Basingstoke: Palgrave MacMillan.

Winship, J. 1987. *Inside women's magazines*, London: Pandora.

Wykes, M. & Gunter, B. 2005. *The media and body image: If looks could kill*. London: Sage.

5 Flexible Work, Flexible Selves?
The Impact of Changing Work Practices on Identity

Carol Linehan

INTRODUCTION

We have become fascinated by the impetus to change. Organizations seek to restructure, delayer, and blur boundaries. Government policy exhorts us to move to a knowledge-based economy in the interests of national competitiveness. In the rush to remake organizations and economies, what impacts might such changes have on ourselves? This chapter seeks to engage in debates about the creation of, and consequences for, employee identity in relation to new forms of work and organization. Identity is a focus that resonates with both employers and employees. Employers hope for staff who will identify with the organization and, it is thought, be more committed, motivated and ultimately perform at a higher level. For employees, what you do, where you work, and under what conditions can be a defining feature of your identity.

Identity is a popular concept used to describe how a person can 'identify' with organizational aims. Simultaneously, it can describe difference or resistance. For example, how a different ethnic or gender identity can be subversive within normative organizational discourse. Of course, differences in understandings of identity range beyond definitions of the concept to concerns about the impacts of changing managerial and organizational practices on our identities, our characters and our selves. To address the debate about the impacts of new work practices on identity, I start by examining 'pro-identification' arguments in relation to workplace change, and move on to consider 'anti-identification' viewpoints, where commentators have pointed to the problems of identifying more closely with work/organizations. The chapter then attempts to bring a fresh perspective to this debate by drawing on Bakhtin's work on the self and subjectivity (1993, 1986). This perspective is illustrated with data drawn from one manager's (Hannah) dilemma as she attempts to construct an 'answerable' self in a precarious organizational environment. This example, it is hoped, will demonstrate the potential of some Bakhtinian concepts to add to our dialogs around the impact of new work practices on our selves. Conceptually, this chapter seeks to explore the issue of subjectivity, which is at the heart of the debates about the creation of, and consequences for, identity in new work contexts.

CHEERLEADERS FOR CHANGE:
PRO-IDENTIFICATION ARGUMENTS

A common theme in discussions of organizational change is that because of reduced bureaucratic controls and routines, there is a need for greater employee commitment and flexibility to successfully deliver organizational performance. Parry and Tranfield (1998 in Cooke, Hebson and Carroll, 2005, 179) noted that many UK companies' change programs were directed at increasing employee commitment. It appears that with reduced regulation and increased levels of flexibility the onus falls more and more on employees' discretionary efforts at work. Perhaps, following from the 'culture of excellence' movement (e.g., Peters and Waterman, 1982) of the 1980s, managers feel that the route to securing employees' discretionary efforts is through building employee identification with the organization and its aims. For example, literature on high-commitment or high-performance work systems has argued for 'bundles' of human resource management practices to deliver employee identification with organizational values, commitment and, consequently, performance (e.g., Appelbaum, Bailey & Berg, 2000; Huselid, 1995; Pfeffer, 1998).

The 'holy grail' is for employees to identify so completely with the organization that the need for external regulation and control is made redundant.

> Increasingly, an organization must reside in the heads and hearts of its members. Thus, in the absence of an externalised (sic) bureaucratic structure, it becomes more important to have an internalised (sic) cognitive structure of what an organization stands for and where it intends to go—in short, a clear sense of the organization's identity. (Albert, Ashforth and Dutton, 2000, 13).

This quote is fairly representative of a position that perceives (or, in some cases, advocates) the necessity of employees identifying with corporate objectives, aims and strategies. Thus the desired outcome of improved performance, particularly in a context of greater organizational flexibility, is often the driving force toward a focus on employee identity. But how is identity conceptualized in such approaches?

Accounts of identity in the managerialist tradition have tended toward assuming stable, coherent, internal accounts of who we are, based around an enlightenment view of self

> which is a view of the individual as a 'coherent, integrated, singular entity whose clear cut boundaries define its limits and separate it from other similarly bound entities'. (Sampson, 1993, 17 in Baxter, 2004, 2)

Based on such a view of identity, forms of language are used that portray identity as residing somehow "inside" the employee. These accounts lead to questions such as how employees identify with the organization or internalize dominant discourses around identity, e.g., following Social Identity Theory perspectives (see Ashforth & Mael, 1989; or Dutton, Dukerich & Harquail, 1994). For example, questions such as Dutton's as to "when a person's self-concept" may contain "the same attributes as those in the perceived organizational identity" (Dutton et al. 1994, 239).

In this vein, for example, Albert et al.'s (2000) conceptualization of identity seems to be one centered on stability and relative fixedness of identity categories, which are thrown into confusion by what is perceived to be an era of rapid change in organizational work practices. The identification process is thought to be complicated by the reduction of bureaucratic rules and structures and yet paradoxically more necessary than ever in the absence of such stable rules. Alvesson, Lee Ashcraft & Thomas (2008, 8) summarize the thrust of such work as

> how identity and identification may hold an important key to a variety of managerial outcomes and thus the potential to improve organizational effectiveness.

They categorize such work on identity as a 'functionalist/instrumental' approach. Perhaps it is not surprising then, that within such streams of work there are questions around how managers/managerialist discourses can attempt to regulate employees' identities. As Williams (2007) points out, whether this trajectory in workplace change is labeled as a shift from bureaucratic to postbureaucratic management, from 'hard' to 'soft' HRM, from 'low-road' to 'high-road' strategies, the common focus is near enough always on the transition from external to internal control that is, from compliance to commitment management strategies. The crux of such concerns seems to be with how individuals identify (or not) with the goals, and values, of organizations and how this identification may ultimately improve worker performance.

FOCUS ON 'YOU': SUGGESTED RESPONSES TO THE CHANGING WORK LANDSCAPE

Thus far, we have seen how changes in organizations and our consequent discourses about managing change (and those workers implicated in the changes) have assumed that employees who more closely identify with organizational aims and objectives are likely to perform better and need less supervision/regulation to do so. However, many writers in this area posit that through successful adaptation both employees and organizations stand to benefit. A mutual benefit model of change and greater identification, if you will.

The landscape of changing work practices including restructuring, delayering, greater use of alliances/networks, flexible specialization, etc., is presented as offering new opportunities to workers willing to embrace the changes. Many writers exhort individuals to think of themselves and their careers in an increasingly flexible manner and to focus on their employability. What follows should, I hope, give you a flavor of some of these approaches. For example, Handy (1995) encouraged workers to think of themselves as 'portfolio people', mobile and portable rather than fixed to a corporation. Drucker (1999, 100) stated that

> with opportunity comes responsibility. Companies today aren't managing their employees' careers; knowledge workers must, effectively, be their own chief executive officers. It's up to you to carve out your place, to know when to change course, and to keep yourself engaged and productive during a work life that may span some 50 years.

This is a common thread in such accounts—to think of yourself as an 'entrepreneur' or 'CEO' in charge of your own career. Indeed, there is work in this area that very much advocates that employees should work on their identity in terms of engaging in 'personal branding' to maintain employability. For example,

> Those of us—starting with me!—who want to survive The Flood will grasp the gauntlet of personal reinvention . . . before we become obsolete (Peters, 1999, 22 in Oswick & Robertson, 2007, 31).

As Oswick and Robertson (2007) point out in their interesting analysis of the explosion of such 'personal branding' literature, most start by inducing anxiety about the threat of job loss, and then, of course, attempt to alleviate this anxiety by selling a vision to the reader of how to create a successful 'brand you'. What could be dismissed as simply 'self-help' style airport literature does, however, seem to have some resonance with employers' views of employability. Brown and Hesketh (2004) in describing UK graduate employers' views of 'employability' talk of the 'new aesthetics' where perceptions of employability are based as much on certain attributes of self-presentation as they are on formal qualifications and evidence of skills.

Thus some common themes emerge in the pro-identification literature, which include the importance of employee identification to improve performance and navigate uncertainties in the more flexible work landscape, employees taking greater responsibility for their own careers, being more proactive about their learning and development, and thinking in terms of performance/contribution rather than longevity or loyalty, etc. The impact for employees is a move from an emphasis on a fairly static knowledge or skill set (know-how) to flexibility and continuous change (learn-how) to now in terms of the 'new aesthetics' of employability knowing 'who' will be attractive to employers (Brown & Hesketh, 2004). Underlying all of these recommendations is the message (sometimes explicitly stated) that there are no 'jobs for life' anymore, and that thinking in terms of a long-term relationship with one organization is outdated. Common in pro-identification accounts are terms like commitment, engagement, involvement, or more prosaically 'greater discretionary effort'. However, underpinning the calls for greater employee identification at work and the increasing focus on employability is the assumption that employment relationships have changed from the relational (aligned with traditional, long-service models) to the transactional (short-term alliances based on mutual benefit). There appears to be a potential double whammy here for employees—in moving from compliance to commitment models of employment, the employee needs to not only do their job but also **internalize,** and identify with, management/organizational goals while paradoxically the organization seeks to reduce its responsibility for individuals' careers and job security—this is now being **'externalized'** to individuals; it is now your responsibility to make sure you are employable. Which brings me to the other side of the story—the dark side of change.

THE DARK SIDE OF CHANGE: ANTI-IDENTIFICATION ARGUMENTS

The flip side of this story of committed, flexible, high-performing employees mastering organizational change is a much darker one. A story of employees being knowingly or unknowingly co-opted into intensifying their efforts for the good of the organization without their commitment being reciprocated by organizations (for example, in terms of job security, pensions and other benefits). If the old employment contract was with an organization, the new 'protean' contract is with the self and one's work (Hall, 1998). For example, Rubery, Earnshaw, Marchington, Cooke and Vincent (2002, 646) in discussing the psychological impacts of organizational change posit that:

> More unstable career patterns and the increased passing on of risk to employees are recognised (sic) to be creating problems for organizational commitment and for the trust relation at the heart of the psychological contract.

There appears to be a growing unease about the tension between the importance of employees' contribution to organizations, on the one hand, and their perceived vulnerabilities to change, flexibility, job insecurity etc., on the other (e.g., Victor & Stephens, 1994; Castells, 1996; Marchington, Grimshaw, Rubery & Willmott, 2005). For example, Brown and Hesketh

(2004) discuss the abandonment in newly flexible organizations of "the contract of loyalty for job security, along with the prospect of career progression for white collar workers" (18). Felstead and Jewson (1999, 3) see a pattern in new work practices that involves a push to lower wage costs "coercive management, intensified labor (sic) process, unsocial hours, and high rates of job turnover". Others see language about engaging the 'hearts and minds' of workers as cynical and manipulative attempts to intensify work. For example, Gorz (1999, 31, in Williams, 2007, 167) portrays moves encouraging workers to identify totally with the interests of the company leading them in effect to becoming 'the proud vassal' of the organization. Concerns about the move from compliance to commitment-based people management strategies are echoed in Rose's (1990) 'governing the soul', Thrift's (2005, 113) 'conviction capitalism' and Ciulla's (2000) claim that postbureaucratic management seeks to 'unlock the soul of the worker'. This trend seems to create what Bunting (2004) describes as 'willing slaves'.

Talk of identities being regulated inevitably calls out for a resistance movement (e.g., Elsbach, 1999; Collinson, 2003). The anti-identification camp portrays managerial initiatives and new work practices aimed at creating committed, perhaps even passionately engaged subjects as 'head-fixing'—an extension of control by stealth, brainwashing and increased regulation of employees. In this movement, authors such as Sennett (1998) or Wallulis (1998) would claim that new work practices and organizational forms are corrosive of character. Yet are such views overly nostalgic for a fleeting (if ever existent) time and place where stability and routine were a protection for employees, supportive of building character? Thompson and Warhurst (1998, 11) quite sensibly point out that "in this area (it is too easy) to confuse managerial ambition with outcome". That is, that there is a healthy dose of employee skepticism regarding the new managerial agenda of identified, committed selves (Gallie et al., 1998 in Cooke, Hebson & Carroll, 2005).

Here we approach the nub of the matter—it is difficult to unequivocally label any new work practice as supportive or exploitative of workers in an acontextual manner. First, the organizational changes wrought by any new work practice are constrained by the legal, social and economic contexts in which they occur. Second, work has not just economic and legal dimensions, but personal and psychological ones as well. While we can debate macro-level economic figures or employment trends, this is a hollow exercise without considering the impact of such changes on peoples' perceptions, and experiences, of work. For example, in times of high unemployment any job may seem like a 'good job'. Conversely, when conditions are better, then people may expect more from work than a basic pay packet. However, the point is that while labor market (and socioeconomic conditions) provide an important backdrop to peoples' perceptions of work, such conditions alone do not determine identity and experience at work. To understand the personal consequences of workplace change, we have to get inside the 'black box' of employee identity at work.

FROM IDENTIFICATION (PRO- OR ANTI-)
TO MULTIPLE IDENTITY POSSIBILITIES

It could be argued that both pro-identification and critical views alike take too limited a view of subjectivity. Both positions tend to portray identity as a relatively stable and enduring phenomenon. There is a risk with work that focuses on regulation for instrumental reasons or even resistance for that matter—that these represent an either/or account of identity that situates agency either with dominant managerial discourses or employee resistance (see Gabriel, 1999 for a critique).

What alternative view of identity can be offered? One which may help us not only to see worker subjectivity in a more complex way, but which may also illuminate more fully the complexity of workers' responses to new work practices. Identity is, of course, about who we are and who we are not, but it is never entirely fixed, nor solely individually defined. In the pro- and anti-identification camps, worker identity only seems to be important to the extent that workers identify with, or resist, organizational aims. Thus identity is framed only with respect to the degree of assimilation or resistance to organizational aims\managerial goals. However, the wealth of work on various aspects of worker identity calls this dichotomy into question. For example, one can identify (or disidentify, or be somewhere in between) with elements of task, role, coworkers, team, client, customer, etc. For example, studies of more highly skilled workers tend to show that such individuals identify more with their occupation or professional group rather than employing organization (Cooke, Hebson & Carroll, 2005). Recent work on organizational identity (e.g., Gallie, White, Cheng & Tomlinson, 1998; Sveningsson & Alvesson, 2003) has recognized that workers display multiple identities and that these shift over time and in specific contexts. Indeed, many would suggest that rather than focus upon the concept of 'identity', which has connotations of being one thing rather than another, we should think in terms of 'identifications'. This shift in language moves us from an entitative (an identity) to a more processual view of identifications.

BUILDING A SENSE OF 'IDENTITY':
IDENTIFICATIONS AND DIS-IDENTIFICATIONS

In essence, my work joins those who approach identity "as a temporary, context-sensitive and evolving set of constructions rather than a fixed, abiding essence" (Alvesson, Lee Ashcraft and Thomas, 2008, 6; or see Alvesson & Willmott, 2002). Part of my aim in this chapter is to build on such work by exploring themes in Bakhtin's writing (1986, 1993) that may help us to develop even richer accounts of identity work. Bakhtin's writing has influenced work in the social constructionist (Gergen, 1989;

Shotter, 1989, 1993) stream and cultural theory (Reckwitz, 2002). The key value of social constructionist work on identity is to recast situated identity work as a creative space from which multiple possibilities can emerge. There is, however, a particular sense of 'being' that is missing from social constructionist accounts of the emergence of self. Discursive events are not just sites of possibility, but also acts in which multiple centers of emotional/valuational/cognitive consciousnesses meet. It is the person's situated identity work that is the focus of interest, and how she or he takes up, rejects and interweaves life history with situated discursive possibilities. Bakhtin's (1993) writing on the 'novelistic self' is relevant here. His contribution is to present a dialogic, agentive account of our participation in discursive interaction. There is some resonance between Bakhtin's position and the social constructionist focus on the human agent in the social process of creating and using meaning within social relationships. However, relating his writing to contemporary studies of identity would entail a theoretical focus on the acting/thinking/feeling person in relationship with others (rather than, for example, identifying 'dominant discourses). The 'person' may be constituted by discourses, yet she is still capable of critical historical reflection and is able to exercise some choice with respect to the discourses and practices she takes up in ongoing interactions. The following section draws on empirical examples (both from my own research and that of others) of situated identity work to illustrate the potential of some Bakhtinian concepts to add to our understanding of identification processes. In these accounts the person is portrayed not as a passive consumer of dominant discourses or a militant hero eschewing all managerial machinations, but a feeling/thinking/acting person struggling with day-to-day experiences.

CONFLICTING CENTERS OF VALUE

This section seeks to illustrate the creative, dialogic space of identity work with reference to some empirical studies of workers' identities. I begin with a short example where Ainsworth and Hardy (2004) discuss a study of a 'Big Six' accountancy firm by Covaleski, Dirsmith, Heian and Samuel (1998) in which the researchers explored two management techniques, mentoring and management by objectives, and how these relate to the development of differing managerial identities for novice accountants, the 'autonomous accounting professional' and the 'business person'.

> the existence of incomplete and contradictory discourses provides employees with opportunities to 'counter-identify (sic) or dis-identify(sic) with managerial formulations of their identity' (Holmer-Nadesan, 1999, 50) regardless of how much 'identity regulation' in which managers engage (Ainsworth & Hardy, 2004, 166).

The novice accountants could creatively respond to differing centers of value in their discursive domain and in so doing construct differing identities. Drawing on work like Covaleski et al. (1998) and Currie and Brown (2003), we can see contestation and struggle occurring in identity work—not because 'an organizational identity' is being resisted in some either/or fashion—but because there are many fractured, incomplete and contested narratives, which can be taken up in enactments of self.

Sims (2003) addresses just such tensions in emergent identities with his account of middle managers. Given the precarious, and possibly contested, position of middle managers, Sims examines the difficulties faced by people in fashioning a coherent narrative or sense of self in such circumstances. Sims highlights how the middle managers' narratives are especially vulnerable to attack by subordinates, to competitive undermining from peers, and to lack of importance by seniors. Even ultimately falling foul of their own 'bullshit detectors' to seem unreal, inauthentic and insincere to themselves (see also Costas & Fleming, 2009). The novice accountants in Covaleski et al.'s (1998) work could draw on competing discourses and yet these different discourses appeared legitimate to participants. In contrast, the manager in Sims' work faces a more difficult challenge, she is in transition—her identity work is contested through competing forces and values.

I will move on now to give an example from a study of health service managers' accounts of their evolving identities in a context of public sector change and the dilemmas they face in creating a coherent account of what it means to be a manager in that setting.[1] Time and again their stories resonate with the kind of middle management dilemmas presented in Sims' work. This group (of health service managers) are particularly interesting as at a 'middle-management' level they seem to have difficulties reconciling competing discourses that they are supposed to represent. My approach here will be to choose one story, recounted by a manager, one in which 'density and concreteness' to draw on a Bakhtinian perspective (Lacasa, del Castillo & Garcia-Varela 2005) can be found.

THE MANAGER'S DILEMMA

The manager in question 'Hannah', is a director of public health nursing (DPHN) in one region of the health service. In that position she reports to the general manager of the region and, in turn, a number of assistant directors of public health nursing report to her. The job description for a DPHN includes

> . . . to achieve service goals in the area of community nursing. The position requires a strategic approach to the development of services and structures, embracing continuous quality improvement and the management of change necessary to achieve organizational objectives.

As part of the program of change and modernization in the public service discourses of new public management have taken hold, reflected in the language of 'strategic approach' or 'management of change' above. Thus, much like the accountants in Covaleski's et al. (1998) research, in crafting identities a manager in the health service can draw on

- Clinical discourses relating to specialist knowledge and expertise, patient care and so on, and/or
- Management discourses relating to strategy, service plans, budgetary responsibility, etc.

However, while we can identify such competing discourses—for example, in recent health service documents, such as strategic statements, or job descriptions (as above)—stopping there would not allow us to engage with or understand the sense of struggle in identity work for some individuals, like Hannah, in this setting. To understand her sense of vulnerability in her identity work, I draw on a story she told me of a dilemma she was faced with.

As part of her set of responsibilities, Hannah oversees the provision of a home help service to thousands of elderly people in her region. Her duties include managing the budget allocated to this service, attempting to improve the quality and flexibility of the service, and liaising with the assistant directors of nursing who oversee the home help organizers and, in turn, the hundreds of frontline home help workers. She recounted to me how recently she had been told in no uncertain terms by her senior manager that:

> when the service had exceeded the budget allocated to it that this would be redressed without any reflection on the senior management department.

Reflections, such as politicians' letters, phone calls from irate clients who now would have a cutback in their level of care and so on, were received. In other words, she was expected to deal with the budget overrun in the home help service as covertly as possible, so as not to create a fuss among frontline staff and service users.

> In addition, there are also high expectations and demands on staff to provide this service to clients who do not appreciate that there have to be any restrictions in the service.

In simple terms, Hannah experiences both upward and downward pressure relating to this budget. Her senior manager wants her to remain within budget and, at times, cut back the budget and associated service (without of course this reflecting negatively on him). Simultaneously, there is increasing demand from service users and frontline staff. Users and staff demands are partly because of increasing dependency and need among some existing elderly clients. Overall, increasing numbers of elderly people require the service and also a take up by frontline staff of the language of 'quality of care', 'continuous improvement of service' etc., which are peppered throughout any official communications to staff.

> The key issue here is the competing priorities of both groups, the senior manager does not want any fallout from a reduction in service because of the need to amend the budget overrun. Frontline staff on the other hand is (sic) unhappy at what they perceive as a reduction of service to vulnerable clients and they do not want to be in the position of reducing service to any client.

As she spoke, Hannah's sense of frustration, confusion and anger were palpable. She really struggles with the dilemma of how to respond to such pressures and competing demands. Also by opting for a given course of action, she realizes that this defines her role as manager and her self in that setting. Her struggle seems to me to be more complex than simply a matter of choosing between (or identifying with) discourses, such as the nurse as 'professional carer' or manager as 'efficient budget controller'. Hannah does not frame her dilemma as being between coolly adopting a ruthless budget-cutting stance nor resisting cuts with recourse to a 'professional' concern with care. Hannah's identity work is not that simple. She recognizes that there are many competing demands and she attempts to 'answer' those demands both in her actions and to herself—how will her course of action come to form part of her ongoing narrative of identity?

> The real fallout from this . . . related to the issue of trust specifically, belief in my ability to redress this difficulty and trust that the reality of demand on the service in question was real . . . I felt that there was a lack of trust by both the senior manager and by frontline staff in my ability to meet the needs of either party albeit this was never expressed in any manifest form.

Hannah's talk of 'trust' reveals a sense of vulnerability on her part—arising from a sense that her story of service demands is not believed or seen as legitimate by her senior manager and that frontline staff also do not trust her to meet either their needs or those of service users. Much like Sims' (2003) participants, this manager is in the invidious position of having to make sense for many audiences (including herself), none of whom seem to believe in the legitimacy of her claims and position.

Hannah's story, for me, illustrates that an account of identities being regulated or resisted in a dichotomous fashion is not sufficient to capture the struggle in her identity work. Nor is a social-constructionist account, with a focus on multiple discursive possibilities and co-constructed realities sufficient. It does not adequately capture the sense of Hannah's need to make sense of this situation in a way that she deems 'answerable' both to herself and others. That is where the Bakhtinian concern with answerability, with what matters to thinking/feeling persons in their search for meaning, is useful to give a rich and vivid account of Hannah's identity struggles.

> Obligation and responsibility arise in and respond to each particular situation in a way that cannot be adequately generalized without depriving it of its very essence." (Lacasa et al. 2005, 299).

Bakhtin's (1993) work is directly concerned with what it means to be a moral agent responsive to discourses that reflect differing centers of value. The difficulties and vulnerabilities faced by Hannah (and other middle managers) bring into sharp focus the struggle of the self attempting to forge coherent identities in a space "defined by distinctions of worth" (Taylor, 1985) or 'multiple centers of value' from a Bakhtinian perspective. For if this were just a space where 'anything goes' (without the weightiness of 'what matters' to us) then surely the middle manager would benefit from their ambiguous positioning, he or she could play with different discourses and narrative possibilities. Yet this space is not one of playful possibilities, but one of potential risk and vulnerability. Bakhtin wrote of the 'nonalibi in being' that is, there is no escaping our own responsibility for ourselves even though there is a sense of openness and unfinalizability to any self (see also Sullivan and McCarthy, 2004). Drawing on concepts such as answerability and nonalibi in being allows us to explore the "actually experienced fact of my actual participation" (Bakhtin, 1993, 49) and also to give voice to what can be experienced as heartfelt dilemmas for the person, such as Hannah.

DISCUSSION

Bakhtin's ideas bring to our understanding of identity a number of rich possibilities. First, is the sense of illuminating that moment of interaction/dialog as the space in which we come to be. Second, that this coming to be is ongoing and is never complete without the other (real or imagined). What is also valuable is the sense that what is coming to be is an acting/feeling person for whom things matter. Constructionist, fluid or processual accounts of identity have sometimes been criticized on the grounds that within such terms 'anything goes', and that such positions necessarily result in moral relativism. In ontologic terms, it does follow that if we deem our social realities to be constructions then it is possible that anything could be created, changed, emerge, etc. Yet recognizing that anything is possible (in an ontologic/philosophical sense) does not preclude the lived experience of what may matter to us at a given moment. Nor does it preclude the sense that some realities and identities will be deemed more legitimate and others more contested because of the socially, historically and culturally situated nature of interactions. Interactions involve multiple centers of value some of which unproblematically interweave with our life narratives, some of which we struggle with.

Highlighting the moral status or legitimacy of identity narratives resonates with Bakhtin's ideas of relations of value and possibly also Sennett's (1998) ideas about self/character and value and the difficulties creating a stable narrative within today's discourse of change and impermanence. I brought together the themes of identity, existing in a space defined by distinctions of worth, and notions of multiple centers of value, because for me these themes seem to resonate very strongly with the way managers talk of their lived experiences—experiences of uncertainty, fragmentation and of being torn between competing possibilities for enacting their identities. If workers were simply 'on message' with a managerialist identity or were actively resisting this, then would there be the same sense of struggle that emerges from stories of their identities? To take this point further, in any moment of experience, we cannot 'excuse' ourselves from this process of coming to be. As McCarthy, Sullivan and Wright (2006) point out

> . . . it is through the uniqueness of our feelings and moral valuing that we occupy an irreplaceable place in being or a 'non-alibi' in being (Bakhtin, 1993). (429)

Our being or uniqueness is not in spite of our participative existence but is enacted and disclosed through that very participation. A dialogic account of the individual in interaction does not have to 'distance' the individual from social conditions in the organization, but rather presents the individual in an ongoing process of responding to social conditions, and trying to do so in an 'answerable' manner.

CONCLUSION

Without doubt, new ways of organizing work and work practices impact on our identities. Identity continues to offer a useful lens to interpret, and reflect on, the experiences of individuals and their lives in organizations—one that resonates for workers, management and academics. I believe it is useful, indeed vital, to continue our debates about the impacts of new work practices on organizations, management practices and individuals. Impacts can include changes in labor market trends, material outcomes, performance in organization, etc. However, if we begin to discuss impacts in terms of worker commitment, engagement, or resistance (whether from a pro- or anti-identification perspective), then this raises the issue of worker subjectivity. Both pro- and anti-positions fundamentally seem to focus on the instrumental outcomes associated with identity positions, for example, to what degree workers' increased commitment and identification contributes to driving up profitability and productivity (and, thus on the anti-identification side work intensification becomes evidence for greater worker exploitation). As I have argued earlier, both views seem to take quite a limited view of subjectivity. This chapter draws on more contemporary ideas about identifications to explore the multiple identity possibilities that arise in relation to any work practice. The nature of work may indeed be changing for managers and workers, but what is crucial is how workers make sense of these changes and their 'project of self' (to borrow a term from Grey, 1994) in relation to such changes.

NOTES

1. The empirical work drawn on here stems from a much larger study of a particular region's 'home help' service within the Irish Health Service. The service provides assistance with domestic chores and, where appropriate, personal and sometimes medical care, to support elderly people remaining in their own homes. The research commenced in 2002 and was initially focused on gaining an understanding of frontline home help staff views on issues of flexibility, work–life balance and communication issues in a changing service context. At that time the researcher met with 80 'frontline' home help workers from across four locations in the region. In addition four group interviews were conducted with those at supervisory and management levels (public health nurses, home help organisers and assistant directors). Over time, I became increasingly interested in the stories of the middle managers in this setting.

REFERENCES

Ainsworth, S. & Hardy, C. 2004. Discourse and identities. In *The Sage handbook of organizational discourse*. Eds. D. Grant, C. Hardy, C. Oswick and L. Putnam. London: Sage. 153–174.

Albert, S., Ashforth, B. & Dutton, J. 2000. Organizational identity and identification: Charting new waters and building new bridges. *Academy of Management Review* 25(1), 13–17.

Alvesson, M. & Willmott, H. 2002. Identity regulation as organizational control: Producing the appropriate individual. *Journal of Management Studies* 39(5), 619–644.

Alvesson, M, Lee Ashcraft, K. & Thomas, R. 2008. Identity matters: Reflections on the construction of identity scholarship in organization studies. *Organization* 15(1), 5–28.

Appelbaum, E., Bailey, T. & Berg, P. 2000. *Manufacturing advantage: Why high performance systems pay off.* Ithaca: ILR Press.

Ashforth, B. & Mael, F. 1989. Social identity theory and the organization. *Academy of Management Review* 14(1), 20–39.

Bakhtin, M.M. 1986. *Speech genres and other late essays.* Eds. McGee, V. (Tr.) Emerson, C. & Holquist, M. . Austin: University of Texas Press.

Bakhtin, M.M. 1993. *Toward a philosophy of the act*. Eds. Liapunov, V. (Tr.) Lianpunov, V. & Holquist, M. Austin: University of Texas Press.

Baxter, L.A. 2004. Relationships as dialogues. *Personal Relationships* 11(1), 1–22.

Brown, P. & Hesketh, A. 2004. *The mismanagement of talent: Employability and jobs in the knowledge economy*. Oxford: Oxford University Press

Bunting, M. 2004. *Willing slaves: How the overwork culture is ruling our lives*. London: Harper Collins.

Castells, M. 1996. *The rise of the network society*. Oxford: Blackwell.

Ciulla, J. 2000. *The working life: The promise and betrayal of modern work*. London: Random House.

Collinson, D. 2003. Identities and insecurities: Selves at work. *Organization* 10(3), 527–547.

Cooke, F.L, Hebson, G. & Carroll, M. 2005. Commitment and identity across organizational boundaries. In *Fragmenting work: Blurring organizational boundaries and disordering hierarchies*. Eds. M. Marchington, D. Grimshaw, J. Rubery and H. Willmott Oxford: Oxford University Press, 179–198.

Costas, J. & Fleming, P. 2009. Beyond dis-identification: A discursive approach to self-alienation in contemporary organizations. *Human Relations* 62(3), 353–378.

Covaleski, M.A., Dirsmith, M.W., Heian, J.B. & Samuel, S. 1998. The calculated and the avowed: Techniques of discipline and stuggles over identity in Big Six public accounting firms. *Administrative Science Quarterly* 43(2), 293–327.

Currie, G. & Brown, A.D. 2003. A narratological approach to understanding processes of organizing in a UK hospital. *Human Relations* 56(5), 563–586.

Drucker, P. 1999. *Management challenges for the 21st century*. New York: Harper Collins.

Dutton, J.E., Dukerich, J.M. & Harquail, C.V. 1994. Organizational images and member identification. *Administrative Science Quarterly* 39(2), 239–263.

Elsbach, K.D. 1999. An expanded model of organizational identification. *Research in Organizational Behaviour* 21, 163–200.

Felstead, A. & Jewson, N. Eds. 1999. *Global trends in flexible labour*. Hampshire: MacMillan.

Gabriel, Y. 1999. Beyond happy families: A critical re-evaluation of the control-resistance-identity triangle. *Human Relations* 52(2), 179–203.

Gallie, D., White, M., Cheng, Y. & Tomlinson, M. 1998. *Restructuring the employment relationship*. Oxford: Clarendon Press.

Gergen, K. 1989. Warranting voice and the elaboration of self. In *Texts of identity*. Eds. J. Shotter & K. Gergen London: Sage, 70–81.

Grey, R. 1994. Career as a project of the self and labour process discipline. *Sociology*, 28(2), 479–498.

Hall, D.T. 1998. The new protean career contract: Helping organizations and employees adapt. *Organizational Dynamics* 26(3), 22–37.

Handy, C. 1995. *The empty raincoat: Making sense of the future*. London: Arrow.

Harre, R. 1998. *The singular self*. London:Sage.

Huselid, M. 1995. The impact of human resource management practices on turnover, productivity and corporate financial performance. *Academy of Management Journal* 38(3), 635–672.

Lacasa, P., del Castillo, H. & Garcia-Varela, A.B. 2005. A Bakhtinian approach to identity in the context of institutional practices. *Culture and Psychology* 11(3), 287–308.

Marchington, M., Grimshaw, D., Rubery, J. & Willmott, H. Eds. 2005. *Fragmenting work: Blurring organizational boundaries and disordering hierarchies*. Oxford: Oxford University Press.

McCarthy, J., Sullivan, P. & Wright, P. 2006. Culture, personal experience and agency. *British Journal of Social Psychology* 45(2), 421--439.

Oswick, C. & Robertson, M. 2007. Personal branding and identity: A textual analysis. In *Exploring identity: Concepts and methods.* Eds. A. Pullen, N. Beech & D. Sims Hampshire: Palgrave MacMillan, 26–43.

Peters, T. & Waterman, R. 1982. *In search of excellence.* New York: Warner communications.

Pfeffer, J. 1998. *The human equation: Building profits by putting people first.* Boston: Harvard Business School Press.

Reckwitz, A. 2002. Toward a theory of social practices: A development in culturalist theorizing. *European Journal of Social Theory* 5(2), 243–263.

Rose, N. 1990. *Governing the soul: The shaping of the private self.* London: Routledge.

Rubery, J., Earnshaw, J., Marchington, M., Cooke, F. & Vincent, S. 2002. Changing organizational forms and the employment relationship. *Journal of Management Studies* 39(5), 645–672.

Sennett, R. 1998. *The corrosion of character: The personal consequences of work in the new capitalism.* New York: W.W.Norton & Co.

Shotter, J. (1989). Social accountability and the social construction of 'you'. In *Texts of identity.* Eds. J. Shotter & K. Gergen. London: Sage, 133–151.

Shotter, J. 1993. *Conversational realities: Constructing life through language.* London: Sage.

Sims, D. 2003. Between the millstones: A narrative account of the vulnerability of middle managers' storying. *Human Relations* 56(10), 1195–1211.

Sullivan, P. & McCarthy, J. 2004. Toward a dialogical perspective on agency. *Journal for the Theory of Social Behaviour* 34(3), 291–309.

Sveningsson, S. & Alvesson, M. 2003. Managing managerial identities: Organizational fragmentation, discourse and identity struggle. *Human Relations* 56(10), 1163–1193.

Taylor, C. 1985. *Human agency and language.* Cambridge: Cambridge University Press.

Thrift, N.J. 2005. *Knowing capitalism.* London: Sage.

Victor, B. & Stephens, C. 1994. The dark side of new organizational forms: An editorial essay. *Organization Science* 5(4), 479–482.

Wallulis, J. 1998. *The new insecurity.* Albany: State University of New York Press.

Williams, C. 2007. *Rethinking the future of work: Directions and visions.* Hampshire: Palgrave MacMillan.

6 New Working Practices
Identity, Agency and the Emotional Experience of Remote Working

Jennifer Wilkinson and Carol Jarvis

INTRODUCTION

Within management studies remote working is becoming an increasingly popular topic and research within the area has grown over the last 10 years. However, with a few exceptions (cf. Fineman, Maitlis and Panteli, 2007; Tietze and Musson, 2002a), little has been specifically written about the emotional experience of remote working from the perspective of remote workers. This chapter develops critical debate about the emotional experience of remote workers by exploring the interplay between identity and perceptions of agency and the ensuing emotions. However, in assembling such substantive themes of identity, agency and emotions in the context of remote working, which itself has a breadth and depth of writing, it is impossible to give a comprehensive account of the literature within one relatively short chapter. Rather, our aim is to introduce the practice of remote working and the themes of identity, agency and emotions before outlining the approach to research; we then explore the interplay between identity, perceptions of agency and emotions. In the context of this chapter, the notion of agency is explored in relation to how remote workers perceive their level of choice in whether, and/or when, to work remotely. In conclusion, we argue that, while there are tensions in bringing together such substantive themes in the remote working context, the unveiling of the apparent interplay between them contributes to our understanding of the way in which this working practice is experienced, and, more specifically, this unveiling offers a platform from which to try to improve the experience of work for those concerned.

LITERATURE REVIEW

Remote working is defined and interpreted in a number of different ways that are both comparable and disparate. Terms such as teleworking (e.g., Daniels, Lamond & Standen, 2001; Tietze, 2002; Baruch, 2001; DiMartino & Wirth, 1990), virtual office (e.g., Helms & Raiszadeh, 2002), virtual working (e.g., Jackson, 1999), telecommuting (e.g., Tomaskovic-Devey, &

Risman, 1993), home working (e.g., Baruch & Nicholson, 1997; Tietze & Musson, 2002b) and location independence working (e.g., Shapiro, 2000), are used, often interchangeably, to depict a way of working that is carried out outside of the office of the employing organization. As such, those who explore this type of working practice are ultimately discussing a pattern of work that does not take place solely in one building of the organization. While acknowledging that 'hot-deskers' may have similar experiences, we are not exploring 'hot desking' (Warren, 2006), where employees are solely located in one organization building, yet do not have a permanent desk. For the type of working practice we are looking at, which we have labeled 'remote working', much of the literature suggests that we rely on three core concepts: organization, location and technology (e.g., DiMartino & Wirth, 1990; Baruch, 2001; Tietze, 2002). Daniels et al. (2001) propose that a fourth core concept, knowledge, can be added as it identifies a specific type/level of cerebral work that is undertaken. Thus, understanding the working practice we are exploring as being one which contains some (if not all) work being undertaken outside the organization's physical parameters raises questions as to how remote workers know they work for an organization, bringing to the fore issues of identity.

Identity, Agency and Emotions

As with remote working, one of the challenges of research into identity is its ubiquitous nature, with it being prevalent within and across a multitude of disciplines and philosophies, each of which attribute their own meaning to it. Thompson (1995, 674) defines identity as "the quality or condition of being a specified person or thing" and as unique to individuals, while Knights and Willmott (1999, 19) state that "the identity of an individual (or a group) is dependent on how s/he is regarded and represented by others," suggesting not only that identity is unique, but that it is also borne out of comparative interaction with others. Thus, who we are—our sense of self—is a product of the society and culture with which we engage (McLeod, 1994, 1999), where identity is not fixed but rather constantly evolving (Hall, 2000). As such, changing the way work is organized requires remote workers to adapt to the 'culture' and 'society' with which they engage. Thus, for remote workers, identity is under continual (re)construction as they adapt to the multiple cultures, such as home and work, which previously simply would not have infringed on each other in the way that a remote working practice physically enables. As such, identity has started to emerge as 'a multi-dimensional and socially constructed phenomena' (Richardson, 2006, 479). This leads us to consider, how, in their removed physical state, remote workers identify with their organization. Hall, Schneider and Nygren (1970) suggest that at an organizational level identity is achieved through consistency in personal and organization orientation. Thus, when remote workers compare their own orientation to that of the organization and conclude they 'want the same things' (have consistent orientation), it can be argued the remote worker perceives s/he has choice in "producing, understanding and transforming the social and natural world" (Knights & Willmott, 1999, 163) of the organization. Thus, in understanding identity as being centered on the perception of choice, it is possible to argue that identity, through the medium of choice, is about power:

> . . . is the key to understanding the ways that individuals come to view themselves, and their relation to their work and work relationships (Dick & Hyde, 2006, 550).

Indeed, the idea that '[p]ower is understood to transform human beings into subjects that identify with the ideas and practices through which power is exercised' (Knights & Wilmott, 1999, p.31) suggests that power and identity are interrelated concepts. Moreover, it can be argued that power is also central to agency, a notion presented by Giddens (1984, 9) when he states that:

> . . . agency refers not to the intentions people have in doing things but to their capability of doing those things in the first place (which is why agency implies power . . .).

He further states:

> Action depends upon the capability of the individual to 'make a difference' to a pre-existing state of affairs or course of events. [where] An agent ceases to be such if he or she loses the capability to 'make a difference', that is, to exercise some sort of power (Giddens, 1984, 141f).

What we are suggesting here is that a remote worker's identity centers on the conscious perception that they have a choice in 'producing, understanding and transforming the social and natural world' (Knights & Willmott, 1999, p.163) of the organization. Hence, their identity also centers on them being aware that they have the power to engender this change (Dick & Hyde, 2006). This capability of the individual remote worker to perceive that they have the ability to make a difference (Giddens, 1984) creates a sense of agency borne out of choice in action. Thus, for the remote worker, identity is about the perception of choice, which is intimately bound up with issues of power and which, in turn, implicates agency.

Highlighting this interplay between identity and agency leads us to question how this manifests itself for the remote worker. Literature (cf. Sanchez-Burks & Huy, 2009; Seo, Taylor & Hill, 2007) along with our own experiences and the experiences of remote workers, tell us that undertaking identity work, and thus perceptions of agency, elicit emotional responses. However, while the emotional experience is acknowledged within the remote working literature, it is often not its focus. During data analysis, we became aware that participants often made references to emotions that appear to intermingle with notions of agency. Thus, in understanding organizations as emotional arenas (Fineman, 2000), where:

> Workaday frustrations and passions—boredom, envy, fear, love, anger, guilt, infatuation, embarrassment, nostalgia, anxiety—are deeply woven into the way roles are enacted and learned, power is exercised, trust is held, commitment formed and decisions made. Emotions are not simply excisable from these, and many other, organizational processes; they both characterize and inform them (Fineman, 2000, 1).

Giddens (1984, 9) notion that 'agency refers not to the intentions people have in doing things but to their capability of doing those things in the first place' suggests that the everyday emotions experienced by remote workers are an interplay with their perceptions of agency and the identity work they undertake. In the following section, we outline how we explored this interplay through a consideration of our participant's emotional experience of remote working.

RESEARCH APPROACH

Here we explore and provide a depth of insight into the everyday emotions experienced by remote workers and their interplay with how participants perceive their level of choice in whether, and/or when, to work remotely (i.e., different perceptions of agency). During interviews, techniques from within the information-centered approach of Clean Language (Grove & Panzer, 1989) were used so as to provide the space for participants to voice the 'everydayness' of their experiences.

Purposive sampling (Bryman, 2008) was used to select participants and 15 individuals who consider themselves remote workers volunteered to participate. Of these, 9 were male and 6 were female. Five were employed within the public sector in specialist/professional roles. The remaining 10 worked within the private sector, where 8 had sales-based roles and 2 had technology-based roles.

Participants attached a range of meaning to remote working. For all it meant working at home at some point, coupled with working in a main office of the organization and/or client sites. The frequency with which remote working was undertaken ranged from twice a month (3 participants), to three times a week (2 participants), to 'all day, every day' (10 participants).

In trying to understand the experience of remote working from the participant's own frame of reference, we use interviews, mind maps and diaries. It was stated at the beginning of each interview that the research was interested in:

- 'The *emotional* experiences of remote working.'

Using a semistructured approach, the interview began with:

- 'Tell me about your experiences of remote working'.

Three additional questions were then asked at different stages of the interview:

- 'How do you know that you belong/are a member of the organization?'
- 'Is there anything you can tell me about trust?'
- 'Is there anything you can tell me about knowledge sharing?'

During interviews, notes were taken in the form of a simple mind map (Buzan, 1995; Mento, Martinelli & Jones, 1999) that captured emergent themes; these were developed collaboratively (Reason, 1999) with the participant post-interview. Template analysis and thematic coding (King, 2004) was undertaken in order to identify patterns within the data. In the following sections, we report on our findings and discuss the implications of these for both theory and practice.

FINDINGS AND DISCUSSION

Building on the discussion developed in the previous literature review section, here we present our findings exploring the interplay between identity, agency and the everyday emotions of the remote worker. First, we explore how remote workers undertake identity work and the alternative social cues they seek (cf. Fineman et al., 2007; Hall, 1996). Here we consider the interplay between remote workers' perception of agency and how they undertake identity work through alternative social cues. We then investigate the emotions experienced by remote workers and the interplay of these emotions with perceptions of agency. Finally, within this section we draw together the interplay between perceptions of agency, identity work and expressed emotions for remote workers.

Identity Work and Agency

All participants in our research, to varying degrees, work remotely, and thus have to cope with the less frequent physical presence of their colleagues and with not seeing them regularly. The removal of visual social cues and organization stimuli, paraphernalia or artefacts (Schein, 1985) means that remote workers have to speculate about what colleagues are doing and be more proactive in generating, or uncovering, organizational stimuli than those who work in a more traditional office environment. Illustrating our thematic nomenclature, the following interview extract typifies responses from participants:

Duncan: How does anybody know that they work for an organization? Good question. Because you are mentioned in dispatches, because you are required to be involved; your businesses interacts with you. They pay you, so that must mean something [TANGIBLE SIGNS]. But as general rule you can become pretty anonymous [VISIBILITY]. But I guess it's just through interactivity really, you know you work for a business because people [SOCIAL RELATIONSHIPS] have got demands on you.

For remote workers, losing their 'social barometer' can leave them "feeling unsure of themselves and less confident in their abilities" (Mann, Varey & Button, 2000, 679). The above quote highlights three alternative social cues that emerged from the data: tangible signs, social relationships and visibility that remote workers engage with to undertake identity work.

The sense of belonging created through the trappings of organization enable the remote worker to identify with their employing organization. Participants explicitly referred to cues such as:

Pay:

Neil: when I get paid every month that helps me to . . . recall that I do work for a company.

Organization logos/branded material:

Sadie: I definitely do feel a part of my own organization . . . we are using sales materials . . . so that is always reinforcing the brand name.

Office furniture/ location:

Diane: I have my own little office . . . you have to have your space, that has your poster, and has your calendar, and all your bits and pieces and all your files in that room and that is where you shut the door at the end of the day.

We have grouped these alternative social cues together and labeled them *Tangible Signs*. Here the identity work undertaken by remote workers is to seek out organizational artefacts (or signs), which have some kinesthetic, or tangible, value (i.e., they can be physically touched or seen by the remote worker). Thus, the remote worker has physical proof of their belonging to an organization, which reinforces their organizational existence.

The second grouping of alternative social cues that enabled remote workers to identify with their employing organization we have labeled *Social Relationships*. These are illustrated through references to the various people in their support network, such as:

Friends/ family members:

Elliott: Where I live, it's a little cul-de-sac; every other house is working from home. It's great, the guy opposite will pick up my post . . . the lady next door (she's from marketing) so she'll pick up the post. So it's almost the old office network of going in and seeing people in the city center . . . in a 'desperate housewives' type cul-de-sac situation.

Intraorganizational relationships:

Sally: I am still working with other people, I am working as part of a team and I am actually, particularly with this one but also the other one, I am working with people who are in the organization. I am not working with people outside of the organization. I would think that that would make a [difference], you would much more strongly identify

Interorganizational relationships:

Kieran: I now find myself almost adopting different [client] firms as my people who I'll go to and talk to when things aren't going so well in [the organization] and so there has been a small shift in allegiance from my employer to my [clients].

Thus, for remote workers, social relationships are another alternative social cue that appear to be a necessity of identity and which involve 'a securing of self through an instrumental participation in social relations' (Knights and Willmott, 1985, 27).

The final grouping of alternative social cues we have labeled *Visibility*. This refers to how participants highlighted contact with intraorganizational members as a way they create visibility so as to identify with their employing organization:

Marie: I've been around the HR team for about 5 years now . . . I couldn't do [remote working] on a permanent basis because . . . people need to know my face and know who you are . . . If you went down that road [remote working] they would tend to know you by name rather than that this is what she looks like . . . so I think that you do need to have some visibility there.

In the above, Marie clearly links intraorganizational contact and visibility as she considers how she knows she is part of the organization. Indicating that intraorganizational visibility is an alternative social cue remote workers use to reestablish their 'social barometer' (Mann et al., 2000).

The above suggests that in undertaking identity work, remote workers seek alternative social cues of tangible signs, social relationships, and visibility. We now explore the suggestion that there is interplay between this and the remote workers perceptions of agency.

When discussing identity, participants embedded the issue of choice within discussion. Using Giddens' (1984) concept of agency, and its link to power when participants perceive that they choose to work remotely, we suggest they experience having agency in relation to remote working:

Sally: Well it is my choice to work from home.

When they perceive that remote working has been imposed upon them, we suggest that their experience is one of lacking agency in relation to remote working:

Kieran: while we weren't told the offices were going to shut we all pretty much believed that they were but we didn't know what was going to happen to us.

Where they sway between perceptions of remote working as choice and as imposition, we suggest their experience is one of having and lacking agency in relation to remote working:

Neil: When I was working at [the organization] they decided in order to cut costs they would do away with the local area office and all the consultants would work from home [LACK AGENCY] . . . you might not have a spare room and you have to work on the kitchen table . . . one of the guys has to do that and they were forced to do it as well, but I mean, I have the choice you see, I can either work in the office or work from home [HAVE AGENCY].

As we started to see different approaches to undertaking identity work being used by various remote workers, we began to wonder if this had any interplay with their perceptions of agency. As we explored this, patterns started to emerge between perceptions of agency and how participants engage in identity work. Clear patterns emerged between the social cues used by participants and how agency was perceived. Intra-organizational contact as a way of creating 'visibility' is mentioned extensively by those participants perceived as having agency, whereas tangible signs and social relationships are not referenced to the same extent. For example, Sally indicates the role of visibility (via intra-organizational contact) in how they undertake identity work with the organization:

Sally: I think the key thing is to work with other people. You occasionally have a week where you are at home all week and it is fantastic because I can really get a lot of things done . . . but I would find by the end of the week that you sort of you need to speak to other people and you need to get some input . . . Even if you can speak to them on the phone it does help.

However, those participants perceived as lacking agency do most of their identity work around social relationships, supporting the argument made by Knights and Willmott (1985, 27) that social relationships are a necessity of identity and involve 'a securing of self through an instrumental participation in social relations'. This is suggested by friendships (social relationships) being mentioned extensively by all of these participants in relation to identity, while tangible signs and visibility are not referenced to the same extent. For example, Elliott made the following comment:

Elliott: a number of my people, like college friends, would be working from home or working for themselves or a combination of the two and you might say well we'll meet up and play 9 holes of golf one night in the week, whereas if you were in the office you could never have done that.

Moreover, those participants perceived as having and lacking agency do most of their identity work around tangible signs. This is suggested by the extent to which pay and office location/ furniture are referenced by these participants in relation to identity, whereas social relationships and visibility are referenced to a lesser extent. For example, Ivan highlights these in the following:

Ivan: Hopefully my monthly salary check keeps arriving; that is the most definitive thing [telling me I work for the organization], but also my travel subsistence gets paid. . . . I have one room, reserved a bedroom, for working from home, I have two filing cabinets, a desk, a telephone, fax, a computer PC—a desktop and I also have a lap-top when I am working away from home.

In losing their social barometer (Mann et al., 2000), remote workers (re) create social cues and support identity work by reestablishing opportunities for comparison (Knights & Willmott, 1999). In this way, we suggest that the identity work undertaken by remote workers varies in relation to the remote workers' perception of their agency. Where those who perceive they have agency tend to make most reference to issues of visibility, those who perceive they lack agency tend to pay more attention to social relationships and those who perceive they both have and lack agency tend to focus on tangible signs. This exploration also highlighted a variety of emotions that remote workers experienced, which also appeared to relate to perceptions of agency. This is considered in the following section.

Agency and the Emotional Experience of the Remote Worker

In the above we have explored: (1) how remote workers undertake identity work which saw the emergence of the alternative social cues of tangible signs, social relationship and visibility; (2) whether they perceive they have or lack agency; and (3) the interplay between how they undertake identity work with their perceptions of agency. Here, we turn our attention to the emotional experience of remote workers and how these also interplay with perceptions of agency.

The following interview extract captures four dominant emotions that emerged from the data and highlights the emotions explored within this chapter (thematic coding in parenthesis):

Duncan: [I find not working with colleagues face to face] a little bit frustrating because . . . people can say no very easily across the telephone but face to face and you get that pressure and they can't find it quite as easy to say that, so perhaps a level of frustration to get them to do things for you [FRUSTRATION] . . .

. . . I think that many of my colleagues who are home based, we all share in that same experience when we come together. It is almost like we are ravenous to share information, and talk to each other about things because we haven't seen each other for ages; it is like long lost friends and there can be often 2 or 3 weeks go by before we actually do see each other [ISOLATION] . . .

. . . perhaps for people who are office based it is about freedom isn't it? Working from home [FREEDOM], but in actual fact it works the opposite way for me, I must feel guilty, but I have to sort of overwork to compensate for that [GUILT].

It is through the emotions of guilt, isolation, frustration and freedom, which emerged from the data, that the emotional experiences of remote workers are considered in relation to whether, for the remote worker, there is interplay between these emotions and different perceptions of agency (Giddens, 1984). Participants are divided into two groups: have agency and lack agency, as noted previously. Through analysis of the data in relation to emotional experience, we have been able to identify emotions in relation to one or the other of a participant's state of perceived agency. Hence, we have not used a third group of those that both have and lack agency.

Patterns emerged between the emotions expressed by participants and how agency was perceived. Participants perceived as having agency expressed feelings of isolation, in the sense that they felt there was an imbalance between the way they were treated by the organization and the way nonremote workers were treated by the organization. For example, the perception that they may not be getting as much information as nonremote workers was highlighted by Duncan in the following extract:

Duncan: From the wider business perspective I think 'out of sight out of mind' is definitely applicable. You see things that bypass you, that just because you are not there they tend to forget about you . . . so visibility is probably an issue.

The notion that there is some imbalance between the way remote workers and nonremote workers are treated is supported by the suggestion that remote workers can experience social and professional isolation as a result of the 'loss of the social barometer' (Mann et al., 2000) through the practice of remote working, and also by Baruch and Nicholson (1997, 23) when they refer to remote workers as feeling that "out-of-sight means out-of-mind". This interaction between agency and isolation is outlined by Julie in the following extract:

Julie: it is not something I would want to do all the time [she would want to have agency] . . . I think that . . . it is nice to all come together in meetings and put your own thoughts on stuff that is happening and coming up, so I think that you would feel isolated . . . well I would feel isolated.

Thus for remote workers, the practice of remote working can create a perception of imbalance between the treatment of remote workers and nonremote workers resulting in feelings of isolation. Findings suggest that this appears more often for those participants that perceive they have agency. This could be a reaction to an underfulfilled psychological contract (Sparrow & Hiltrop, 1994), as in choosing to work remotely, especially if the organization has 'sold it' to their employees as a positive way of organizing work. Hence, it is possible that they did not expect to experience feelings of loss, thus giving rise to feelings of isolation. However, this is speculative and requires further research.

Participants who perceived they had agency also expressed feelings of guilt in the sense that they were in some way misleading someone (i.e., the organization or partner) if they enact this agency and make a decision to do something that person may not 'approve' of. This is highlighted by Diane in the following:

Diane: [I] feel that finishing before 5 would be cheating the company and colleagues and there's lots to do! Basically [I] would feel guilty if [I] finished before 5.

As such, clock-based temporal ordering (Tietze & Musson, 2003) was used by participants to avoid guilt, with participants suggesting they keep a note of the hours they worked and 'make sure' they do more rather than less. Furthermore, the relationship between guilt and agency was noted explicitly by Sally who, post-interview, stated that:

Sally: it's important that it's your own decision to work from home and that it's not forced: that stops feelings of guilt; I have chosen to do this.

Taken alone, Sally's comment above appears to contradict the claim that feelings of guilt are heightened for participants who perceive they have agency. However, the context in which it was mentioned refers to how remote working enables her to do more work than if she were in the office, which prevent feelings of guilt. In turn, this enables her to attend to non-work commitments.

The freedom afforded through the structural flexibility of working from home is a reason for which remote working is often undertaken. Yet it is this very freedom that can leave remote workers feeling guilty and that they need to 'justify' or 'prove' that they are doing their job, especially if they enact their agency and take time off to undertake personal tasks at times when they think 'other' people would expect them to be 'at work'. The following extract supports the notion that remote workers feel that they need to prove (and be believed) that they are at work when they are at home:

Duncan: you get sick of listening to that: 'Sorry to bother you, you must be out in the garden or a similar story'. Perhaps for people who are office based it is about freedom, isn't it, working from home; but in actual fact it works the opposite way for me, I must feel guilty, but I have to sort of overwork to compensate for that . . . [to] dismiss that feeling of guilt when you do a little bit of work when you do your DIY or whatever.

Pervasive throughout explicit and implicit references to guilt is the idea that somehow participants are misleading someone and it is this sense of misleading that elicits the -feelings of guilt. Moreover, it is possible to suggest that guilt is the tension the remote worker appears to be holding between the home–work interface (e.g., see Tietze, 2002; Tietze & Musson, 2002a, 2002b, 2003; Baruch, 2001; Harris, 2003; Helms & Raiszadeh, 2002), and their perception that through working at home they are doing something 'wrong'. It can be argued that the emotions remote workers experience when they feel they should not be doing something they are, for example, they should not, for example, be finishing before 5, looking after the kids and be assembling a bike, is tempered through the emotions they experience because they are doing something they want to, for example, they are finishing before 5, looking after the kids and assembling a bike. Thus remote working can heighten the tension between home–work interface increasing the possibility of feelings of guilt and our findings suggest that this happens most for those remote workers who perceive they have agency. Of course, this also raises some really interesting questions around self-regulation at work (Knights & McCabe, 2003), the 'Protestant' work ethic (Weber, 1930) and whether work should ever be fun! Moreover, it also raises the possibility that by choosing to work in a way that is perceived as more enjoyable (and that potentially may provide more autonomy) the rules must somehow be being broken and remote workers are experiencing 'guilty pleasures' borne out of their work organization—an area worth future exploration.

Participants who lacked agency experienced feelings of freedom through the perceived structural flexibility of the remote working practice. For example, Neil perceives remote working as imposed by the organization and, therefore, is interpreted as lacking agency:

Neil: It [remote working] is great, I love it; it is the freedom, the free-dom to do what you want, when you want, within reason.

However, it can further be seen that participants perceived as lacking agency in the decision over whether to work remotely have, in some way, had their hopes disappointed (Thompson, 1995). For example, Duncan was aware when he took the job that it would mean working remotely. However, he notes that when he moved south the only jobs he could apply for were all home based, yet he would rather be office based and, in this sense, he lacks agency. In the following he describes his experience of remote working:

Duncan: [remote working is] A little bit frustrating because . . . people can say no very easily across the telephone but face to face and you get that pressure and they can't find it quite as easy to say that, so perhaps a level of frustration to get them to do things for you.

Suggesting that his hopes for his working relationships have been disap-pointed, leading to feelings of frustration. This is supported by Mike:

Mike: Many times when I have not been in working from my own branch, a day or so, and I come back to my own branch to the head office and I am expected to know stuff that has been dropped in quite casually . . . it does become frustrating.

Thus, the practice of remote working can leave remote workers feeling as though the hopes for their working life have been disappointed, resulting in feelings of frustration. We suggest that this appears more often for those participants who perceive they lack agency.

In the above, we propose that there is interplay between the emotions remote workers expressed and their perceptions of agency, where those who have agency experience feelings of guilt and isolation more so than those who lack agency; and those who lack agency experience frustration and freedom more so than those who have agency. Previously, we proposed that there is interplay between how remote workers undertake identity work and their perceptions of agency.

In bringing these two propositions together, we thus suggest that there is interplay between how remote workers undertake identity work and their expressed emotions, mediated through their perceptions of agency. As such, remote workers who have agency, experience guilt and isolation the most and when undertaking identity work, these participants attempt to recreate comparative opportunities to benchmark themselves with others (Knights & Willmott, 1999) through intra-organizational contact so as to create visibility within their organization. Furthermore, remote workers who lack agency, experience frustration and freedom the most and when undertaking identity work, these participants attempt to re-establish their social barometer (Mann et al., 2000) through friendships and inter-organizational relationships so as to (re) establish social relationships.

CONCLUSION

In seeking to develop critical debate around the emotional experience of the remote worker from the perspective of the remote worker, we suggest that there appears to be some interplay between the way in which remote workers undertake identity work and their perceptions of agency in the choice over whether or not to work remotely. We also suggest that their perception of agency, and thus the way in which they undertake identity work, interplays with the emotions they experience. The implications of these findings for both theory and practice are wide ranging. Notably, for practitioners, it would suggest that changing to, or maintaining, a remote working practice necessitates an understanding of the interplay between remote workers engagement in undertaking identity work and their perceptions of agency and how these interplay with remote workers feeling guilty and isolated or free, yet frustrated. In theory, these findings open up the avenue to explore the interplay between perceptions of agency and the undertaking of identity work specifically for remote workers and their emotional experience, an area which is currently under-researched.

However, future work is required to develop the emergent ideas presented. In particular, we suggest further research, which identifies remote workers' states of agency in relation to undertaking identity work, and also research which looks at mapping the identity work undertaken by remote workers onto their emotional experience.

REFERENCES

Baruch, Y. 2001. The status of research on teleworking and an agenda for future research. *International Journal of Management Reviews* 3(2), 113–129.

Baruch, Y. & Nicholson, N. 1997. Home, sweet work: Requirements for effective home working. *Journal of General Management* 23(2), 15–30.

Bryman, A. 2008. *Social research methods*. 3rd ed. Oxford: OUP.

Buzan, T. 1995. *The mind map book*. 2nd ed. London: BBC.

Daniels, K., Lamond, D. & Standen, P. 2001. Teleworking: Frameworks for organizational research. *Journal of Management Studies* 38(8), 1151–1185.

Dick, P. & Hyde, R. 2006. Consent as resistance, resistance as consent: Re-reading part-time professionals' acceptance of their marginal positions. *Gender, Work and Organization* 13(6), 543–564.

DiMartino, V. & Wirth, L. 1990. Telework: A new way of working and living. *International Labour Review* 129(5), 529–554.

Fineman, S. 2000. *Emotion in organizations*. London: Sage.

Fineman, S., Maitlis, S. & Panteli, N. 2007. Virtuality and emotion. *Human Relations*, 60(4), 555–560.

Giddens, A. 1984. *The constitution of society: Outline of the theory of structuration*. Cambridge: Polity.

Grove, D. & Panzer, B. 1989. *Resolving traumatic memories: Metaphors and symbols in psychotherapy*. New York: Irvington.

Hall, S. 1996. Who needs identity? In *Questions of cultural identity*. Eds. S. Hall, and P. du Gay. . London; Sage.

Hall, S. 2000. Who need identity? In *Identity: A reader*. Eds. P. du Gay, J. Evans, and P. Redman. London: Sage.

Hall, D., Schneider, B. & Nygren, H. 1970. Personal Factors in Organizational Identification. *Administrative Science Quarterly* 15(2), 176–190.

Harris, L. 2003. Home-based Teleworking and the employment eelationship: Managerial challenges and dilemmas. *Personnel Review* 32(4), 422–437.

Helms, M. & Raiszadeh, F. 2002. Virtual offices: Understanding and managing what you cannot see. *Work Study* 51(5), 240–247.

Jackson, P. 1999. *Virtual working: Social and organizational dynamics*. London: Routledge

Knights, D. & McCabe, D. 2003. Governing through teamwork: Reconstituting subjectivity in a call centre. *Journal of Management Studies* 40(7), 1587–1619.

Knights, D. & Willmott, H. 1985. Power and identity in theory and practice. *Sociological Review* 33(1), 22–46.

Knights, D & Willmott, H. 1999. *Management lives: Power and identity in work organizations*. London: Sage.

King, N. 2004. Using templates in the thematic analysis of text. In *Essential guide to qualitative methods in organizational research*. Eds. C. Cassell, and G. Symon. London: Sage.

Mann, S., Varey, R. & Button, W. 2000. An exploration of the emotional impact of tele-working via computer-mediated communication. *Journal of Managerial Psychology* 15(7/8), 668–691.

McLeod, J. 1994. *Doing counselling research*. London: Sage.

McLeod, J. 1999. Counselling as a social process. *Counselling* 10(3), 217–222.

Mento, A., Martinelli, P. & Jones, R. 1999. Mind mapping in executive education: applications and outcomes. *Journal of Management Development* 18(4), 390–407.

Reason, P. 1999. Integrating action and reflection through cooperative inquiry. *Management Learning* 30(2), 207–226.

Richardson, J. 2009. The manager and the flexworker: An interpretive interactionist perspective. *Management Revue* 20(1), 34–52.

Sanchez-Burks, J. & Huy, Q N. 2009. Emotional aperture and strategic change: The accurate recognition of collective emotions. *Organization Science* 20(1), 22–34.

Schein, E. 1985. *Organizational culture and leadership*. 2nd ed. . San Francisco: Jossey Bass.

Seo, M-G., Taylor, M.S. & Hill, N.S. 2007. The role of affect and leadership during radical organizational change. *Academy of Management Proceedings* p1–6.

Shapiro, G. 2000. '*Good practice case study': Introducing location independent working with RM consulting.* Centrim: University of Brighton.

Sparrow, P. & Hiltrop, J-M. 1994. *European human resource management in transition.* Prentice-Hall: London.

Thompson, D. Ed. 1995. *The concise oxford dictionary*: English. 9th ed. Oxford: Clarendon.

Tietze, S. 2002. When 'work' comes 'home': Coping strategies of teleworkers and their families. *Journal of Business Ethics* 41(4), 385–396.

Tietze, S. & Musson, G. 2002a. Working from home and managing guilt. *Organizations & People* 9(1), 34–39.

Tietze, S. & Musson, G. 2002b. When 'work' meets 'home': Temporal flexibility as lived experience. *Time & Society* 11(2/3), 315–334.

Tietze, S. & Musson, G. 2003. The times and temporalities of home-based work. *Personnel Review* 32(4), 438–455.

Tomaskovic-Devey, D. & Risman, B. 1993. Telecommuting innovation and organization: a contingency theory of lab or process change. *Social Science Quarterly* 74(2), 367–385.

Warren, S. 2006. Hot-nesting: A visual exploration of the personalization of workspace in a hot-desking environment. In *The speed of organization.* Eds. P. Case, S. Lilley & T. Owens .Liber, CBS, 119–146.

Weber, M. 1930. *The Protestant ethic and the spirit of capitalism.* London: Unwin University Book.

7 Flexwork in Canada
Coping with Dis-Ease?

Julia Richardson

INTRODUCTION

As the title of this book suggests, changes in organizational processes and practices have given rise to an increasingly diverse menu of work arrangements and experiences. Some of these arrangements can be described as 'flexible work practices' such as flexitime, flexwork, a compressed work week, telecommuting and remote working (Johnson, Andrey, & Shaw, 2007; Kelliher & Anderson, 2010; Lautsch, Kossek, & Eaton, 2009; Tremblay, Paquet, & Najem, 2006). Exploring one such practice, this chapter focuses on the experiences of group of 'flexworkers' in a MNC in the high-tech industry in Canada. Drawing on Gergen's (1991) conceptions of 'saturation of the self' and 'dis-ease', it explores the extent to which these concepts might be used to understand participants' experiences of flexwork.

Flexwork is one example of the broader category of 'telecommuting' practices which, according to Maxwell, Rankine, Bell and MacVicar (2007, 138), involves "any policies and practices, formal or informal, which permit people to vary when and where work is carried out" . It is a situation where, like telecommuting, "workers are given opportunities to work from home rather than reporting to a centralized office location on a daily basis" (Shia & Monroe, 2006, 456). The participants in the study are, therefore, part of the growing number of employees who are conducting some portion of their work outside the traditional space of a designated office (Galinsky, Bond, & Sakai, 2008; Grote & Raeder, 2009; Kossek & Van Dyne, 2008; Lautsch et al., 2009; Schokley & Allen, 2007). Indeed, according to one U.S.-based study (SSHRM, 2008), 59% of HR professionals said their employees had access to flextime. A further 37% reported that employees had access to a compressed work week. Reflecting a similar trend, a study of three large Canadian cities (Montreal, Toronto and Vancouver) reported that 3.9% of employed adults between the ages of 15 and 74 work at home for pay, representing 6% of the labor force in the respective cities (Moos & Skaburskis, 2007). The same study also found that business and other services in Canada had the largest number of homeworkers followed by finance, insurance and real estate.

In 2006, Schweitzer and Duxbury expressed concern about a paucity of research on Canadian teleworkers. Since that time, however, there has been increasing scholarly and political interest in flexible work practices in Canada and, particularly, in their impact on/connection to employee well-being, work–life balance, and organizational and individual performance (see, for example, Johnson et al., 2007; Korabik & Lero, 2003; Lanoie, Raymond & Schearer, 2001; Lero, Richardson & Korabik, 2009; Schweitzer & Duxbury, 2006; Tremblay et al., 2006). Tremblay et al. (2006), for example, have explored the growing number of Canadians who are working from home and whether their motivations to do so are driven by family responsibilities. Other Canadian studies have explored individual experiences of telework, the perceived implications for men versus women and the 'blurring' of boundaries between work and home domains (see, for example, Johnson et al. 2007; Tremblay 2002). This interest, alongside the concomitant growth in the number of empirical studies in the field, echoes similar trends in the U.S., Europe and Australasia as evidenced by other studies in this volume.

Taken as a whole, the current body of literature on flexible work practices reflects a complex and dynamic field of study replete with complementary and contradictory findings. Employers offering opportunities to work from home are frequently characterized as socially responsive and 'employee friendly'. Indeed, being able to work from home has been widely understood as one of the precursors to achieving work–life balance, having less work–family conflict and more work satisfaction (Fang & Lee, 2008; Galinsky & Backon, 2007; Kelliher & Anderson, 2010; Kossek, 2005; Lautsch et al., 2009). Thus, for example, in a recent study of 220 working adults in the U.S., McNall, Masuda and Nicklin (2010) reported that flexible working arrangements facilitate greater 'enrichment from work to home', which the authors also found was associated with higher job satisfaction and lower turnover intentions. Kelliher and Anderson (2008) also found that UK teleworkers moved fairly seamlessly between fulfilling the demands of home and work, which suggests that employers might also stand to benefit from increased employee productivity, satisfaction and organizational commitment, as well as reduced turnover and real-estate costs (e.g. Bloom & Reenen, 2006; Crandall & Gao, 2005; Kelliher & Anderson, 2010). Allowing employees to work from home also reduces traffic congestion and urban pollution (Manoocherhri & Pinkerton, 2003; Tremblay, 2003). Alongside these positive themes, however, some scholars have recommended a more cautionary approach. Harris's (2003) UK study of a work from home initiative stressed the need for perceived mutual gain and described how teleworkers (particularly men with young children) faced challenges in marking out the boundaries between work and home. Other authors (Tietze, 2005; Tietze & Musson, 2003) also contend that removing the boundaries between work and home exposes the employee and their family to economically driven forces and increased stress. Drawing on discourse analysis, Tietze (2005) argues that because the home (or family) is a context of love and nurturing, whereas work is a context within which making money is the primary objective, their co-presence creates challenges for individuals and their families. Suggesting a similar theme, Mann and Holdsworth (2003) also found greater levels of mental-health problems for employees who worked from home.

Acknowledging and embracing the complexity of the field, this chapter explores how Canadian flexworkers learn to manage the interdependency of their work and home 'selves' by deconstructing and then redrawing the boundaries between their work and home lives. This theme echoes other studies (e.g., Tietze & Musson, 2003, 442), positing that flexwork, like telework, creates a situation where 'work comes home' and is, therefore, "characterized by the meeting of two previously distinct meaning worlds". It also echoes the work of scholars who have highlighted the connectivity between teleworking, identity construction and the development of the self (see, for example, Brocklehurst, 2001; Grote & Raeder, 2009; Tietze, 2002). The chapter develops a further line of enquiry by drawing on Gergen's (1991) conception of 'the saturation of the self' and 'dis-ease' and the extent to which those concepts might be used to understand participants' experiences of flexwork.

THE POSTMODERN SELF: AN AFFIRMATIVE APPROACH

According to Holstein and Gubrium (2000, 56), there are "two options for the postmodern self". Affirmative approaches, as reflected by Gergen (1991), see the self as socially constructed and located in a world that "multiplies and hybridizes our identities" (Holstein & Gubrium, p, 56). From this perspective, the self continues to exist albeit as an evolving entity that is consistently challenged by a multitude of experiences and interactions. This perspective can be distinguished from the more skeptical or radical postmodern approaches that see the self as merely an image (e.g., Baudrillard, 1983). By adopting the affirmative perspective, Gergen (1991) suggests that, caught up with the ever-increasing demands of contemporary life, we are experiencing a 'saturation of the self'. We are pulled, he says, "in myriad directions, inviting us to play with such a variety of roles that the very concept of an 'authentic self' with knowable characteristics recedes from view" (Gergen, 1991, 6–7). "This", he continues, "makes it increasingly difficult for us to maintain a sense of 'unity', thus creating the condition of 'multiphrenia' and 'dis-ease' and leaving us to struggle to meet the competing (and often contradictory) demands for attention and domination".

Drawing on Gergen's work, this chapter considers the extent to which, in seeking to meet the needs of diverse identities and responsibilities, flexworkers experience 'saturation of the self', 'dis-ease' and 'multiphrenia'.

It will explore whether the flexworkers who took part in this study were, indeed, "pulled in myriad directions" (Holstein & Gubrium, 2000, 58) when managing the demands of their 'home and work selves'. Given that flexwork invariably involves the blurring of boundaries between one's 'work self' and one's 'home self', it will examine whether they felt a sense of 'dis-ease' and if so how they coped with it—i.e., did they seek to alleviate it and if so how? A key concern here will be whether 'blurring of boundaries' between one domain and another is also a source of 'dis-ease'.

Although maintaining a predominantly exploratory stance, then, the chapter considers the following questions:

- How useful are conceptions of a 'home' self and a 'work' self for understanding participants' experiences of flexwork?
- How useful are conceptions of 'saturation of the self' and 'dis-ease' for understanding participants' experiences of flexwork?
- How do participants' satisfy the responsibilities of different 'selves' that are likely to evolve in the context of flexwork?

DATA COLLECTION

Sampling

This self-selected sample comprised 76 flexworkers in the Canadian subsidiary of a MNC in the high-tech industry. All participants were working from home 2 or more days per week. Although self-selection may attract individuals with an agenda of complaints or praise, most accounts contained positive and negative themes. All participants had a laptop and IT support to allow them to work at home or elsewhere. They were employed in a diverse range of departments, which provides a broad range of perspectives and experiences. Fifty participants had access to a 'hot desk' or temporary work cubicle in the main office. Tenure at the organization ranged from less than 1 to over 10 years. Twenty-seven participants had a managerial or leadership role. Ages ranged from 20 to 56, although most were between 36–50 years old. A majority had 1 or more school-age children currently living at home.

Data Analysis

All interviews were transcribed verbatim and coded using template analysis (King, 2004) with the computer-assisted qualitative data analysis software Nvivo. This involved creating lists of 'nodes' representing themes contained in the data. Some of the themes, such as blurred boundaries between home and work domains, managing multiple identities/selves, and the impact of technology on participants' experiences of flexwork were identified *apriori* from the existent literature. Others, such as maintaining a 'visible work self', 'implications of flexworking for career advancement' and the 'learning curve' of flexwork were added during analysis. Parallel coding captured the overlap and connections between themes. As analysis progressed, dominant and subsidiary themes were identified. For example, 'maintaining a visible work self' was a dominant theme, because it was mentioned extensively by the majority of participants. However, it could also be broken into subsidiary themes such as 'maintaining a visible work self for relationships with managers', 'maintaining a visible work self for relationships with peers' and 'connections with career advancement'. Coding reports identified which participants had 'contributed' most (or least) to specific 'nodes'.

Limitations

Focusing on one organization has provided an in-depth and instructive case study. Yet, the findings may not be applicable to smaller organizations or organizations in other countries, particularly given the reported differences in managerial support for flexworkers in different national contexts (Peters & Den Dulk, 2003). Indeed, flexworkers in other companies in Canada may also have quite different experiences. Furthermore, the organization at the center of this study is technology-based and has extensive expertise to support flexworking. To that extent, having the technological capacity to support teams of flexworkers may set it apart from other organizations, which tend to use more individualized teleworking arrangements (Tremblay, 2002).

FINDINGS

Managing Multiple Selves in a Context of Blurred Boundaries

The idea of a 'home self' and a 'work self' operating in closer proximity permeated all interviews. Moreover, the majority of participants described how they might be simultaneously required to be 'different selves'. This notion of living the home and work self at once, or at least in closer proximity, echoes Tietze and Musson's (2005) contention that when employees work from home, the boundaries between home and work become blurred. Yet, rather than being a cause for concern, the majority of participants believed that over time (and with further customizing according to their individual circumstances) the blurring and then *redrawing* of those boundaries added to their sense of well-being. More importantly, having a flexwork arrangement was a positive experience precisely because they could *customize* the boundaries between home and work and thus between their home and work selves.

Alongside these positive themes, however, most participants did express some concern that flexwork and the concomitant blurring of boundaries could detract from their "sense of direction" or "purpose". Some, but particularly those with managerial responsibility, reported being "overwhelmed" by the need to satisfy their responsibilities to their work and home selves simultaneously rather than in what one participant described as "a more compartmentalized way". These descriptions have some synergy with Gergen's (1991) notion of 'living all our selves at once' and the subsequent 'saturation of the self' and 'dis-ease'. Several participants, for example, said that when they first started flexworking they were living both their home and work selves at once, which left them feeling "overwhelmed" or "swamped". Jean, for example, described an "adjustment period":

> When I started out, I'd vacuum or do my laundry when I was on a conference call. But you cannot do that and remain focused. I couldn't, so I had to structure my day and some of my colleagues told me 'you have to structure your day if you're working from home just like you were going to the office' and that's what I started to do and that's where I'm finding my success. The only thing is that I carry that throughout my day. So I have to remember to shut-off at a certain time.

Jean's description of the need to "remain focused" and "shut-off" reflects the challenges that she and many other participants faced during the initial stages of redrawing the boundaries between their home and work selves. Their descriptions of this challenge reflect Gergen's concern about being "pulled in myriad directions at the same time" (Holstein & Gubrium, 2000, 58). Reflecting on his own experience as an academic, for example, Gergen (1991, 1) describes feeling overwhelmed by the multiple demands of his professional and personal life ranging from demands from publishers, students, administrative staff and colleagues to responsibilities to friends requiring 'relational time'.

Yet, there was also an interesting contradiction where many participants said that they had requested a flexible work schedule precisely in order to "eliminate" or "deconstruct" the boundaries between their home and work selves. In other words, they had started out wanting to work in what several participants described as "a more holistic fashion". There was also widespread agreement that "eliminating" or "deconstructing" those boundaries allowed them to be more effective in the multiple domains of their lives. Despite the initial sense of being "overwhelmed", then, the majority of participants said that once they had got used to flexworking they learned to manage their multiple roles and respective selves more effectively. This learning process enabled them to avoid the 'dis-ease' and 'saturation of the self' that Gergen (1991) has described.

Interestingly, the majority said that some managers (and organizations) resist flexwork initiatives through fear of the 'home self' being accorded more importance (and, hence, more time and energy) then the 'work self'. However, if this is indeed true, such fears may be unfounded because all participants, including those with children, created strategies to ensure that they fulfilled their responsibilities to **both** the home and work self. In fact, there was also widespread evidence that **not** being able to fulfill those responsibilities also created a strong sense of 'dis-ease'. Tina, a senior sales manager, for example, had introduced a rule in her household that if she was working in the basement her children had to play in their bedrooms. Her concern was to focus on fulfilling the responsibilities of her 'work self' rather than being distracted by those of her 'home self'. Michael, a flexworker of many years, also described having "laid down some ground rules" for his family precisely because he wanted to fulfill his responsibilities to his 'work self':

> My kids and wife would think that I'm working from home so it's like 'let's go shopping!' I had to make a point of saying 'this is work time and this is personal time. I've got to fulfill my responsibilities to my work and then I can be with you'.

On a related theme, virtually all participants with small children used childcare facilities so that they could engage fully with their 'work selves' during the day and their 'home selves' outside of work hours. Indeed, several interviewees (males and females) emphasized that although working from home allows parents to spend more time with children, using childcare facilities outside of the home is essential.

Thus far, we have seen how the majority of participants described their concern to accord each self what they believed was the "right" amount of attention. This included both avoiding a situation where the 'home self' "took over" at the expense of the 'work self', and preventing the 'work self' from becoming too dominant, which would mean that they were "working all the time". This concern reflected a widespread desire to maintain "work–life balance"—in this case, understood as a balance between the 'work self' and the 'home self'. Most participants took a task-oriented approach to achieving this balance, pointing out the need for certain skills or competencies. Although several skills were identified, time management was accorded most importance. Participants like Jane and Melanie, for example, said time management was essential for maintaining both balance and "focus and direction":

> You definitely have to have time management skills, I think it's very important and you have to try and be an organized person because you no longer have an office to keep your paperwork in or stuff like that. I guess I've now reduced my paper load because I now keep everything electronically and I guess multitasking. (Jane)

> Self-discipline and organizational skills, thinking carefully about 'what am I going to do today, during what time?' You know, being able to prioritize, prioritize between certain types of work that you need to get

done throughout the week and what you can do when you're working from home most effectively. (Melanie)

"Effective planning" was another "essential' skill, as suggested by Penny, below:

> One of the things you have to do is think ahead. 'Ok, who am I going to meet? Where am I going to be working tomorrow, is it home? Is it the regular office? Is it the other office?' and then 'What am I going to need for that day?' So I'll be thinking a couple of days ahead. I think beyond that, I've really gotten organized on my email and my planning so that I know what has to be done and when.

It is notable here that Penny adopts a very specific strategy to avoid being overwhelmed by the blurring of boundaries between her home and work selves. Like most other participants, she seemed aware of the potential of 'dis-ease'. What is particularly interesting here is how these participants empha-size the need for order and separation of the work and home self even though some had requested a flexible work schedule precisely so that the boundaries between them might be more blurred. For example, Penny wanted to plan ahead in order that she could fulfill the responsibilities of her 'work self'. Yet, later in her interview she also accorded equal importance to "being my home self". The process of planning described by Penny, and others, reflected a clear concern to avoid what many described as the "confusion" and "chaos" of trying to live both selves at once. Yet, they also enjoyed being on a flex-work schedule because it allowed them to live a more "holistic" life where home and work were not operating as two separate domains.

Although just under a quarter of participants felt that their employer should provide them with training and support to manage the boundaries between work and home, most said that it is ultimately up to the indi-vidual. Indeed, some participants said that if the employer does intervene then it detracts from the necessarily individualized nature of flexwork as evidenced by Seamus, below:

> I believe people see how I manage voice-mail, how I manage commu-nications, how I manage the structure piece of it. Whether they say 'hey, that seems to work for Seamus maybe I'll try that', I don't know. I think that given the complexity of our jobs and the volume of work that we're asked to contribute to I think everybody has to find out what works for them. . . . it also depends on your own individual situation and life circumstance.

Preserving the 'Professional/Work Self'

The need to "preserve" a 'professional' or 'work self' dominated most interviews and usually involved ensuring that they were seen by either

office-based managers, other flexworkers or colleagues whom participants wanted to impress or at least gain acceptance from, as suggested
by Tina, below:

> It's the informal meetings where you talk and, you know, have a coffee
> with somebody. I just had a coffee with my VP of sales, today and he
> says 'I don't really know you very well' and I thought—'mmm, not a
> good sign!'

Just over one-half of non-managerial participants stressed the importance
of ensuring that their 'work self' was particularly visible to office-based
managers. They were especially concerned about the implications of not
being visible for performance evaluations, career opportunities and/or
professional networks. Conversely, flexworking managers seemed more
concerned with ensuring that their 'work self' was visible to subordinates
rather than other managers. Their major concern was maintaining what
one manager referred to as a "strong physical and emotional presence
with my direct-reports". This finding identifies other employees (be they
flexworkers, managers or office-based employees) as 'significant others'
because they are individuals, whom participants respect, want acceptance
from or identify with (Richardson, 2009). Echoing Tremblay's (2002) study
of teleworkers in Canada, which suggested that for individuals with career
aspirations maintaining professional visibility in the office is important,
fifteen participants in this study said they went into the office *specifically*
in order to maintain "visibility" for career development.

Rob and Michael clearly identify this need for visibility particularly
emphasizing the importance of face-to-face contact with office-based and
flexworking peers as well as with senior management:

> Another advantage of being in the office versus working from home
> from time to time is to be able to walk in and check in with people
> and to put yourself into those social situations within the corporate
> community and take advantage of that. If you're working from home
> 100% of the time you've just removed yourself from that part of the
> equation. (Rob)

> For me, it's important to have face-time with my manager, face-time with
> my peers and, in fact, sometimes maybe meet up socially when you're
> done. You can walk next door to somebody's office, you know, you can get
> a 5-minute coffee, talk about business and so forth. So when you have a
> local office versus when you are away from the office you have to find time
> to build that relational piece in with customers and your peers. (Michael)

The need to maintain and preserve one's 'work self' also arose in discussions about relationships with family members, neighbors or friends. The

specific concern here was how family members accord more importance to the 'home self' because it is that self with which they are most familiar. Linda, for example, said that when she started flexworking, her husband assumed that because she was home all day they wouldn't need childcare facilities so she deliberately "promoted" her 'work self' by emphasizing that she stayed home to meet work rather than family responsibilities. She described having to sit down with him to describe her work responsibilities, whereas when she was office-based she did not feel any obligation or need to do so. Len provides a further example of this theme:

> My family and friends who don't have a work from home option, they don't really understand the fact that I'm actually working and people might stop by in the afternoon. Like even my dad will stop by on occasion and I'll be on a conference call for 2 hours and I'll have to say 'look, I can't talk for 2 hours. . . . Just because I'm home, it doesn't mean that I'm accessible or have time or am working less'.

The reactions and behaviors of Len's family and friends suggests that they may be somehow unable (or unwilling) to accommodate his 'work self' within the home domain. Connecting this finding directly with the notion of 'dis-ease', what we observe here is how participants like Len and Linda were concerned to promote their 'work self'—to their family members. Indeed, it was the prospect of their 'work self' not being recognized by family members which seems to be a potential source of 'dis-ease'.

'Technologies of Saturation'

All participants in this study had access to an 'instant messaging system', email and conference calls/videos and were required to participate in interactions using all media as an integral part of their work life. Many suggested that they could fulfill most of their work responsibilities without ever going into the office. Ashley, captures this theme explicitly:

> There's very little that can't be done at home that can be done only at the office. We've invested substantially in technology that allows us to be able to work from home. Any application, any piece of data, anything I need, can be done so there really is no compelling reason to go into the office.

This finding suggests that technology enables flexwork by specifically creating situations where multiple selves coexist. However, Gergen's (1991) notion of 'technologies of saturation' also provides a useful framework here because it suggests that with rapid technological development comes the potential of 'informational overload' and the requirement to manage different selves simultaneously. Several participants, such as Chandra below, indicated that they had created mechanisms for managing how they used the technology, particularly the instant messaging system and email, specifically in order to avoid being "overwhelmed" or "swamped":

> You have to take control of it otherwise work never ends and I guess it depends on the nature of the work you do but especially in the IT world, it's becoming more and more difficult to turn off because the technology is becoming more and more dominant in our everyday lives. So you have a blending of the personal and your business. You've got all these devices that are converging in on us.

The majority of participants were acutely aware of what many referred to as the "danger" of allowing email and communications with work colleagues to interfere with their personal lives. There was also a strong awareness that not managing the technology effectively would allow their 'work self' to dominate their 'home self'. In this regard we observe how technology can indeed operate as a source of dis-ease, unless it is managed appropriately.

CONCLUSION

Whereas the different dimensions of our lives are unlikely to ever be completely separate, this chapter suggests that flexworkers are simultaneously challenged to manage their 'work selves' alongside their 'home selves'. That each of these selves may have quite diverse characteristics, demands and responsibilities adds further to the complexity of the challenge. Drawing on Gergen's (1991) affirmative postmodern perspective (Holstein & Gubrium, 2000) of the self, the chapter has explored whether flexwork creates a 'saturation of the self' culminating in a sense of 'dis-ease' (1991). It has also explored the strategies that individuals may use to cope with or avoid that 'dis-ease'.

Although not denying the potential for 'dis-ease' in contemporary living, Holstein and Gubrium (2000, 222, 223) have criticized Gergen for failing to take into account that rather than living "all their circumstances at once" individuals "take the moral order in circumstantial doses". Yet, some of the participants who took part in this study had requested a flexwork arrangement precisely because they thought it would allow them to live their different selves at once, or at least blur the boundaries between them. Having said that, however, they also felt a sense of 'dis-ease' during the initial stages of flexworking, precisely because the boundaries had been blurred. A major source of their 'dis-ease' was the possibility of what Johnson et al.(2007, 152) refer to as "leakage of home and household into the work domain". They were reluctant to allow too much leakage between their 'work self' and their 'home self' for fear that it would create problems in both their home and work domains. To counter this 'dis-ease' they then *redrew* the boundaries—but according to their own individual circumstances. Therefore, although flexwork may indeed create 'saturation of the self' and the concomitant spiral into 'dis-ease', it can be avoided (or at least managed) by allowing individuals to customize the boundaries between the different domains of their lives. Indeed, it is notable that all participants felt that they were more effective in both the work and home domains precisely because they were on a flexible work arrangement that was more attuned to their individual circumstances.

The majority of participants indicated that flexwork provided them with opportunities to live their lives "more fully", "holistically" or "together". Just over one-third said that the advantage of working from home (albeit on a part-time basis) was that they could construct a 'whole life' rather than a life which one participant described as "disjointed, flipping between home and work", where home and work selves are more physically removed from one another. Therefore, although the potential for 'dis-ease' should be acknowledged, it seems most likely during the earlier stages of flexworking before participants adopted 'coping mechanisms' to help them manage domain boundaries. The mechanisms they described echo those used by teleworkers (Tietze, 2002, 2005; Tietze & Musson, 2003), thus demonstrating the similarities between flexworkers and teleworkers. This finding suggests that whereas 'saturation of the self' and 'dis-ease' is a potential risk for the neophyte flexworker, it applies less to their more experienced counterpart.

Reflecting Gergen's (1991) notion of the self as evolving and socially constructed and maintained, participants were able to 'stand outside themselves' by taking on the role of the other (in this case senior managers or other 'significant others' in the office). This led them to actively "promote" and "preserve" their 'work self' for the attention of what one participant described as "interested parties". Thus, for example, many were concerned about becoming "invisible", particularly new employees with limited organizational connections and networks, employees looking for promotion and flexworking managers. This finding also suggests Cooley's notion (1972) of the 'looking-glass self' where participants looked 'away from and out of' themselves to understand how they might be perceived and evaluated by others. It also echoes widely reported concerns about home-based employees feeling isolated from office-based colleagues and management (e.g., Bailey & Kurland 2002; Crandall & Gao 2005; Harris 2003).

Concerns about the potential problems associated with flexwork notwithstanding, this study has a number of important practical implications. First, flexworkers should be encouraged to develop their own mechanisms for managing the boundaries between their work and home selves. Second, whereas organizations should be concerned about the potential of 'dis-ease' they should acknowledge that flexwork offers an important opportunity for employees to redraw those boundaries according to their own individual circumstances and that it is this more *customized redrawing* that they seem to enjoy and benefit from most.

REFERENCES

Bailey, D.E. & Kurland, N.B. 2002. A review of telework research: findings, new directions, and lessons for the study of modern work. *Journal of Organizational Behavior*, 23(4), 383–400.

Baudrillard, J. 1983. *Simulations*. New York: Semiotexte(e).

Bloom, N. & Reenen, J.V. 2006. Management practices, work-life balance, and productivity: A review of some recent evidence. *Oxford Economic Policy* 22(4), 457–482.

Brocklehurst, M. 2001. Power, identity and new technology homework: Implications for new forms of organizing. *Organization Studies* 22(3), 445–466.

Crandall, W.R. & Gao, L. 2005. An update on telecommuting: Review and prospects for emerging issues. *SAM Advanced Management Journal, Summer*, 30–37.

Fang, A. & Lee, B. 2008. Work-friendly benefits and labour market outcomes. Paper presented at the *2008 Western Academy of Management Meetings Proceedings*, March 26–29.

Galinsky, E. & Backon, L. 2007. *When work works*: Alfred P. Sloan Foundation.

Galinsky, E., Bond, J. & Sakai, K. 2008. *2008 National Study of Employers*. Retrieved September 17th, 2010, from the World Wide Web: http://familiesandwork.org/site/research/reports/2008nse.pdf

Gergen, K. J. 1991. *The saturated self: Dilemmas of identity in contemporary life*. New York: Basic.

Grote, G. & Raeder, S. 2009. Careers and identity in flexible working: Do flexible identities fare better? *Human Relations* 62(2), 219–244.

Harris, L. 2003. Home-based teleworking and the employment relationship. *Personnel Review* 32(4), 422–437.

Holstein, J. A. & Gubrium, J. F. 2000. *The self we live by*. New York: Oxford University Press.

Johnson, L., Andrey, J. & Shaw, S. 2007. Mr. Dithers comes to dinner: Telework and the merging of women's work and home domains in Canada. *Gender, Place and Culture* 14(2), 141–161.

Kelliher, C. & Anderson, D. 2008. For better or for worse? An analysis of how flexible work practices influence employees' perceptions of job quality. *International Journal of Human Resource Management* 19(3), 419–431.

Kelliher, C. & Anderson, D.A. 2010. Doing more with less? Flexible working practices and the intensification of work. *Human Relations* 63(1), 83–106.

King, N. 2004. Using templates in the thematic analysis of text. In *Essential guide to qualitative methods in organizational research*. Eds. C. Cassell & G. Symon. London: Sage, 256–270.

Korabik, K. & Lero, D.S. 2003. A multi-level approach to cross cultural work-family research. *International Journal of Cross Cultural Management* 3(3), 289–303.

Kossek, E.E. 2005. Workplace policies and practices to support work and families: Gaps in implementation and linkages to individual and organizational effectiveness. In *Workforce/workplace mismatch, work, family, health and well-being*. Eds. S. Bianchi & L. Casper & R. King. Mahwah, NJ: Lawrence Erlbaum Associates.

Kossek, E.E. & Van Dyne, L. 2008. Face-time matters: A cross level model of how work-life flexibility influences work performance of groups and individuals. In *Handbook of Work-Family Integration: Research, Theory and Best Practices*. Eds. K. Korabik & D.S. Lero & D.L. Whitehead. New York: Academic Press, 305–330. .

Lanoie, P., Raymond, F. & Schearer, B. 2001. Work sharing and productivity: Evidence from the firm level. *Applied Economics* 33, 1213–1220.

Lautsch, B.A., Kossek, E.E. & Eaton, S.C. 2009. Supervisory approaches and paradoxes in managing telecommuting implementation. *Human Relations* 62(6), 795–827.

Lero, D.S., Richardson, J. & Korabik, K. 2009. *Cost-benefit review of work-life balance practices—2009*: Canadian Association of Administrators of Labour Legislation.

Mann, S. & Holdsworth, L. 2003. The psychological impact of teleworking: Stress, emotions and health. *New Technology, Work and Employment* 18, 196–211.

Manoocherhri, G. & Pinkerton, T. 2003. Managing telecommuters: Opportunities and challenges. *American Business Review* 9–16.

Maxwell, G., Rankine, L., Bell, S. & MacVicar, A. 2007. The incidence and impact of flexible working arrangements in smaller businesses. *Employee Relations* 29(2), 138.

McNall, L.A., Masuda, A.D. & Nicklin, J.M. 2010. Flexible work arrangements, job satisfaction, and turnover intentions: The mediating role of work-to-family enrichment. *The Journal of Psychology* 144(1), 61–82.

Moos, M., & Skaburskis, A. 2007. The characteristics and location of home workers in Montreal, Toronto and Vancouver. *Urban Studies* 44(9), 1781–1808.

Peters, P. & Den Dulk, L. 2003. Cross cultural differences in managers' support for home-based telework. *International Journal of Cross Cultural Management* 3(3), 329–346.

Richardson, J. (2009) Geographical flexibility in academia: A cautionary note. *British Journal of Management*, 20, 160–170.

Schokley, K.M. & Allen, T.D. (2007). When flexibility helps: Another look at the availability of flexible work arrangements and work-family conflict. *Journal of Vocational Behaviour* 71, 479–493.

Schweitzer, L. & Duxbury, L. 2006. Benchmarking the use of telework arrangements in Canada. *Canadian Journal of Administrative Sciences* 23(2), 105–117.

Shia, S.M. & Monroe, R.W. 2006. Telecommuting's past and future: A literature review and research agenda. *Business Process Management Journal* 12(4), 455–482.

SSHRM. 2008. *2008 Employee benefits survey*. Retrieved September 17th, 2010, from the World Wide Web: http://www.shrm.org/hrresources/surveyspublished/2008%20Benefits%20Survey%20Report.pdf

Tietze, S. 2002. When "work" comes "home": Coping strategies of teleworkers and their families. *Journal of Business Ethics* 41(4), 385–397.

Tietze, S. 2005. Discourse as strategic coping resource: Managing the interface between "home" and "work". *Journal of Organizational Change Management* 18(1), 48–62.

Tietze, S. & Musson, G. 2003. The times and temporalities of home-based telework. *Personnel Review* 32(4), 438–455.

Tietze, S. & Musson, G. 2005. Recasting the home-work relationship: A case of mutual adjustment? *Organization Studies* 26(9), 1331–1352.

Tremblay, D.G. 2002. Balancing work and family with telework. *Women in Management Review* 17(3/4), 157–170.

Tremblay, D.G. 2003. Telework: a new mode of gendered segmentation? Results from a study in Canada. *Canadian Journal of Communication* 28(4), 461–476.

Tremblay, D.G., Paquet, R. & Najem, E. 2006. Telework: A way to balance work and family or an increase in work-family conflict? *Canadian Journal of Communication* 31(3), 715–731.

Understanding Processes of Individual Resistance to New Working Practices

The Case of Deciding Not to Embrace Telework

Daniel Wade Clarke

INTRODUCTION

One strand of thought holds that younger workers/managers, more accustomed to Information Communication Technology (ICT), are more amenable to teleworking. This chapter explores this idea and seeks to pursue an understanding of individual resistance to telework, explored through the critical themes of place (Tuan, 1991; Brown & O'Hara, 2003), aspiration and identity (Pratt, 2000; Thornbarrow & Brown, 2009). The chapter reports the findings of an original piece of qualitative research conducted in a Scotland-based new business venture, called FifeX, engaged in the design and manufacture of high impact, interactive, hands-on, educational scientific exhibits used in schools and science museums.

In 2006, FifeX moved into new business premises in Tayport. The relocation presented the two owner-managers, Craig and Ken, with the opportunity to consider new ways to work. Acting in my capacity as a full participant–observer (Waddington, 2004), I helped with the relocation and took part in many of the conversations in which this opportunity was discussed. This signaled the beginning of my "placeful" (O'Hara et al., 2003, 72) exploration of home and mobile working and marked my entry into the world of place-making, relocation and workplace management.

Craig and Ken both lived in St. Andrews at the time of the relocation and moving to Tayport, which was closer to Dundee than it is to St. Andrews, added an extra 15 miles each way to their daily commute. Before moving to Tayport, FifeX operated out of one office in the St. Andrews Technology Centre, best described as a University-owned and managed Incubation Unit for small "spin-out" business ventures. Nearly all of FifeX's manufacturing, however, was done off-site.

This chapter suggests that an understanding of individual resistance to telework also requires an understanding of, and empathy with, place, aspirations and identity. The intention of the chapter, therefore, is to propose concepts to help cast fresh light on what happens when individuals resist new ways to work; that is, the social processes that bring resistance into being, how resistance is played out and how it is constituted. Although literature has shed some light on the different rationales underpinning resistance to telework it has not addressed the 'doing' and 'meaning' of individual resistance. This chapter seeks to address this gap, thereby adding to our understanding of teleworking in a "diversity of situations" (Baruch & Yuen, 2000, 524). It is notable, however, that my interest in this work is not to present strategies to help overcome individual resistance, or to offer concepts to see if we can find evidence of them in the data. Rather, similar to Brown and O'Hara (2003, 1580), I am interested in the different ways in which these concepts can "inspire us to look at the data and make sense of the meanings" people attribute to the spatiality of telework, or lack thereof.

REVIEW OF THE LITERATURE ON TELEWORK

Home-based work and the idea of the electronic worker are not new. According to Huws (1991), the idea of the electronic homeworker made its way into public consciousness in the early 1970s in the context of the energy crisis. With the realization that the era of cheap, limitless supplies of fossil-fuel-based energy was over, home-based working offered a way of saving fuel, and was discussed in terms of the 'telecommunications/transportation tradeoff'. By the mid-1970s, researchers (Nilles, 1976; Harkness, 1977) had produced detailed estimates of how many millions of barrels of oil would be saved per annum for each percentage of the U.S. workforce working from home; the word 'telecommuter' was coined (adapted from Huws, 1991).

Since then, a whole range of words and phrases such as home-based-, distance-, remote-, and off-site worker have all been used interchangeably to describe what Baruch and Yuen (2000, 522) and Baruch (2001, 114) refer to as 'teleworkers'. For them, teleworkers are defined as "employees who perform all or a substantial part of their work physically separate from the location of their employer, using IT for operation and communication".[1] Yet, Baruch (2001, 114) cautions that it is a mistake to regard telework as a single, fixed form of employment.

Acknowledging Baruch's (2001, 114) argument, broadly speaking, there are four forms of telework: home-based telecommuting, use of satellite centers, neighborhood work centers, and mobile working (Kurland & Bailey, 1999). This range of flexible work options available to knowledge workers is well broadcast in both popular (Myerson & Ross, 2003) and academic (Donnelly, 2006) literatures, government policy documentation (Department of Trade & Industry [DTI], 2003) and the images popularized by Western media (identified in Mirchandani, 2000).

It is generally accepted that teleworking offers benefits to not only individual employees and organizations, but also to families and society at large (Harpaz, 2002, van Gelderen et al., 2008). Most of these accounts seem to agree on the following: that telework can help lower real estate costs, improve productivity, increase employee flexibility, help retain employees and attract new staff. Other oft-cited benefits are improved work–life balance, more leisure time (i.e., reduced commuting) and reductions in carbon emissions.

In his review on the status of research on teleworking, Baruch (2001, p. 116) notes that "[M]ost of the early writing on teleworking was focused on its innovative and positive influence (or expected impact)". As such, there is no shortage of indications in the literature on how organizations (DTI, 2003) and managers (Helms & Raiszadeh, 2002; Johnson, 2004; Illegems & Verbeke, 2004) can facilitate the implementation of flexible work arrangements. Since the 1990s, however, more balanced research has emerged (Baruch, 1996; Fairweather, 1999; Harris, 2003) which has acknowledged the difficulties, dilemmas and challenges facing both organizations and managers who manage remotely. It would appear that the "rosy picture constructed by past research" (Redman et al. 2009, 172) might be fading.

THE DARKER SIDE OF TELEWORK

Critical perspectives have provided insights into telework in a number of different ways, but mainly in terms of technology (Ahmadi et al., 2000; Vos & van der Voordt, 2001; Towers et al., 2006), surveillance and control (Fairweather, 1999; Kurland & Egan, 1999). Continuing in this critical line of inquiry, there have been more concentrated efforts to heed unheard voices speaking to the negative experiences of teleworking, which, in turn, have drawn attention to the practice of teleworking itself.

Brocklehurst (2001, 456), for example, notes that following a move to homework, many homeworkers engage in "recreating a work identity . . . [that is] . . . convincing to both themselves and to others". In addition, the negative impact of flexible work on identity construction has become the object of several more recent studies (Tietze, 2005; Pini & McDonald, 2008). By researching how people struggle for space to work at home, construct their identity, manage anxiety, "do" family and socialize in the same space, and how they learn to cope with ambivalence (Taskin & Devos, 2005), this body of research has usefully addressed the "darker side" of flexible working.

Elsewhere in the literature, research has examined professional isolation (Pratt, 1984; Ward & Shabha, 2001), the shifting boundaries between home and work (Surman, 2002; Towers et al., 2006), flexibility (Hjorthol & Nossum, 2008), work–life balance (Roberts, 2008), the meaning of teleworking spaces for teleworkers themselves (Brown & O'Hara, 2003;

Surman, 2002) and the non-teleworkers left behind in the office (Golden, 2007). Home-workers families' and/or co-residents' coping strategies for dealing with both the co-presence of sometimes conflicting and competing work and family demands, and the (negative) impact of telework on family life have also been addressed (Sullivan & Lewis, 2001; Tietze, 2002, 2005; Tietze & Musson, 2005; Hilbrecht et al., 2008).

The arguments presented here differ somewhat from other critical accounts of telework. While more recent literature has recognized resistance to new working practices (Baruch, 2001; Peters & Den Dulk, 2003) it has not explored how that resistance is played out. This chapter will, therefore, seek to address this gap by examining the 'doing' and 'meaning' of individual resistance telework.

Having introduced some of the key themes in the literature, I turn now to the theoretical framework within which this chapter is located.

PLACE AS THEORETICAL FRAMEWORK

> The phenomenon of flexible working can, and ought to be, studied from a variety of theoretical perspectives and frameworks (Baruch, 2001, 116).

> I now urge that speech and the written word be considered integral to the construction of place, and therefore integral to the geographer's understanding of place (Tuan, 1991, 694).

Work, no matter what type of work it is, be it "agricultural", "industrial", "cultural", "knowledge" or "creative", is always carried out in some kind of place. Place and the making of place(s) should be a central concern for scholars of telework because according to Brown & O'Hara (2003, 1574), work (and I would argue telework) inescapably and unavoidably involves some kind of place making. Indeed, according to Brown & O'Hara (2003, 1574), "Mobile work does not just 'take place' but rather 'makes place', . . .". Yet, while these authors address practiced space, or "actual" places, they do not address "imagined spaces" (Taylor & Spicer, 2007) understood in this context as space intended for telework that has not yet been created. The idea that teleworking "makes" place is important because it draws our attention to the possibility of making "new" places for teleworking.

Gajendran & Harrison (2007, 1525) note that there is a "substitution of place involved in telecommuting" whereby home replaces the office. However, even before a home is renegotiated or reconstructed as an office, it is a house. After all, home is a house infused with meaning (Tuan, 2004; Mallet, 2004), so to become an office, it must become infused with yet another layer of meaning(s). The creation of a home office, therefore, is the result of material transformations to the physicality of the house itself. Physical space is transformed by the addition of new furniture and the installation of ICT. In preparing for the move to telework, aspiring teleworkers are likely to consult their colleagues and friends in other teleworking organizations in order to try to establish *the* best way of going about it. Alternatively, they might consult the practitioner-oriented literature for step-by-step guides to "make the virtual leap" a successful one (Barron, 2007).

Turning to the teleworker him or herself, when the time comes for the imagined space for teleworking to be translated into an actual place, neophyte teleworkers might speak with professional office outfitters, the employer's facilities management personnel or whomsoever has been tasked with helping bring their imagined telework place into being.

For Tuan (1991, 684), language is "integral to the construction of place, and therefore integral to the geographer's understanding of place". He also contends that "It is simply not possible to understand or explain the physical motions that produce place without overhearing, as it were, the speech—exchange of words—that lie behind them" and reminds us that as well as producing place, language, or words, can "**destruct**" it (p. 693, my emphasis in bold). This invites the question, if our employer, or business partner, for example, denies us the opportunity to work from home and to undertake these seemingly trivial and superficial "design" and place making activities (Clarke, 2008), to what extent might we say that s/he is "destructing" (Tuan, 1991) imagined spaces for teleworking?

Brown and O'Hara (2003, 1570) note that " . . . there are still many unanswered questions regarding mobile work—in particular, surrounding the management of location, and the role which place plays for mobile workers". By concentrating on the power of language to "destruct" (Tuan, 1991, 693) imagined places for teleworking, and combining this focus with an interest in how aspirations can shape individual resistance to the opportunity to telework, this chapter responds directly to the call to study flexible working arrangements "from a variety of theoretical perspectives and frameworks" (Baruch, 2001, 116).

In summary, this chapter casts fresh light on how conversations centered around places, aspirations and identities, and, more specifically, how language itself, can 'kill' the idea of teleworking before it even gets off the ground. It also explores how that resistance is played out, and how it is experienced from the point of view of the person in favor of a move to telework.

NARRATIVES ON DECIDING NOT TO EMBRACE TELEWORK

The context of place making in the case of FifeX provides a contextual anchor for examining the social processes of resistance to the opportunity to embrace telework. Therefore, as in the larger 8-month ethnographic study on place making (Clarke, 2008) upon which this chapter draws; narrative is used as a form of data and theoretical lens. The narratives comprise extracts taken from digitally recorded interactions and extensive field notes collected during the study. Because of space limitations in this chapter, not all the stories told can be represented. As such, the decision to include some narratives at the expense of others constitutes a key analytical element of organizing the data.

Field notes and interview transcripts were revisited and remined in order to cull perceived meaningful connections between relations, situations, events and actions concerning the research participants and their surroundings. From this, the following key moments and incidents were identified to create the overall narrative.

In the following section, some selections from interviews and transcripts from fieldwork with the research participants are used to first illustrate some of the possible reasons for wanting to move to telework; second, how aspirational identity can get in the way to prevent that from happening.

PART ONE: MEANING OF MAKING
THE MOVE TO TELEWORK FOR KEN

From an operational standpoint, FifeX had outgrown the Incubation Unit. Reluctantly, contracts were being turned down because there was no room to do the work. From this, it was generally felt that the lack of space was preventing the company from growing.

The move to Tayport not only meant that there might be more opportunities for both Craig and Ken to work from home, but for Ken there were several other advantages in relocating:

> This place [Tayport] is further away from home than St. Andrews. . . . I can't just pop home and be there in a couple of minutes. It has made the organization of my time much more formalized. And one other thing, I like the drive into work in the morning. It's a way to get focused for the day ahead. In the past, I did not have that.
>
> Now that we are here [in Tayport], I have actually got my own space which is a big thing for me . . . , having the privacy. It takes out the issue of micro-managing each other.

We observe in the excerpt below, for example, how Ken attributes particular importance to having privacy. It is not surprising, therefore, that the opportunity to work from the privacy of his own home was especially appealing precisely because it enabled him to work without interruption from his business partner, Craig:

> The design process is an enormous thing. Because I did most of the [design] work here, in our [St. Andrews] office, Craig could see all my working. He was constantly looking over my shoulder and telling me what to do. 'Change this. Do that. Why are you doing it like that? Why

don't we have it like this . . . ?' In design work, you do a little to get the thing up and running before you show the client. Craig was like the annoying client you get from time to time. Despite thinking he is a good decision maker, he is actually poor. He jumps in too quickly.

Although Ken did not explicitly state that he wanted to prevent Craig from looking over his shoulder, and neither did he openly admit to favoring flexible working arrangements; his latent desire to make the move to telework became somewhat more tangible in the following excerpt in which he spoke about his passion for music and his identity outside the organizational context.

> I know that Craig has an issue with my music [i.e., frequency of live performances]. He thinks that I do too much outside of FifeX and that it gets in the way of my work . . . and he tells me this. I mean. . . . , ok, from time to time . . . , I do take long lunch breaks because I am rehearsing for a concert I am organizing at the University. . . . But during the weekends, when Craig is away, or off doing his thing . . . , whatever he does, I am either working at home, or in [the St. Andrews offices] here. Mid-week, I might not get back from a lunch-time rehearsal until gone 2 or 3 pm, but Craig goes home at 5 pm. . . . Pretty much . . . , well, quite often, I am in here until 7, 8 pm at night . . . [. . . and I send . . .], shit loads of emails from home [during . . .] the mornings, evening time, and during the weekend. But Craig does not see that!

A lot of what FifeX does can be carried out independently of their location. Indeed, their use of work-extending technologies (i.e., information communication technology, such as "caller divert" and Blackberrys) and broadband internet access meant they could both easily work from home. Moreover, given Ken's concerns about his lack of privacy and interference from Craig, telework seemed to be an attractive option. However, Craig was strongly opposed to such a move. The form his opposition took will be explored next.

PART TWO: MEANING OF CRAIG'S RESISTANCE TO NOT MAKING THE MOVE TO TELEWORK

The source of Craig's resistance to telework reflected multiple and diverse concerns, including his personal preference for working and concerns about the image of the organization as a whole. For example, Craig felt that when people visited FifeX for the first time in the St. Andrews Technology Centre, they were often "disappointed" to learn that it operated out of just one of the many offices in the Incubation Unit rather than owning the whole building, as suggested below:

> One thing that surprises me most about our office space [at St. Andrews Technology Centre] is . . . , when clients visit us, they often ask if they

can see where we manufacture our products. They mistake the whole of the St. Andrews Technology Centre for our business premises. Then they always seem disheartened and let down when we bring them into the building and take them to the door leading to our small office.

The importance Craig attributes to FifeX's image becomes clearer in the following excerpt:

While Tayport doesn't have the same appeal as St. Andrews, people can instantly see just how big we are when they visit us here [in Tayport]. And if we still want the nice restaurants and bars to entertain our clients, St. Andrews is only 15 min down the road.

Throughout the study, Craig often spoke openly about what daily life might be like in companies, such as Google. He also mentioned his desire to turn FifeX into a holding company, like Virgin and spoke fondly of Google, forwarding images and case studies illustrating how working life is reported to be inside its offices. Throughout our conversations, Craig conveyed the idea that FifeX ought to have "funky offices" (van Meel & Vos, 2001), openplan, heavily populated, creative, friendly and welcoming workspaces, just like Google, as suggested in the excerpt below:

This is my long term vision. I see massive potential. If you [. . .] are interested in Education . . . , I think there are opportunities [. . .] under the banner of FifeX. I see FifeX as a holding company . . . , kind of like Virgin. Under Virgin Holdings you have Virgin Records, Virgin Trains, Virgin Airways, Virgin Mobile, etc. If one of those goes bust, the centre is not affected. FifeX [in Tayport, now] has the space, the established business relations and funding if we need it. That's no problem. . . . We just need the right people . . . [. . .] to do it with . . . and . . . I want to work with my friends. . . .

This excerpt clearly reflects the extent of Craig's aspirations for both how the organization would function and its ultimate development.

DISCUSSION AND ANALYSIS

I turn now to the subject of how teleworking would get in the way of what Craig was trying to create, particularly if viewed from Ken's perspective.

Place

Viewed through the lens of 'place making', Craig's fascination with Google and concern about FifeX's public image provide some explanation for his resistance to telework. More specifically, in order to realize his dream to turn FifeX into a future Google or Virgin, he had to "destruct" (Tuan, 1991, p. 693) Ken's imagined places for teleworking. This 'destruction' frequently took the form of emphasizing the centrality of the current office space and office hours to his daily work activities with comments such as: "I have been in since 8:50 am" (when Ken arrived at 9:45 am), or "If you need me for anything, just call, I will be here until 5 pm" (when Ken was leaving the office at 4 pm).

Aspiration

Listening to Craig talk about Google, Virgin, the future of FifeX, and the need for both Ken and himself to be in the office all day, everyday (see below), I was struck by his ability to create expectations by resorting to discourses of managerial identity: namely, that of the visible (present) versus the invisible (absent) manager; and aspirational identities (Pratt, 2000; Thornbarrow & Brown, 2009). More specifically, because it was important for him that others see for themselves "just how **big** we are" and "what we have achieved", by drawing on conceptions of social identity and 'aspirational identities' we can see how scale and visibility was important for Craig, as symbolized through the size of the new business premises in Tayport and constant presence of two managing directors. All this was central to his self-concept, aspirational identity and what he ultimately wanted FifeX to become. In aspiring to be 'big' and dreaming of all that FifeX could achieve, Craig was constantly reminded of what he did not have (i.e., busy offices, owning the entire building) and of what he had both at a personal and organizational level. In other words, his aspirational identity served as a constant reminder of what he was yet to achieve.

Viewed from Craig's standpoint, by not being fully present at all times, Ken was not making himself physically available to satisfy the needs of the business, existing clients and potential new customers. Moreover, by not being physically present in the office during what he felt were regular business hours (i.e., times when customers might come to the office), Craig felt that Ken was making FifeX look even smaller and thus even further away from his ultimate goal for the company. In Craig's eyes, when Ken is absent and he (Craig) is left to meet customers alone, FifeX looks like "one-man-and-his-shed", which, he feels is an inaccurate portrayal of what FifeX is and (perhaps more importantly) has the potential to be. For Craig, then, FifeX's organizational identity and potential must be protected by resisting the move toward teleworking and, in particular, ensuring that Ken is on the premises (at least during business hours). This resistance also, by necessity, involves him seeking to manage and, in some instances, seeking to regulate (Gotsi et al., 2010) Ken's identity by influencing how he presents himself to customers and clients—i.e., at a minimum by ensuring that Ken is physically visible to customers. Through talking to and wanting to act out the role of a 9–5 pm managing director with Ken, and in an effort to make sense of the organization and form an identification with FifeX, Craig's deidentifaction with "one-man-and-his-shed" outfits was an ongoing attempt to create a specific image for FifeX. Furthermore, it might also be that, in aspiring to imitate Richard Branson, or for FifeX to be like Virgin, Craig was seeking to "vicariously gain the qualities of the other" (Ashforth & Mael, 1989, 22).

Identity

As Ken is the production director, he must visit existing clients and potential new customers at their place of work. For Craig, Ken already spends enough time out of the office as it is. And so, if teleworking became an option, Craig's major fear is that Ken would become even more 'invisible'. From an image management perspective, as far as Craig is concerned, such a situation would be problematic if not untenable, because it would undermine Fifex's ability to display its two most important assets, i.e., it's managing directors. In light of Craig's aspirational identity for both FifeX and himself, we can see the importance he attributes to Ken being present at all times but specifically during 'working hours'.

Speaking, then, from an (aspirational) identity point of view, if Ken is not around, FifeX will appear (to both Craig and others) to be even further from its potential status as a big, friendly, creative, 'funky' office space, filled with like-minded people. What we see here then, is how Craig's aspirations for FifeX, have created an "identity standard" (Stets & Burke, 2000, 232) which he feels he must maintain and which, in turn, results in his resisting Ken's efforts toward teleworking. Yet, on the other hand, Ken is no pawn in the turn of events. Indeed, throughout the study it was clear that he also displayed clear resistance, but, in this instance, toward Craig's aspirations for the company:

> "I mean [. . .] we are not as big as Craig likes to think. I don't know what Craig thinks of us and I don't know exactly what he tells other people, but we are definitely not this big [. . .] company he seems to like to think that we are!"

Since FifeX is not perceived by Ken and others to be as big as Craig would like it to be, Craig is constantly confronted with a disparity between his current and aspired identity.

For Ken, however, the idea that he should make himself available between 9 am–5 pm, 5 days a week, just in case somebody drops by with a question that they would like the production director to answer, was equally untenable. In this regard we see how, in supporting the move toward teleworking he was attempting to 'destruct' Craig's imagined space of an office where they were both located during office hours:

... it is not as if new and existing clients are visiting us on a daily basis, definitely not at 9 am on Wednesday mornings. Most people who visit us come at a specific time because they set an appointment.

The idea of not being a visible 9 am–5 pm director both undermines Craig's conception of what it means to work and his conception of the place of work. By showing that he was not prepared to let Ken vacate the role of a 9–5pm production director because the notion of the invisible managing director is anathema to his own self-concept and social relations, Craig was resisting the opportunity to embrace telework. In an attempt to usurp Ken's sense of self with his ideal self, when Craig told Ken, "If you need me for anything, just call", Ken's sense of self was being devalued.

For Ken, however, work is an activity and not a place. The main attraction with working from home was that he could avoid the gaze of Craig and "work around" (Brown & O'Hara, 2003, 1576) his music life. Echoing previous research findings, this theme reflects one of the main advantages of working from home in that it makes it more difficult to be configured or controlled (at least in theory) by others (Brown & O'Hara, 2003, 1582). However, through failing to plan and persuade Craig of the perceived importance of working from home, the linguistic creation (i.e., naming) of Tayport as a 9–5 pm workspace simultaneously spelled the destruction of places for teleworking and the denial of any potential for embracing telework practices on a more formal level.

From the above account and discussion, and consistent with previous discussions in the literature on telework which address issues of control and monitoring (Taskin & Devos, 2005, 18), an important finding we see here is how the whole notion of "visibility" and "presence" permeates Craig's discussions with Ken. However, rather than appealing to the need to be seen to be working (i.e., visibility) so that Craig could control and monitor Ken, Craig's appeal for Ken to be "present" was based upon his aspiration to create a different kind of business organization. Craig set out to name Tayport as the **place** of work in order achieve his **aspirational** self through his relationship with Ken and other organizations (i.e., by comparing "one-man-and-his-shed" outfits with Google and Virgin). Viewed from Ken's perspective, it would appear, then, that Craig seeks to find "meaning that originates from a sense of discontentment about who one is" (Pratt, 2000, 464) and to shape Ken's own **identity** as a 9–5 pm production director.

CONCLUSION

The findings suggest that resistance to new ways of working simultaneously constitutes the destruction of imagined places for telework, the maintenance of actual (lived) places of work, and a site for identity work. In particular, we have seen how Craig's identity work got in the way of

Ken's spatial imaginings and subsequently prevented him from formally adopting teleworking practices. Thus, along with his work/place relationship, Ken was "configured" (Brown & O'Hara, 2003, 1582), by Craig as he managed to successfully decrease home as a place to work during the hours of 9 am–5 pm.

This chapter has sought to add to Brown and O'Hara's work (2003) on the "placeful" dimension of telework. I have contributed to this debate by exploring how individual resistance to telework unfurls and I have provided a conceptual framework through synthesizing the critical themes of place, aspiration and identity to assist us in that. I conclude though, by saying that the conceptual framework that I have provided is one that resonates loudly with Craig and Ken's experience and helps me explain and make sense of their feelings. It is by no means fixed and other critical themes could have been used.

NOTES

1. For alternative definitions and a detailed analysis of what constitutes telecommuting / teleworking, that is, the variety of remote work options, see Mokhtarian (1991).

REFERENCES

Ahmadi, M., Helms, M. M. & Ross, T. J. 2000. Technological developments: Shaping the telecommuting work environment of the future. *Facilities* 18(1/2) 83–89.

Ashforth, B. & Mael, F. 1989. Social identity theory and the organization. *The Academy of Management Review* 14(1), 20–39.

Bailey, D.E. & Kurland, N.B. 2002. Review of telework research: Findings, new directions and lessons for the study of modern work. *Journal of Organizational Behavior*, 23, 383–400.

Barron, M. 2007. Making the virtual leap: Ten issues to consider about telecommuting. *Industrial and Commercial Training* 39(7), 396–399.

Baruch, Y. 1996. Homeworking—attention is needed. *Facilities* 14(3/4), 49–51.

Baruch, Y. 2001. The status of research on teleworking and an agenda for future research. *International Journal of Management Reviews* 3(2), 113–129.

Baruch, Y. & Yuen, Y. K. J. 2000. Inclination to opt for teleworking. A comparative analysis of United Kingdom versus Hong Kong employees. *International Journal of Manpower* 21(7), 521–539.

Brocklehurst, M. 2001. Power, identity and new technology homework: Implications for 'new forms' of organizing. *Organization Studies* 22(3), 445–466.

Brown, B. & O'Hara, K. 2003. Place as a practical concern of mobile workers. *Environment and Planning* 35, 1565–1587.

Clarke, D. W. 2008. *The social poetics of place making. Challenging the control/dichotomous perspective* (unpublished doctoral thesis), University of St. Andrews. Available from http://research-repository.st-andrews.ac.uk/bitstream/10023/691/6/Daniel%20W%20Clarke%20PhD%20thesis.pdf

Department of Trade and Industry (DTI). 2003. *Telework guidance* (DTI Publication No. 6856/10k/08/03/NP). London: UK. Crown Copyright. Retrieved from http://webarchive.nationalarchives.gov.uk/+/http://www.berr.gov.uk/files/file27456.pdf

Donnelly, R. 2006. How "free" is the free worker? An investigation into the working arrangements available to knowledge workers. *Personnel Review* 35(1), 78–97.

Fairweather, N. B. 1999. Surveillance in employment: The case of teleworking. *Journal of Business Ethics* 22, 39–49.

Gajendran, R. S. & Harrison, D. A. 2007. The good, the bad, and the unknown about telecommuting: Meta-analysis of psychological mediators and individual consequences. *Journal of Applied Psychology* 92(6), 1524–1541.

Golden, T. 2007. Co-workers who telework and the impact on those in the office: Understanding the implications of virtual work for co-worker satisfaction and turnover intentions. *Human Relations* 60(11), 1641–1667.

Gotsi, M., Andriopoulos, C., Lewis, M. W. & Ingram, A. E. 2010. Managing creatives: Paradoxical approaches to identity regulation. *Human Relations* 63(6), 781–805.

Harkness, R. C. 1977. *Technology Assessment of Telecommunication / Transportation Interaction*, Menlo Park, CA: Stanford Research Institute.

Harpaz, I. 2002. Advantages and disadvantages of telecommuting for the individual, organization and society. *Work Study* 51(2), 74–80.

Harris, L. 2003. Home-based teleworking and the employment relationship. Managerial challenges and dilemmas. *Personnel Review* 32(4), 422–437.

Helms, M. M. & Raiszadeh, F. M. E. 2002. Virtual offices: Understanding and managing what you cannot see. *Work Study* 51(5), 240–247.

Hilbrecht, M., Shaw, S. M., Johnson, L. C. & Andrey, J. 2008. 'I'm Home for the Kids': Contradictory implications for work–life balance of teleworking mothers. *Gender, Work and Organization* 15(5), 444–476.

Hjorthol, R. & Nossum, Å. 2008. Teleworking: A reduction in travel or just increased flexibility? *The Journal of E-working* 2, 81–94.

Huws, U. 1991. Teleworking: Projections. *Futures* 23, 19–31.

Illegems, V. & Verbeke, A., 2004. Telework: What Does it Mean for Management? *Long Range Planning* 37, 319–334.

Johnson, J. 2004. Flexible working: Changing the manager's role. *Management Decision*, 42(6), 721–737.

Kurland, N. B. & Bailey, D. E. 1999. Telework: The advantages and challenges of working here, there, anywhere, and anytime. *Organization Dynamics* Autumn, 53–68.

Kurland, N. B. & Egan, T. D. 1999. Telecommuting: Justice and control in the virtual organization. *Organization Science* 10(4), 500–513.

Mallett, S. 2004. Understanding home: A critical review of the literature. The Editorial Board of *The Sociological Review*, 62–89.

Mirchandani, K. 2000. "The best of both worlds" and "cutting my own throat": Contradictory images of home-based work. *Qualitative Sociology* 23(2), 159–182.

Mokhtarian, P. 1991. Telecommuting and travel: State of the practice, state of the art. *Transportation* 18(4), 319–342.

Myerson, J. & Ross, P. 2003. *The 21st century office*. London: Laurence King Publishing.

Nilles, J. 1976. *The telecommunications-transportation tradeoff*. New York: John Wiley.

O'Hara, K., Brown, B. & Perry, M. 2003. Mobile work, technology and place. In *Proceedings of mobile communication: Social and political effects*, Budapest, Hungry. Retrieved from http://www.ict.csiro.au/staff/kenton.ohara/papers/Ohara_mobilecomms.pdf

Peters, P. & Den Dulk, L. 2003. Cross cultural differences in managers' support for home-based telework. *International Journal of Cross Cultural Management* 3(3), 329–346.

Pini, B. & McDonald, P. 2008. Men, masculinities and flexible work in local government. *Gender in Management: An International Journal* 23(8), 598–612.

Pratt, J. H. 1984. Home teleworking: A study of its pioneers. *Technological Forecasting and Social Change* 25, 1–14.

Pratt, M. G. 2000. The good, the bad, and the ambivalent: Managing identification among Amway cistributors. *Administrative Science Quarterly* 45(3), 456–493.

Redman, T., Snape, E. & Ashurst, C. 2009. Location, location, location: Does place of work really matter? *British Journal of Management* 20, 171–181.

Roberts, E. 2008. Time and work–life balance: The roles of 'temporal customization' and 'life temporality'. *Gender, Work and Organization* 15(5), 430–453.

Stets, J. E. & Burke, P. J. 2000. Identity theory and social identity theory. *Social Psychology Quarterly* 63(3), 224–237.

Surman, E. 2002. Dialectics of dualism: The symbolic importance of the home/work divide, *ephemera* 2(3), 209–223.

Sullivan, C. & Lewis, S. 2001. Home-based telework, gender, and the synchronization of work and family: Perspectives of teleworkers and their co-residents. *Gender, Work and Organization* 8(2), 123–145.

Taskin, L. & Devos, V., 2005. Paradoxes from the Individualization of human Resource management: The case of telework. *Journal of Business Ethics* 62, 13–24.

Taylor, S. & Spicer, A. 2007. Time for space: A narrative review of research on organizational space. *International Journal of Management Reviews* 9(4), 325–346.

Thornbarrow, T. & Brown, A. D. 2009. 'Being regimented': Aspiration, discipline and identity work in the British parachute regiment. *Organization Studies* 30(4), 1–22.

Tietze, S. 2002. When "work" comes "home": Coping strategies of teleworkers and their families. *Journal of Business Ethics* 41, 385–396.

Tietze, S. 2005. Discourse as strategic coping resource: Managing the interface between "home" and "work". *Journal of Organizational Change Management* 18(1), 48–62.

Tietze, S. & Musson, G. 2005. Recasting the home-work relationship: A case of mutual adjustment? *Organization Studies* 26(9), 1331–1352.

Towers, I., Duxbury, L., Higgins, C. & Thomas, J. 2006. Time thieves and space invaders: Technology, work and the organization. *Journal of Organizational Change Management* 19(5), 592–618.

Tuan, Y. 1991. Language and the making of place: A narrative-descriptive approach. *Annals of the Association of American Geographers* 81(4), 684–696.

van Gelderen, M., Sayers, J. & Keen, C. 2008. Home-based internet businesses as drivers of variety. *Journal of Small Business and Enterprise Development* 15(1), 162–177.

van Meel, J. & Vos, P. 2001. Funky offices: Reflections on office design in the 'new economy'. *Journal of Corporate Real Estate* 3(4), 322–334.

Vos, P. & van der Voordt, T. 2001. Tomorrow's offices through today's eyes: Effects innovation in the working environment. *Journal of Corporate Real Estate* 4(1), 48–65.

Waddington, D. 2004. Participant observation. In *Essential Guide to Qualitative Methods in Organizational Research*. Eds. C. Cassell, & G. Symon. London: Sage, 154–164.

Ward, N. & Shabha, G. 2001. Teleworking: An assessment of socio-psychological factors. *Facilities* 19(1/2), 61–70.

9 Telecommuters

Creative or Exhausted Workers? A Study into the Conditions Under Which Telecommuters Experience Flow and Exhaustion

Pascale Peters and Marijn Wildenbeest

INTRODUCTION

To remain competitive in fast-changing global markets, organizations increasingly focus on employees' human capital, instead of more traditional sources which used to provide competitive advantage, such as technology or economies of scale (Pfeffer, 1994). In particular, employees' skills that are more difficult to imitate, such as creativity and innovativeness, are currently seen as organizations' core values (Becker & Huselid, 1998; Vittersø, Akselsen, Evjemo, Julsrud, Yttri & Bergvik, 2003). This has set the trend for new ways of organizing work and new work practices, in which employees are given a greater span of control and accountability (cf. Reich, 1992).

Telecommuting, also termed tele(home)working, is one of the outstanding contemporary and newly emerging work practices, that is believed to have the potential to enhance both organizational competitiveness and employees' quality of working life. In 2005, the share of telecommuters among European workers, including self-employed home-office workers, averaged about 8% (European Foundation for the Improvement of Living and Working Conditions, 2007). Although diffusion of telecommuting practices varies across countries, telecommuting is generally expected to become one of the main pillars of working life in the Information Society (European Commission, 2000).

In view of the anticipated spread of telecommute practices, the present study aims to contribute to the scientific debates on positive and negative outcomes of telecommuting (Bailey & Kurland, 2002; Gajendran & Harrison, 2007) and to stimulate better implementation of telecommute policies and practices in organizations. We assess the effects of working conditions on two work outcomes, work-related flow and exhaustion as perceived by employees working from home for part of their contractual working hours, in the remainder of this chapter, are referred to as telecommuters. The focus is on the Netherlands, one of the front-running West-European service sector economies with regard to telecommuting: in 2007, 32% of the workers (including the self-employed) worked at home at least 1 hour per week (Beffers & Van den Brink, 2008).

'Work-related flow' can be viewed as a potential positive telecommute outcome (cf. Peters & Wildenbeest, 2010). Flow is a psychological concept generally defined as "The state in which people are so intensely involved in an activity that nothing else seems to matter; the experience itself is so enjoyable that people will do it even at great cost, for the sheer sake of doing it (Csikszentmihalyi, 1992, 4)". Flow may relate to any activity perceived as useful and meaningful and which makes one feel good. Work-related flow is defined as a short-term peak experience, or a positive feeling, which is characterized by three dimensions: absorption, work enjoyment and intrinsic work motivation (Bakker, 2008). Absorption refers to a situation of full concentration in which people are fully engaged in their work. Work enjoyment indicates that workers enjoy the work activity, which then leads to a higher quality of working life. Intrinsic work motivation relates to people's wish to be engaged in the work activity, just for the sake of the activity itself and to continue doing it (ibid.). Flow may be a purpose in itself, but it may also enhance other positive work outcomes, such as creativity (Amabile, Conti, Coon, Lazenby & Herron, 1996). During a flow experience a worker feels satisfied and happy (Csikszentmihalyi, 1992), which opens up the possibility to be more creative and innovative (Csikszentmihalyi, 1998), and to perform better, and, ultimately, to enhance competitive advantage (Becker & Huselid, 1998; Pfeffer, 1994).

Exhaustion can be viewed as a negative work outcome which, under certain work conditions, may also be influenced by telecommuting (Golden, 2006; Peters & Wildenbeest, 2010). Exhaustion implies that workers suffer from extreme fatigue (Schaufeli & Bakker, 2004) and is viewed as the most important component of burnout (Wright & Cropanzano, 1998). Burnout may lead to a loss of commitment, long-term sick-leave and turnover (More, 2000), which brings about costs for both the employer and employee.

To assess the working conditions under which telecommuters experience flow and exhaustion, this quantitative study employs the Job Demands–Resources Model (JD–R model) (Demerouti, Bakker, Nachreiner & Schaufeli, 2001) to develop testable hypotheses. The JD–R model has been used in previous studies on flow (Bakker, 2008; Mäkikangas, Bakker, Aunola & Demerouti, 2010), but to the best of our knowledge, it has only been applied to flow and burnout of telecommuters on one previous occasion (Peters & Wildenbeest, 2010). In fact, to date, telecommuting research that includes either flow (cf. Manssour, 2003) or burnout (cf. Golden, 2006) is scarce.

THEORY AND HYPOTHESES

The Job Demands–Resources Model

The JD–R model, initially used to explain burnout (exhaustion and mental distance), distinguishes between two broad categories of working conditions: job demands and job resources. Moreover, it describes two central mechanisms: the exhaustion process and the motivation process (Demerouti et al., 2001).

In the exhaustion process, *job demands* continuously use up energy reserves which, in the long run, leads to exhaustion. Job demands may refer to physical, psychological, social or organizational aspects of work, which require physical or mental effort of the worker (ibid.). Demands become stressors when time to recover is insufficient. In that case, too much effort leads to exhaustion (ibid.). Important job demands mentioned in the literature are: work overload (Bakker, 2008), working hours and commuting time (Peters & Van der Lippe, 2007), physical and emotional demands (cf. Bakker & Geurts, 2004) and work–home interference (Bakker & Geurts, 2004).

In the motivation process, *a lack of job resources* leads to mental distance towards work (Demerouti et al., 2001). Resources are defined as those physical, psychological, social, or organizational aspects of work which are useful with regard to: (1) the achievement of work-related goals; (2) the reduction of demands and associated costs; or (3) the enhancement of personal development (Demerouti et al., 2001). When job resources are insufficient, goals cannot be realized, negative demands are not compensated and personal growth not stimulated (ibid.). As a consequence, workers may experience failure and frustration. To cope with this, workers may develop a detached attitude toward their work. In the literature, several categories of job resources are distinguished: (1) resources at the organizational level; (2) the interpersonal level; and (3) the job level (Schaufeli & Bakker, 2004). Important resources available at the organizational level are possibilities for personal growth and career options (Bakker, 2008; Bakker & Geurts, 2004). The most important resources at the inter-personal relationship level are support from colleagues (Bakker, 2008) and support from the manager (Bakker, Demerouti, Hakanen & Xanthopoulou, 2007). An example of a resource at the job level is job autonomy (Bakker, 2008; Bakker & Geurts, 2004).

Whereas the JD–R model was initially used to study burnout, in more recent studies using this model, positive psychological work outcomes related to optimal performance and employee well-being have gained importance (Schaufeli, Salanova, González-Romá & Bakker, 2002). In these studies, the motivation process is increasingly seen as a positive process: instead of emphasizing the negative effects resulting from a lack of resources, current research also looks into positive effects of job resources, such as work-related flow (cf. Bakker, 2008). With regard to flow, it is assumed that workers experience flow when job demands are not too high and when job resources are sufficiently present (Salanova, Bakker, & Llorens, 2006).

Although it is recognized that job demands may also facilitate flow and job resources may prevent exhaustion (cf. Bakker & Geurts, 2004), generally, job demands are more likely to affect exhaustion than flow. In a similar vein, the relationships between job resources and flow are expected to be stronger than the relationships between job resources and exhaustion.

Based on the mechanisms described above, the present study looks into the effects of job demands and resources, on both telecommuters' perceived levels of exhaustion and work-related flow. The job demands distinguished in this study are: overtime, work overload, commuting time, distractions from work in the workplace office and in the home office and work–home interference. The job resources examined are: job autonomy and supervisory and collegial support. Below, the hypotheses to be tested in this study are developed.

Hypotheses

Overtime

Time–spatial flexibility is often associated with ongoing work intensification (cf. Appelbaum, Bailey, Berg & Kalleberg, 2000). Under these conditions, telecommuters may feel that they have to reciprocate by giving employers who offer their employees time–spatial flexibility something in return (cf. Fleetwood, 2007), for instance, working longer hours (Peters & Van der Lippe, 2007). Indeed, telecommuters may work overtime and skip their lunch or tea breaks when working at home (Bailey & Kurland, 2002). In that case, telecommuters may find it difficult to fully recover from work. In the long run, the lack of 'recreation time' may increase exhaustion (Demerouti et al., 2001), and, maybe, reduce flow. However, as telecommuting allows employees to ignore the standard office hours usually imposed on them, the availability of more time for work in the home office may create room for flow. Based on this, it can be expected that: (1) telecommuters who work more overtime experience more exhaustion. However, (2) the effect of overtime on flow is not straightforward.

Work Overload

Generally, telecommuting allows employees to organize their work in more efficient ways, which may reduce employees' perceptions of work overload (Gajendran & Harrison, 2007). However, the associated lack of alternation and breaks, particularly in the home office, may also increase perceptions of work overload (Walrave & De Bie, 2005). In any case, it can be expected that telecommuters who experience more work overload are (1) more exhausted and (2) experience less flow (cf. Bakker et al., 2007).

Commuting Time

One of the outstanding advantages of telecommuting is that it reduces employees' weekly commuting time (Mann & Holdsworth, 2003; Ory & Mokhtarian, 2007). The energy saved and the reduction of commuting related stress may cause telecommuters to feel less exhausted (Montrieul & Lippel, 2003). Moreover, telecommuting may increase the time that employees have available for concentrated working, which may enhance their flow experience. Studies show that especially employees facing longer commuting hours prefer to telecommute (Peters, Tijdens & Wetzels, 2004). However, most telecommuters only work from home occasionally (Peters & Van der Lippe, 2007), which also implies that among telecommuters longer commuting hours are likely to affect flow and exhaustion levels. Therefore, telecommuters having longer daily commuting times are expected to experience (1) more exhaustion and (2) less flow than telecommuters having shorter commuting hours.

Distractions from Work in the Workplace Office

In the workplace office, employees can easily be distracted from work by surrounding colleagues or customers demanding time and energy (Bailey & Kurland, 2002). These distractions and disruptions may reduce flow. Moreover, factors in the work environment can use up emotional and mental energy and, therefore, enhance exhaustion (Golden, 2006). Since most telecommuters only occasionally work at home, for 1 or 2 days at most (Bailey & Kurland, 2002; Peters & Van der Lippe, 2007), telecommuters still spend the largest share of their working time in the workplace office. Consequently, it can be expected that, also among telecommuters, more work disruptions or distractions from work in the central office enhance (1) exhaustion and (2) reduce flow.

Distractions from Work in the Home Office

Telecommuting has the potential to enhance absorption, which can help employees to focus and meet deadlines. The need for work concentration appears to be one of the outstanding reasons why employees prefer to and why employers allow telecommuting (Peters et al., 2004). At home, however, telecommuters can also be distracted from work (Mirchandani, 2000), for example, by disruptions because of the presence of children, or by the noise produced by other family members, neighbors or machines. Like the workplace office, distractions can engender exhaustion (Golden, 2006). Distractions from work during telecommuting days may also hinder flow. Based on this, it can be expected that telecommuters who report more distractions from work in their home offices experience (1) more exhaustion and (2) less flow.

Work–Home Interference

Telecommuting often causes boundaries between the work and home domains to become blurred. This may enhance work–home interference. The relationship between telecommuting and work–home interference has often been studied (cf. Peters & Van der Lippe, 2007). Since work–home interference is likely to affect exhaustion and to reduce flow (Bakker & Geurts, 2004), it can be expected that telecommuters who experience more work–home interference experience (1) more exhaustion and (2) less flow.

Job Autonomy

Job autonomy allows employees to cope with stressful working demands (Bakker & Demerouti, 2007), which are likely to reduce exhaustion. In addition, a previous study showed job autonomy to lead to more flow (Bakker, 2008). Therefore, it can be expected that telecommuters who enjoy more job autonomy experience (1) less exhaustion and (2) more flow.

Social Support from Colleagues and Supervisor

One major disadvantage of telecommuting is the alleged lack of social contact among co-workers and between telecommuters and their supervisors (Beffers & Van den Brink, 2008). In the JD–R model, social support is also viewed as one of the most important single job resources, since it helps employees to meet work-related goals, and, therefore, to reduce stress and exhaustion (Bakker & Demerouti, 2007). In addition to the more instrumental helping behavior, the emotional aspects of social support can also buffer the impact of job demands. Consequently, workers experiencing social support from their colleagues and supervisors at work may consider their work as more enjoyable. Therefore, telecommuters who perceive their colleagues and supervisor to be more supporting are expected to experience (1) less exhaustion and (2) more flow.

METHODOLOGY

Data

The data used in this study is a subsample of a larger data set collected in 2003 by means of a multistage sample. In the first stage, 30 organizations in the Netherlands, covering both public and private organizations, were selected. For the purpose of the study, knowledge-intensive and larger organizations were oversampled. In each organization, a selected number of employees of two or three job categories (and their managers) were asked to participate. The employees (and their spouses) were interviewed in their homes using both computer-controlled and written questionnaires. The response rate among the employees was 29% (cf. Peters & Van der Lippe, 2007).

In the employee questionnaire, telecommuters were defined as employees who work at home at least part of their contractual working time, excluding overtime performed at home. In the total sample ($N = 1114$), 21.9% of the employees' telecommute days averaged less than 1 day per week; 5% telecommute 1 day per week; 1.4% telecommute 2 days per week; 0.7% telecommute 3 days per week; 0.4% telecommute 4 days per week; and 0.3% telecommute 5 days per week.

In the subsample of telecommuters used in the present study (331 tele-commuters), 87 respondents worked at home 1 day per week, on average, or more. In the subsample 59% of the telecommuters were males and 41% were females. The average age was 40.6 years ($SD = 8.6$). The youngest telecommuter was 24 and the oldest was 63 years old. As a consequence of the selection procedure, the share of higher educated was high (84%). Most telecommuters (78%) were married or cohabiting; only 22% were single. More than one-half of the telecommuters (54%) had a child living at home. Forty six percent of telecommuters' youngest child was less than 13.

Operationalization

Telecommuters' experience of work-related flow was assessed with the Work-Related Flow Instrument (WOLF) (Bakker, 2008). The WOLF-instrument comprises 13 statements referring to the way in which the respondent experienced his or her work during the last 2 weeks (ibid.). Five statements relate to *intrinsic motivation*: I would still do this work, even if I received less pay; I find that I also want to work in my free time; I work because I enjoy it; when I am working on something, I am doing it for myself; I get my motivation from the work itself, and not from the reward for it (ibid.). Four statements refer to *work enjoyment*: My work gives me a good feeling; I do my work with a lot of enjoyment; I feel happy during my work; I feel cheerful when I am working (ibid.). Four statements assess *absorption*: When I am working, I think about nothing else; I get carried away by my work; when I am working, I forget everything else around me; I am totally immersed in my work (ibid.). In the present study, the Cronbach's α of the sum score of all three flow dimensions was 0.89. A higher sum score corresponds with more frequent flow experiences as indicated by the telecommuter (7 = always; 1 = never).

Telecommuters' feelings of *exhaustion* were assessed with a subscale of three items (Cronbach's α = 0.85) (cf. Schaufeli, Leiter, Maslach & Jackson, 1996). One of the items was: "I feel mentally exhausted from work." A higher score corresponds with a higher level of exhaustion (7 = each day; 1 = never).

Telecommuters' perceptions of *work overload* was assessed with a 3-item scale referring to the speed of work and the work load (Van Veldhoven & Meijman, 1994). A higher score corresponds with more work overload (5 = always; 1 = never) (Cronbach's α = 0.67).

Commuting time was assessed with one single question: "How much time on average do you spend commuting to your work". This question relates to one-way commuting time expressed in minutes per day.

Overtime was assessed with one single question: "How often does it happen that you have to do overtime in the evening or in the weekend?" A higher score relates to more frequent overtime in evenings or the weekend (5 = always; 1 = never).

Telecommuters' perceptions of *distractions from work in the central office* were assessed with three items: I suffer from noise because of colleagues talking and walking around; I am distracted from work by my colleagues; I am distracted from work by noise from devices (telephones, fax, computers, etc.). A higher score corresponds with more distractions from work in the central office (5 = always; 1 = never) (Cronbach's α = 0.79).

Telecommuters' perceptions of *distractions from work in the home office* was assessed with three items based on the previous items: I suffer from noise by other persons (neighbors or household members); I am distracted from my work in my home office by other people; I am distracted from my work in my home office by noise from devices. A higher score corresponds with more distractions from work in the home office (5 = always; 1= never) (Cronbach's α = 0.68).

Telecommuters' perceptions of *work–home interference* were assessed with a validated subscale consisting of three items (Geurts, Taris, Kompier, Dikkers, Van Hooff & Kinnunen, 2005), for example, "How often does it happen that your work schedule makes it difficult for you to fulfill your domestic obligations?" A higher score corresponds with higher levels of negative work–home interference (5 = always; 1 = never) (Cronbach's α = 0.65).

Telecommuters' perceptions of *job autonomy* was assessed with three items concerning freedom of action in accomplishing formal work task (Bakker, Demerouti, Taris, Schaufeli & Schreurs, 2003). A higher score corresponds with more job autonomy (5 = always; 1 = never) (Cronbach's α = 0.69).

Telecommuters' perceptions of *support from colleagues* was assessed with three items (Bakker et al., 2003), for example: "Can you ask your colleague for help if necessary?" A higher score corresponds with more perceived collegial support (5 = always; 1 = never) (Cronbach's α = 0.80).

Telecommuters' perceptions of *support from supervisor* was assessed with 5 items (Le Blanc, 1994), for example, "I feel appreciated by my supervisor". A higher score corresponds with more perceived support from one's supervisor (5 = fully agree; 1 = fully disagree) (Cronbach's α = 0.89).

Control Variables

The variables used to control for other factors that may affect telecommuters' experienced levels of flow and exhaustion are presented below.

Golden (2006) shows employees' *telecommute frequency* to correlate negatively with exhaustion. In the present study, three telecommuter categories were distinguished (Peters & Van der Lippe, 2007): (1) *occasional telecommuters* working at home on average less than 1 day per week; (2) *light telecommuters* working at home on average 1 day per week; and (3) *heavy telecommuters* working at home on average more than 1 day per week.

Although previous studies show that personal characteristics hardly affect exhaustion (More, 2000), the present study controls for *age, sex,* and *household situation of the respondents.* Women appear to score higher on exhaustion than men (Bakker, Schaufeli & Van Dierendonck, 2000). In the present study, sex was measured with a dummy variable (1 = female). Moreover, single workers are shown to experience more exhaustion than cohabiting workers (ibid.), which may be because spouses can provide support and distraction, which balances factors generating exhaustion. In this study, the cohabiting telecommuters were chosen as the reference group in the analyses. Surprisingly, the presence of children in a household appears to reduce the level of exhaustion (ibid.). In this study, this was measured with a dummy variable (1= child[ren] present).

Analyses

Correlation analysis shows that there was no multicollinearity among the independent variables used in the study (Table 9.1). To test the hypotheses and the influence of the control variables, multiple regression analyses were conducted explaining the variance in the scores of telecommuters on the full-flow and the exhaustion scale. In addition to the adjusted R^2, the standardized coefficients (β) were calculated to compare the magnitudes of the effects of all single independent variables used in this study.

RESULTS

Flow

Multivariate regression analysis (Table 9.2) shows that a large number of independent variables have significant relationships with *flow* (adjusted R^2 = 26%). The significant relationships in the flow model are discussed below.

Contrary to expectations, telecommuters reporting more work overload and more overtime score higher on flow. Also, contrary to expectations, telecommuters who experience more distractions in their home offices report higher flow levels. In line with expectations, however, telecommuters who report more work–home interference experience lower flow levels. In addition, in line with hypotheses, telecommuters having more job autonomy and those reporting more social support from colleagues and supervisors experience more flow.

Furthermore, telecommuters who work from home 1 day per week or more experience more flow in comparison with telecommuters who work from home occasionally. Senior telecommuters also experience more flow.

Table 9.1 Pearson Correlation Analysis between Independent Variables (Job Demands and Job Resources) and Dependent Variables (Flow and Exhaustion) (N = 317)

	1	2	3	4	5	6	7	8	9	10	11	12	13	14	15	16
1. Flow	1															
2. Exhaustion	-.33***	1														
3. Work overload	.09	.27***	1													
4. Overtime	.10	.13*	.25***	1												
5. Distractions in regular office	-.08	.16**	.23***	-.00	1											
6. Distractions in home office	.01	.07	.04	.06	.06	1										
7. Work–home interference	-.21**	.51***	.31***	.18***	.15**	.13*	1									
8. Autonomy	.27***	-.16**	-.02	-.09	-.12*	-.09	-.12*	1								
9. Social support colleagues	.32***	-.17**	-.11*	-.04	-.03	-.07	-.20***	.17**	1							
10. Social support of supervisor	.28***	-.18***	-.08	-.12*	-.13*	-.07	-.21***	.14**	.35***	1						
11. Telecommuting frequency	.14**	-.08	-.08	-.05	-.06	-.05	.04	.08	-.04	-.08	1					
12. Age	.11	-.11*	.07	-.10	-.08	-.07	-.04	.15**	-.12*	-.09	.12*	1				
13. Children at home	.00	-.13**	.03	.09	-.07	.25***	-.03	.06	-.01	-.08	.01	.17**	1			
14. Commuting time	.06	.09	-.01	.01	.00	-.02	.17**	.11*	.00	-.00	.20***	-.05	-.05	1		
15. Sex	-.06	.01	.09	-.07	.11*	-.08	-.08	-.16**	-.00	.09	-.01	-.13*	-.07	-.10	1	
16. Household situation	-.03	-.03	.04	.03	.12	.17***	.11*	.09	-.05	-.10	-.01	.20***	.49***	.05	-.06	1

* $p < 0.05$; ** $p < 0.01$; *** $p < 0.001$.

In conclusion, the standardized effects (Table 9.2) show *support received from colleagues* to be the single most important factor in telecommuters' flow experiences. When ranking all variables by magnitude (β coefficient), this single factor is followed by *work–home interference; support from supervisor; work overload; autonomy; overtime; telecommute frequency; age; distraction from work at home; children at home; commuting time; sex; household situation;* and, finally, *distractions from work in the regular work place.*

Exhaustion

The statistical model explaining exhaustion (Table 9.2) shows that only three independent variables have significant relationships with telecommuters' exhaustion levels: *work overload; work–home interference;* and *job autonomy* (adjusted R^2 = 29%).

Table 9.2   Multivariate Regression Analyses (Unstandardized [B] and Standardized [β]) Regression Coefficients

	Flow		Exhaustion	
	B	β	B	β
Work overload	.19**	.18**	.20*	.11*
Commuting time	.00	.05	.00	.04
Overtime	.13**	.16**	.01	.01
Distractions in regular office	.02	-.02	.06	.04
Distractions in home office	.15*	.10*	.02	.01
Work home interference	-.27***	-.20***	.99***	.43***
Autonomy	.22***	.18***	-.21(*)	-.10(*)
Social support of colleagues	.24***	.24***	-.06	-.03
Social support of supervisor	.20***	.185***	-.13	-.07
Telecommuting frequency 1: Occasional teleworkers *(= Reference group)*	–	–	–	–
Telecommuting frequency 2: Light teleworkers	.26*	.12*	-.03	-.01
Telecommuting frequency 3: Heavy teleworkers	.41**	.14**	-.43	-.09
Sex *(Reference group = man)*	-.07	-.04	.07	.03
Age	.01*	.11*	-.01	-.05
Household situation *(Reference group = alone)*	-.04	-.02	-.12	-.04
Children at home *(Reference group = no children)*	.08	-.05	-.33(*)	-.12(*)

* $p < 0.05$; ** $p < 0.01$; *** $p < 0.001$; (*) $p < 0.05$ when all nonsignificant variables are removed from the regression model.

In line with expectations, telecommuters reporting more work overload and more work–home interference experience more exhaustion. After removing the nonsignificant effects from the model, it is shown that telecommuters reporting more *job autonomy* experience less exhaustion.

Only one single control variable appears to be significant after removing all nonsignificant factors, i.e., telecommuters with *children* experience less exhaustion.

In conclusion, the standardized effects (Table 9.2) show *work–home interference* to be the single most important determinant of exhaustion among telecommuters, followed by the *presence of children in the household*; *work overload*; and *job autonomy*.

CONCLUSION AND DISCUSSION

Introduction

The present study intended to single out working conditions that affect either telecommuters' flow, or exhaustion, or both. Much in line with expectations based on the JD–R model, telecommuters' perceived job resources (i.e., job autonomy and support from colleagues and supervisor) were shown to play a more important role in the motivation process engendering flow, than their perceived job demands. Also, telecommuters' perceptions of work–home interference appeared to negatively affect job demand flow. However, the present study also showed that not all job demands affect the quality of working life negatively (cf. Bakker & Geurts, 2004), as work overload, overtime, and even distractions in the home office as perceived by telecommuters stimulated their flow experiences.

Partly in line with and partly in contrast to expectations, two out of the six job demands analyzed in this study were shown to feed the exhaustion process: work overload and work–home interference. Moreover, job autonomy was the only single job resource having a diminishing effect on telecommuters' exhaustion levels.

Below, the most important results of this study regarding the work conditions related to flow and exhaustion, respectively, are summarized and research and policy implications are discussed.

Conditions Related To Flow Only

The Importance of Social Support

Perceived social support (particularly support received from colleagues) was the single most important job resource in the telecommuters' flow levels. This finding is important, given that a lack of social cohesion in the organization is usually considered one of the most important drawbacks of distributed working (Gajendran & Harrison, 2007; Beffers & Van den Brink, 2008). Often, telecommuters voluntarily choose to work at home in isolation to meet deadlines, or to concentrate on a complex task (Peters et al., 2004). However, this study shows that this does not imply that telecommuters do not need the input and support from others in order to achieve positive work outcomes. In fact, creating and maintaining social cohesion and trust may be one of the biggest challenges for organizations who want to introduce New Ways to Work. Therefore, flexible organizations may need to regularly organize formal and informal meetings, either face-to-face, or virtually, to enable employees, managers, and other stakeholders to communicate and to support each other, such that employees experience sufficient levels of flow during dispersed work activities, in order to achieve the associated positive work outcomes (Csikszentmihalyi, 1992, 1998).

Positive Aspects of Distractions during Work at Home

Telecommuters, in the present study, also experienced more flow when they reported more distractions during work in the home office. This counterintuitive finding suggests that more distraction at home during work stimulates the motivation process. It was assumed, however, that telecommuters want to work in isolation to enable work concentration, to forget about everything else, and, consequently, to achieve flow. It was expected that absorption would be less likely when telecommuters are distracted from work in their home offices, for example, by household members. An explanation for the positive relationship found in this study may be that some distractions by others contribute to telecommuters' work enjoyment. This finding may underline the importance of social contacts in the case of telecommuting (cf. Kurland & Cooper, 2002). An alternative explanation may be that the result reflects a so-called 'selection effect'. Especially telecommuters who experience higher flow levels may consider work discontinuations serious distractions. Both explanations demand further investigation.

Overtime Reflecting Telecommuters' Task Orientation?

Overtime frequency was shown to have a positive relationship with telecommuters' flow levels. Strikingly, however, overtime did not coincide with higher exhaustion levels. Not being hindered by time limits usually imposed by traditional office hours, telecommuters who are able to continue working during evenings and in weekends may focus more on the quality of their work activities. Their task rather than time orientation may result in higher work enjoyment and higher motivation levels. This explanation implies flow to result from overtime. Of course, it should be noted that the cross-sectional design cannot distinguish between cause and effect. In fact, flow may also be a determining factor in overtime. It can be argued that telecommuters who enjoy their work and who are more intrinsically motivated may be prepared to work longer hours, even at the expense of their own leisure time. Future research could elaborate the mechanisms underlying the relationship between overtime and flow in the case of telecommuting.

Conditions Related To Flow and Exhaustion

Balancing Work Overload

Work overload was shown to enhance both telecommuters' flow and their exhaustion levels (cf. Bakker, 2008; Bakker & Geurts, 2004; Demerouti et al., 2001; Schaufeli & Bakker, 2004). Since telecommuting practices are often accompanied by output management, this finding stresses the importance of balancing telecommuters' work load. If the work load is too low, telecommuters' flow levels are low. If their work overload is too high, employees will become exhausted. In the long run, both conditions may lead to costs for the employee and the organization.

Stimulating Job Autonomy

Much in line with earlier studies (Bakker et al., 2007; Bakker & Geurts, 2004), perceived job autonomy had a positive relationship with flow and a negative relationship with exhaustion. Although telecommuting generally coincides with higher job autonomy levels (Mann & Holdsworth, 2003; Gajendran & Harrison, 2007), this may not always be the case, for example, in the instance of lower educated workers. However, the findings suggest that increasing telecommuters' perceptions of job autonomy can be viewed as an important instrument for organizations to stimulate flow and, simultaneously, to reduce exhaustion, which is likely to improve individual and organizational performances.

Avoiding Work–Home Interference

In line with expectations, perceived work–home interference was shown to be an important hindering factor in telecommuters' flow experience. Telecommuters who were able to reduce work–home interference clearly experienced more flow. Moreover, the reported work–home interference was the single most important factor in exhaustion among telecommuters (cf. Golden, 2006). Work–home interference apparently demands a lot of emotional or mental energy. The present study, therefore, underlines the importance of work–life balance in new work environments, such as home offices. Organizations and managers, therefore, may support telecommuters in gaining a better work–life balance as it improves their flow levels and reduces exhaustion. Both outcomes will improve telecommuters' work performance in the short and long run and, hence, the performance of the organization. For some employees, telecommuting may be a solution to difficulties in balancing their work and private lives. However, as telecommuting itself may also engender work–life balance problems in some cases (Peters & Van der Lippe, 2007), organizations should monitor whether work does not dominate telecommuters' private lives to the extent that the quality of working life is being affected. Therefore, in order to arrive at sustainable employment relationships, telecommuting organizations have to pay sufficient attention to employees' work–life balance in their human resource policies.

Telecommute Policies

In this study, senior telecommuters experienced higher flow levels than younger telecommuters. One possible explanation may be that senior employees value the time–spatial flexibility, the reduction of weekly commuting time, and the alternative home office better than younger telecommuters. This finding may indicate that the added value of senior workers for the company can be improved by the institutionalization of telecommute programs for senior workers as part of organizations' life-stage aware diversity policies. Of course, to create acceptance for structural telecommuting policies and practices, all stakeholders should be involved in the process underlying the adoption of telecommute policies and practices (Peters, Bleijenbergh & Oldenkamp, 2009).

In fact, the present study showed that telecommuters with higher telecommute frequencies experience more flow in comparison with telecommuters who occasionally work from home. This finding also implies that organizations looking for innovative working conditions to generate more positive work outcomes might consider the adoption of structural telecommute practices as part of a more comprehensive telework program or an element of a New-Way-to-Work strategy, rather than using telecommuting practices as *ad hoc* solutions to problems that employees face in their work or home domains. Higher flow levels among substantial telecommuters may be attributed to them building telecommute routines, or to the presence of better supporting work conditions, such as better technological equipment, or a home office separated from the rest of the home domain (Mirchandani, 2000). These conditions may not be offered by organizations, or arranged by workers themselves, when telework policies and practices are not formalized and when telecommuters only occasionally work from home (cf. Peters & Van der Lippe, 2007).

In conclusion, The JD–R model appears to be a fruitful way of explaining flow and exhaustion of telecommuters. Much in line with previous research, based on the JD–R model, the focus in the present study was on working conditions (job demands and resources) and work outcomes (flow and exhaustion) as *perceived* by telecommuters. This shows that organizations that aim to improve both employees' quality of working life and organizational competitiveness by implementing New Ways to Work have to be aware of the fact that the success of such interventions and the realized practices very much depends on employees' perceptions of their own working conditions. Yet, employees' perceived work conditions and realized human resource practices may deviate from those intended by the organization (cf. Bowen & Ostroff, 2004). In order to assess the success and effectiveness of new ways of organizing work, future research may focus on any discrepancies between intended, perceived and realized new working conditions and practices, such as promoted by telecommute policies, and on their intended and unintended work outcomes, such as, work-related flow and burnout.

REFERENCES

Amabile, T.M., Conti, R., Coon, H., Lazenby, J. & Herron, M. 1996. Assessing the work environment for creativity. *Academy of Management Journal*, 39(5), 1154–1184.

Appelbaum, E., Bailey, T., Berg, P. & Kalleberg, A.L. 2000. *Manufacturing advantage: Why high-performance work systems pay off.* Ithaca, NY: ILR Press.

Bakker, A.B. 2008. The work-related flow inventory: Construction and initial validation of the WOLF. *Journal of Vocational Behavior* 72(3), 400–414.

Bakker, A.B. & Demerouti, E. 2007. The Job Demands-Resources model: State of the art. *Journal of Managerial Psychology* 22(3), 309–328.

Bakker, A.B. & Geurts. S. 2004. Toward a dual-process model of work-home interference. *Work and Occupations* 31(3), 345–366.

Bakker, A.B., Demerouti, E., Hakanen, J.J. & Xanthopoulou, D. 2007. Job resources boost work engagement, particularly when job demands are high. *Journal of Educational Psychology* 99(2), 274–284.

Bakker, A.B., Demerouti, E., Taris, T., Schaufeli, W. & Schreurs, P. 2003. A multi-group analysis of the job demands-resources model in four home care organizations. *International Journal of Stress Management* 10, 16–38.

Bakker, A.B., Schaufeli, W.B. & Van Dierendonck, D. 2000. Burnout: Prevalentie, risicogroepen en risicofactoren. In *Psychische vermoeidheid en werk: Cijfers, trends en analyses.* Eds. I. Houtman, W.B. Schaufeli, & T. Taris. Alphen a/d Rijn: NWO/Samson, 65–82.

Becker, B.E. & Huselid, M.A. 1998. High performance work systems and firm performance: a synthesis of research and managerial implications. *Research in Personnel Management and Human Resources Management* 16, 53–101.

Beffers, T. & Van den Brink, I. 2008. *Telewerken, samenvatting resultaten.* Den Dolder: ADV Markt research.

Bowen, D.E. & Ostroff, C. 2004. Understanding HRM-firm performance linkages: The role of the 'strength' of the system. *Academy of Management Review* 29(2), 203–221.

Csikszentmihalyi, M. 1992. *Flow. The psychology of happiness.* London: Rider.

Csikszentmihalyi, M. 1998. *Creativiteit. Over flow, schepping en ontdekking.* Amsterdam: Boom.

Demerouti, E., Bakker, A.B., Nachreiner, F. & Schaufeli, W.B. 2001. The Job Demands-Resources model of burnout. *Journal of Applied Psychology* 86(3), 499–512.

European Commission. 2000. *eWork 2000. Status report on new ways to work in the Information Society.* Retrieved from http://www.eto.org.uk

European Foundation for the Improvement of Living and Working Conditions 2007. *Fourth European working conditions survey.* Loughlinstown, Dublin: European Foundation for the Improvement of Living and Working Conditions.

Fleetwood, S. 2007. Why work-life balance now? *International Journal of Human Resource Management* 18(3), 387–400.

Gajendran, R.S. & Harrison, D.A. 2007. The good, the bad, and the unknown about telework: meta-analysis of psychological mediators and individual consequences. *Journal of Applied Psychology* 92(6), 1524–1541.

Geurts, S.A.E., Taris, T.W., Kompier, M.A.J., Dikkers, J.S.E., Van Hooff, M.L.M. & Kinnunen, U.M. 2005. Work-home interaction from a work psychological perspective: Development and validation of a new Questionnaire, the SWING. *Work and Stress* 19(4), 319–339.

Golden, T.D. 2006. Avoiding depletion in virtual work: Telework and the intervening impact of work exhaustion on commitment and turnover intentions. *Journal of Vocational Behavior* 69(1), 176–187.

Kurland, N.B. & Cooper, C.D. 2002. Manager control and employee isolation in telecommuting environments. *Journal of High Technology Management Research* 13, 107–126.

Le Blanc, P.1994. *De steun van de leiding: Onderzoek naar het leader member exchange model in de verpleging.* [Supervisory support: a study on the leader member exchange model among nurses.] Amsterdam: Thesis Publishers.

Mäkikangas, A., Bakker, A.B., Aunola, K. & Demerouti, E. 2010. Job resources and flow at work: modelling the relationship via latent growth curve and mixture model methodology. *Journal of Occupational and Organizational Psychology* 83, 795–814.

Mann, S. & Holdsworth, L. 2003. The psychological impact of teleworking: stress, emotions and health. *New Technology, Work and Employment* 18(3), 196–211.

Manssour, A.B.B. 2003. Flow in journalistic telework. *Cyber psychology and behavior,* 6(3), 31–39.

Mirchandani, K. 2000. "The best of both worlds" and "cutting my own throat": Contradictory images of home-based work. *Qualitative Sociology,* 23(2), 159–182.

Montreuil, S. & Lippel, K. 2003. Telework and occupational health: A Quebec empirical study and regulatory implications. *Safety Science* 41, 339–358.

More, J.E. 2000. Why is this happening? A causal attribution approach to work exhaustion consequences. *The Academy of Management Review* 25(2), 335–349.

Ory, D.T. & Mokhatarian, P.L. 2007. Does telework really save commute time? Time, distance, and speed evidence from State of Californiaworkers. In *Competing Claims in Work and Family Life.* Eds. T. van der Lippe, & P. Peters. Cheltenham and Northampton, MA: Edward Elgar Publishing, 249–268.

Peters, P. & Wildenbeest, M.E. 2010. Telewerken als hulpbron? 'Flow' en uitputting onder twee telewerkcategorieën vergeleken. [Telework as a job resource: A comparison of 'flow' and exhaustion among marginal and substantial teleworkers]. *Gedrag & Organisatie,* 23(2), 97–117.

Peters, P. & Van der Lippe, T. 2007. The time-pressure reducing potential of telehomeworking: the Dutch case. *International Journal of Human Resource Management* 18(3), 430–447.

Peters, P., Bleijenbergh, I. & Oldenkamp, E. 2009. The telework adoption process in a Dutch and French subsidiary of the same ICT-multinational: how national

culture and management principles affect the success of telework programs. *The Journal of E-working* 2, 1–16.

Peters, P., Tijdens, K.G. & Wetzels, C. 2004. Employees' opportunities, preferences, and practices in telework adoption. *Information and Management* 41(4), 469–482.

Pfeffer, J. 1994. *Competitive advantage through people: Unleashing the power of the workforce*. Boston: Harvard Business School Press.

Reich, R.B. 1992. *The work of nations. Preparing ourselves for the 21th century capitalism*. New York: Vintage Books.

Salanova, M., Bakker, A.B. & Llorens, S. 2006. Flow at work: evidence for an upward spiral of personal and organizational resources. *Journal of Happiness Studies* 7(1), 1–22.

Schaufeli, W.B. & Bakker, A.B. 2004. Job demands, job resources, and their relationship with burnout and engagement: A multi-sample study. *Journal of Organizational Behavior* 25(3), 293–315.

Schaufeli, W.B., Leiter, M. P., Maslach, C. & Jackson, S.E. 1996. The MBI-general survey. In *Maslach burnout inventory manual*. Eds. C. Maslach, S.E. Jackson & M.P. Leitner Palo Alto, CA: Consulting Psychologists Press, 19–26

Schaufeli, W.B., Salanova, M., González-Romá, V. & Bakker, A.B. 2002. The measurement of engagement and burnout: A two sample confirmatory factor analytic approach. *Journal of Happiness Studies* 3(1), 71–92.

Van Veldhoven, M. & Meijman, T. 1994. *Het meten van psychosociale arbeidsbelasting met een vragenlijst: De Vragenlijst Beleving en Beoordeling van de Arbeid (VBBA)*. Amsterdam: Nederlands Instituut voor Arbeidsomstandigheden.

Vittersø, J., Akselsen, S., Evjemo, B., Julsrud, T.E., Yttri, B. & Bergvik, S. 2003. Impacts of home-based telework on quality of life for employees and their partners. Quantitative and qualitative results from a European survey. *Journal of Happiness Studies* 4, 201–233.

Walrave, M. & De Bie, M. 2005. *Mijn kantoor is waar mijn laptop staat. Mythe en realiteit van telewerk*. Antwerpen: Faculteit Politieke en Sociale Wetenschappen.

Wright, T. A. & Cropanzano, R. (1998). Emotional exhaustion as a predictor of job performance and voluntary turnover. *Journal of Applied Psychology* 83(3), 486–493.

10 Innovation in Distributed Teams
The Duality of Connectivity Norms and Human Agency

Paul Collins and Darl Kolb

INTRODUCTION

In this chapter we focus on creativity and innovation management through a lens of "connectivity" and explore how dualities between generative and regenerative knowledge processes match the inherent duality of connectivity, i.e., connects and disconnects (Kolb, 2008). We propose that knowledge is created and maintained within a duality of connects and disconnects and that this duality provides, not just theoretical insights, but also practical implications for creativity and innovation. Underpinning this connective perspective on knowledge creation are the following two premises:

> **Premise 1:** We need to be connected to be creative (generative connection).

> **Premise 2:** Creativity also requires periods of contemplation and reflection (regenerative disconnection).

When these conditions are met, we may experience "requisite connectivity", which means having enough, but not too much connectivity (Kolb, Collins & Lind, 2008).

Following the view that knowledge is socially constructed (Berger & Luckmann, 1967; Giddens, 1984; Pinch & Bijker, 1984), our first premise reminds us that creativity is inherently a social process. Sawyer (2008) has shown that most of the creative breakthroughs in the arts, business, science and engineering were the result of people working in highly collaborative environments. Csikszentmihalyi (1996) persuasively illustrates that creativity consists of ideas, methods and artifacts that are novel and also *meaningful* to some social network. If our own original thoughts are to be useful to ourselves and others, they must fit within existing structures of meaning, i.e., they must make sense to our referent group. Therefore, serious creativity is a highly *social process* (Csikszentmihalyi, 1996). Creativity requires us to connect with others, be it in face-to-face conversations, on the phone, text messages or in virtual, mediated environments.

Our second premise suggests the paradox of creativity: our ability to absorb and adopt new information and knowledge is enhanced by reflective learning, which generally requires some form of *independence*, even brief periods of separation, from others (Sawyer, 2008). In an increasingly interconnected world, most of us still need to disengage somewhat sometimes to make sense of things, or to get perspective (Wyatt, Thomas & Terranova, 2002). We need to let our brain process the never-ending stream of information that comes our way in an ever-increasing variety of media and modes (Carr, 2010; Woolgar, 2002). As Murphy suggests (2007), creative professional work requires a temporary connective "off" switch if we are to keep our creative juices flowing.

Connectivity exists as a duality between connects and disconnects on many technical and social dimensions (Kolb, 2008). Moreover, it is never a fixed state; connectivity comes and it goes (ibid.). As any remote or mobile worker knows, one day you are making great connections (physical and intellectual) and the next you feel disconnected and isolated (Maznevski & Chudoba, 2000). This is indeed a dynamic duality, where the more you connect on one dimension, the more disconnection you may experience in another. For example, the more effort one puts into travel to meet others face-to-face and/or the more one uses computer-mediated communication, the more one's interpersonal, group or organizational connectivity may suffer from connective gaps (Kirkman, Rosen, Tesluk & Gibson, 2004; Turkle, 1995). The crux of the argument here is that, as stated in Premise 2 above, we must accept and manage the disconnects as effectively as we manage the connects, because disconnects contribute significantly to creativity and innovation.

CONNECTIVITY AND INNOVATION
CHALLENGES IN DISTRIBUTED TEAMS

The challenge of managing connectivity is especially problematic for members of distributed project teams engaged in innovation.[1] At first pass, distributed teams seem to have the basic ingredients for innovation: multiple perspectives, deep functional skill sets, broad organizational boundaries and, in some cases, a very external, even global, perspective. Although there is very limited research on the impact of distributed teams on innovation, Gibson and Gibbs' (2006) study of 14 virtual teams in a variety of industries and 56 aerospace virtual design teams established that four characteristics of these distributed teams—geographic distance, electronic media dependence, structural dynamism and national diversity, were *negatively* correlated with their successful development of innovative designs (as judged by internal, downstream functions).

We postulate that unpacking the relationship between distributed teams and innovation requires deeper exploration in the ways and means by which distributed teams manage connectivity. We think that more innovative teams are those that have both the right *kind* and *amount* of team connectivity (Kolb et al., 2008).

Kinds of Connectivity

We consider two fundamental kinds of connectivity: technical and social. Technical connectivity consists of the ways and means that facilitate information and material exchange. In general, in the context of knowledge work and distributed teams, Information and Communication Technologies (ICTs) constitute the media and modes through which we connect with one another. In contemporary knowledge work settings (both distributed and collocated), these media include email, phone, SMS messaging, as well as on-line social media. By our definition, technical connectivity also includes travel, trade, site visits and other physical exchanges that provide face-to-face interaction. Social connectivity refers to the social and psychological relationships that draw and bond individuals, groups, organizations and whole societies together. It may be based upon interpersonal relationships or network ties. Ultimately social connectivity can produce a sense of shared or collective capacity and efficacy (Bandura, 2000) and in mediated environments social and technical connectivity are inherently intertwined (Brown & Duguid, 2000; Kiesler, Seigel & McGuire, 1984).

Generally, the more distributed the team, the more it must rely on an array of information and computer technologies to mediate communication within the team (Boudreau, Loch, Robey & Straud, 1998). Morgan and Liker (2006) contend that well-designed information and computer technologies enable organizational structures and product development processes that are designed for innovation to operate more effectively. For example, shared product data management systems enhance inter-departmental coordination by facilitating the exchange of design information between functions operating along the value stream.

We hypothesize that:

> *Hypothesis 1: The greater the technical connectivity, the more the likelihood that innovation goals will be achieved.*

How can we reconcile this hypothesis with the Gibson and Gibbs (2006) finding that there is a negative correlation between "electronic dependence" and innovation? While their term, electronic dependence, appears similar to our term "technical connectivity", the underlying constructs are substantially different. In their study, dependence was rated as how much a team relied upon electronic vs. other (e.g., face-to-face) media, reflecting a conceptual continuum with high reliance on mediated (electronic) connectivity, on one end, and nonmediated (face-to-face) interaction, at the other extreme. In effect, their measures locate technical (electronic) connectivity and social (face-to-face) connectivity as trade-offs, i.e., you are relatively more dependent on one than the other (rated as low, moderate and high electronic dependence). We believe that this measure might be more indicative of the challenges of team dispersion than it is about the amount and kind of technical connectivity employed, which is our construct of interest. Put simply, we believe our measures of amount and kind of technical connectivity are distinct from Gibson and Gibbs' construct of low vs. highly mediated electronic dependence.

While the impact of technical connectivity on performance may be debatable, the distributed team literature reveals the myriad of social, organizational and cultural barriers experienced by distributed team members that cannot be fully compensated by high levels of technical connectivity (Hinds & Mortensen, 2005; Kirkman, et al., 2004; Nardi & Whittaker, 2002; Olson & Olson, 2000; Olson, Teasley, Covi & Olson, 2002). This is the lingering problem of social connectivity. The lone team member located in a remote facility is unlikely to ever experience the same level of social connectivity as her/his distant team members who happen to be located at the "home site", where several other core team members are within a short walk. Whether it is impromptu hallway meetings or lunches or after-hour celebrations, the home site subgroup will have inherently higher levels of social connectivity. Although the member at the remote location can send emails and participate in weekly teleconference meetings, these media are insufficient substitutes for the fact that home site team members can benefit from spontaneous, face-to-face exchanges. These kinds of problems are compounded among distributed teams whose members are located across multiple time zones or vast geographical, organizational or cultural distance. Thus, the more distributed the team, the more problematic social connectivity becomes.

There is a vast literature on the benefits of high social connectivity for innovation in project teams. Burns and Stalker (1961) were among the first to recognize that high social connectedness among diverse functional experts translates into more effective idea generation and implementation. The cross-functional "heavyweight" product development teams described by Clark and Wheelright (1992) are also characterized by strong social ties. Brown and Eisenhardt's (1995) literature review of project-level predictors of innovation identify several social/organizational variables as key predictors of innovation. While there are no studies that we know of that specifically focus on the relationship between social connectivity and innovation in distributed teams, we expect that the same relationships will hold. Therefore,

Hypothesis 2: The greater the social connectivity, the greater the likelihood that innovation goals will be achieved.

Amount of Connectivity

Managing the right amount of connectivity is also essential for understanding the creative potential of distributed teams. Team connectivity problems range from being "hypoconnected" (i.e., too little connectivity, or disconnected) to "hyperconnected" (i.e., too much connectivity, or overly connected). We contend that the more team members are distributed (time, space, culture, etc.), the more likely they are to experience problems associated with having the right amount of connectivity. While collaborative technologies, such as videoconferencing (e.g., Skype, HP Telepresence) or shared websites (e.g., MS Sharepoint), have begun to address the problem of hypoconnectivity, it may ironically increase members' sense of hyperconnectivity. Whereas before 24/7 videoconferencing, for example, a team member was able to disconnect by default, now his teammates located around the globe who want to "meet" can technically do so at will (subject to time and space availability). The bottom line is that excessive use of connective media has been associated with frustration and inefficiency (Brown & Duguid, 2000), alienation (Turkle, 1995), cynicism (Wyatt, et al., 2002), lost productivity (Murphy, 2007) and fragmented attention spans (Carr, 2010).

Hypothesis 3: The less the hypoconnectivity, the greater the likelihood that innovation goals will be achieved.

Hypothesis 4: The less the hyperconnectivity, the greater the likelihood that innovation goals will be achieved.

EMERGENCE OF CONNECTIVITY NORMS

Partly to help manage problems with the amount and kind of connectivity and partly for social-psychological reasons, distributed teams develop connectivity norms regarding when (responsiveness) and how (modalities) to communicate.[2] These connectivity norms first emerge from the memories and scripts that members bring with them from their previous experiences with distributed teams (Bettenhausen & Murnighan, 1985). Connectivity norms very quickly solidify as members negotiate or learn which norms are supported or seem to generally work best, given the new team's own experiences. Postmes, Spears & Lea (2000) empirically demonstrate that norms regarding both the content and form of computer-mediated communication not only emerge very early in a team's life cycle, but conformity to these norms increase with time. Moreover, they show that these norms are fairly specific to the group and that they are not typically enforced beyond the focal group's boundaries. Thus, connectivity norms are first formed out of the member's own team connectivity scripts, then collectively reshaped and augmented so that they better fit the team's current situations and needs. These connectivity norms play an essential role in helping team members regulate their connections and disconnects.

> *Hypothesis 5: The more widely shared the connectivity norms, the greater the likelihood that innovation goals will be achieved.*

MODERATING EFFECT OF HUMAN AGENCY

Because innovation necessarily involves some degree of ambiguity and uncertainty, strong connectivity norms could inhibit innovation. It is individual team members operating within their own sphere of functional competency, time, location and culture, using whatever electronic media is available to them, who periodically must choose when and how to accept, modify or temporarily ignore the team's norms. Simply put, creativity and innovation depend on human agency to generate the creative sparks that reset norms and move the whole, collaborative team in new directions.

Three elements of human agency that bear on the creativity and innovation problem in distributed teams are: iteration, projection and practical evaluation (Cousins & Robey, 2005; Emirbayer & Mische, 1998). Iteration consists of the application of past ideas, scripts and actions to the new, distributed context. As we approach our new distributed work setting, we selectively apply approaches that have worked for us in the past. Because others are also doing so, we seek to align our individual scripts. This alignment is no longer rooted in the past; we each begin to "project" future ways of acting based on our hopes, fears and future ambitions. Projection is an imaginative space where we "hypothesize" what can work better for us given the circumstances we are now facing. We individually begin to think about where we are going, where we want to go and how we are going to get there. In so doing, we may challenge past scripts, whether they are those now operating as group norms or individualized scripts that apply only to a particular individual. Last, each member must judge the alternative courses of action in response to the challenges and opportunities faced in the ever-changing current situation. This practical evaluative element of agency helps us to contextualize our choices and adapt to real-world circumstances. Thus, we begin with what is expected of us, then confront our own desires and hopes of what we individually want to do, and finally confront the question, "what can we realistically do?" Therefore, in summary, it is the duality of connective norms and individual agency that sets the stage for creativity and innovation.

We would expect connectivity norms to be beneficial to most people much of the time since they ostensibly help the team-at-large more effectively meet its shared objectives (Bandura, 2000). Yet innovation often requires new frames of reference. This is one reason why innovation is more likely to occur as members exercise agency. Agency does not necessarily mean that we reject extant connectivity norms. However, as we confront new challenges and opportunities in our work, we may need to adjust when, how and with whom we connect or disconnect. Perhaps we are expected to respond to an email within a day, for example, and we observe this practice most of the time. In a crisis, however, this norm gives way to the practical evaluative need for a more immediate response. At other times we may need to stay focused on meeting schedule requirements and we choose to wait an additional day to respond, with an apology, of course. From a cognitive psychological perspective, Bandura's core properties of human agency, namely *intentionality, forethought, self-reactiveness* and *self-reflectiveness* (Bandura, 2006), explain how and why individuals with a strong sense of self-efficacy make choices to improve their chances of success. As such, the agency of individuals operating in good faith increases opportunities for creative sparks to become team-based innovation. Therefore, we hypothesize that:

> *Hypothesis 6: The greater the exercise of agency, the more positive the effect of connectivity norms on the achievement of innovation goals.*

AN EXPLORATORY ANALYSIS

The findings reported herein are drawn from initial data gathered as part of a large-scale survey of distributed work teams. The sample is described below in more detail, but basically involves generally global-scale firms with operations across national borders, serving clients and customers around the world. Using our team innovation measures as proxies for creativity, we explore to what extent *both* connection and disconnections are necessary for team innovation. The ability to disconnect from team communication and interaction, we define under a variable called "communication choice", which is based on the notion of human agency (Giddens, 1984). However, our ability to choose if and when to connect with others in a team environment will be, to some degree, contingent on the communication expectations of the team.

RESEARCH METHODS

Sample

Our sample consists of 36 distributed product development or professional service project teams, many of which operate around the globe. We invited all core members of the project team to participate in the study.[3]

There are 151 respondents in the sample for an average of about 4 respondents per core team. Project locations to date include countries such as: Australia, China, India, Indonesia, Ireland, Japan, Malaysia, New Zealand, Sweden, and the United States.

Table 10.1   Sample Characteristics

	Median
Demographics	
English 1st language (mean %)	76.0
Male Gender (mean %)	82.0
Years of Age	35.0
Distributed team experience	
Years employed by company	5.5
Months member of project team	9.0
Percent of time devoted to project	85.0
Years worked in distributed work teams	5.0
Number distributed project teams have been a member	5.0

Most of the sample speaks English as their primary language (76%), are male (82%) and about 35 years of age (Table 10.1 above). Project team members devote about 85% of their time to the project and have been on the project team for 9 months. They have an average of 5.5 years of work experience at their respective companies and have worked in 5 distributed project teams.

MEASURES

Innovation

We measured innovation as the team's average assessment of its innovation performance on two related project outcomes: (a) the extent to which the project met its targeted innovation goals (1 = much worse than target; 5 = much better than target) and (b) in comparison to similar projects in the company, how did the project meet its innovation objectives (1 = much worse than comparison; 5 = much better than comparison). These two items have an α reliability coefficient of 0.83 (Table 10.2). Reported project innovation performance scores ranged from 2.5 to 4.3, with a mean of 3.56. Thus, the typical team met or slightly exceeded its targeted innovation goals.

Dimensions of Connectivity

Connectivity is represented by four related Likert-type scales (see Appendix A below). The first two dimensions represent the *kinds* of connectivity used by the team: (a) *technical*, such as the use of information and communication technologies and (b) *social*, referring to the strength of social ties among team members. All distributed teams use some mix of these inter-dependent components to communicate. Some teams use technologies such as videoconferencing to strengthen the feeling of social presence among members. While social connectivity may be less visible to team members, it is no less important. For example, a high level of social connectivity helps a team member to appropriately interpret a terse email message from his or her boss or peer. Mean *social* connectivity scores (Table 10.2: 2.84) are noticeably lower than *technical* connectivity scores (Table 10.2: 3.6).

The remaining two components consist of the *amount* of connectivity on the team: (c) *hypoconnectivity*, which means having too little connectivity relative project requirements, and (d) *hyperconnectivity*, having too much connectivity in the team relative to project requirements. We theorize that either extreme can have negative, if not disastrous, effects on team performance. Too little connectivity and there is little chance of creative exchanges among members; too much and there is little time for reflection, for getting one's tasks completed in a timely manner. Mean *hypoconnectivity* scores (Table 10.2: 1.75) are somewhat lower than *hyperconnectivity* scores (Table 10.2: 2.07).

Connectivity Norms

We measure two types of connectivity norms: (a) *responsiveness*—shared expectations regarding whether to respond to member or leader messages within the same day, and (b) *shared approach*—shared expectations regarding whether and when it is appropriate to use various modes of communication, such as email or videoconferencing, as well as the length and style of the response.

These norms are an essential test of the duality of connectivity. Making a personal decision to *not* connect with one's boss or peers is especially significant when there are explicit expectations regarding constant availability, for example. If there are few expectations, then the choice is relatively empty, since it has no social consequences. The descriptive data in Table 10.2 show the presence of connectivity norms in most cases. *Responsiveness* norms have a slightly lower mean score (3.59) than *shared approach* to communicating (3.85), indicating that there is less agreement about responsiveness and more about how and when to use information and communication technologies.

Connectivity Choice

Agency is central to the process of personal regeneration, particularly given high levels of team connectivity. Fundamentally, in a distributed team context, agency is the ability to choose when and how to be in contact with others and what media should be used, whether face-to-face or email, for example. For the purposes of this paper, we define agency as "connectivity choice", which consists of four items that range from the ability to choose communication media to being able to work uninterrupted (Appendix A).

Table 10.2 Descriptive Statistics and Correlations

	Innovation	Technical connectivity	Social connectivity	Hypo-connectivity	Hyper-connectivity	Approach	Response	Connectivity choice	Project duration	% Project complete	Project team size
Technical connectivity	0.32†										
Social connectivity	0.21	0.49**									
Hypoconnectivity	-0.48**	-0.68**	-0.53**								
Hyperconnectivity	-0.33*	-0.17	-0.05	0.50**							
Connectivity norms (approach)	0.45**	0.59**	0.43**	-0.62**	-0.28†						
Connectivity norms (response)	0.05	0.39*	0.39*	-0.42**	0.19	0.38*					
Connectivity choice	0.02	0.27	0.11	-0.25	-0.41**	0.16	-0.24				
Project duration	0.01	-0.07	-0.10	0.05	-0.11	0.13	-0.31	-0.25			
Project complete (%)	0.08	0.36†	0.62**	-0.61**	-0.23	0.25	0.56**	0.03	-0.04		
Project team size	-0.31†	-0.10	-0.23	0.15	0.07	-0.35†	-0.12	0.04	0.39*	-0.10	
Mean	3.56	3.56	2.84	1.75	2.07	3.85	3.59	2.19	17.70	65.23	56.13
S.D.	0.47	0.60	0.70	0.44	0.55	0.56	0.74	0.61	9.99	31.69	47.60
α	0.83	0.94	0.87	0.80	0.89	0.77	0.94	0.83	n/a	n/a	n/a

$p \leq 0.10$ † / * $p \leq 0.05$ / ** $p \leq 0.01$

In general, respondents report a moderately low level of communication choice with a mean of 2.19 and a standard deviation of 0.61 (Table 10.2).

CONTROLS

Project Duration

Our first control is the targeted number of months to complete the project. This is an official estimate that is used for budgeting and strategic planning purposes. It also is a good proxy for project scale since larger projects typically take more time. Whether teams end up reducing or exceeding the original time estimate is beyond the scope of this paper. The average duration of the 36 projects was about 18 months (Table 10.2).

Project Completion

This variable captures the estimated percentage of the project that is completed to date. We would expect distributed teams that have spent more months working together to have better connectivity—the result of trial and error learning if nothing else, and stronger connectivity norms since there has been ample time to figure out what does and does not work. We speculate that this variable is also a good proxy of team maturity. The typical project was 65% completed at the time our survey (Table 10.2).

Team Size

We measure team size as the total number of team members, both core and noncore, as well as management assigned to the team. We chose to measure total team size rather than core team size, since core teams are typically small (a median of 11 members in our data set). We think that this likely underestimates a team's actual scale and complexity. Moreover, our tests of the predictive power of core vs. total team size shows that total team size is a better predictor of team outcomes. Controlling for total team size provides a more conservative test of the true effects of size on team dynamics and performance. The average total team size was 56 members (Table 10.2).

RESULTS

Connectivity and Innovation

As predicted, having the right kind and amount of connectivity is essential for innovation in distributed teams; three of four hypotheses on connectivity and innovation are supported. Higher levels of technical connectivity are associated with higher levels of innovation (Table 10.3, Model A: b =

0.31*), thereby supporting Hypothesis 1. Surprisingly, we did not find a relationship between social connectivity and innovation (Table 10.3, Model B: $b = 0.20$ n.s.) and conclude that our exploratory data do not support Hypothesis 2. This might be because of suppressor effects of unmeasured variables, such as differences among our teams in their level of national diversity. As Gibson and Gibbs (2006) established, more nationally diverse teams are typically less cohesive and they find it difficult to share a common world view.

Having the right *amount* of connectivity is essential for innovation in distributed project teams. Having too little or too much connectivity lowers innovation. Of the two extremes, hypoconnectivity has a larger negative effect on innovation (Table 10.3, Model C: $b = -0.53**$) than hyperconnectivity (Table 10.3, Model D: $b = -0.30*$). We speculate that it is easier to say "no" to teammates to regulate excessive levels of communication than to demand to be included in their conversations, for example. These findings offer solid support for Hypotheses 3 and 4.

Our data paint a mixed picture of the direct effects of connectivity norms on innovation. Norms governing expected *approaches* to take in communicating with teammates has a strong, positive relationship with innovation (Table 10.3, Model E: $b = 0.40*$), thereby supporting Hypothesis 5 (i.e., approaches). However, there is no direct relationship between responsiveness connectivity norms and innovation (Table 10.3, Model F: b = 0.04, n.s.), indicating that Hypothesis 5 (i.e., responsiveness) is not supported. To the extent that innovation is the goal, *how* teammates connect is more important than *when* they connect.

The impact of connectivity norms on innovation is moderated by the team's connective choices. The cross-product term between connectivity approach and choice has a significant and positive effect on innovation (Table 10.3, Model I, $b = 4.50**$) and it increases the variance explained in innovation achievements from 22% to 46% (Table 10.3). While norms of responsiveness had no direct effect on innovation, it does have an interaction effect with connectivity choice (Table 10.3, Model K, $b = 3.39**$). These findings not only provide solid support for Hypotheses 6, they also suggest that project leaders and members realize the importance of managing the duality of connectivity by exercising some choice over when and how to connect.

Team Connectivity Norms and Individual Agency

Figure 10.1 provides a more interpretable view of the interactions. There is a negative relationship between connectivity approach norms and innovation for *low*-choice teams—that is, if there is a strong connectivity approach norm and little or no choice, then innovation suffers. High choice, however, has a dramatic double-edge sword effect on the connectivity and innovation relationship. The impact of connectivity approach norms on innovation are magnified when team members have high choice. Closer examination of the intersection of the two slopes in Figure 10.1 reveals that high choice,

Table 10.3 Predictors of Distributed Project Team Innovation

	Models										
	(A)	(B)	(C)	(D)	(E)	(F)	(G)	(H)	(I)	(J)	(K)
Predictor variables											
1. Technical connectivity	0.31•										
2. Social connectivity		0.20									
3. Hypoconnectivity			-0.53••								
4. Hyperconnectivity				-0.30•							
5. Connectivity norms (approach)					0.40•			0.42•	-2.32••		
6. Connectivity norms (responsiveness)						0.04				0.07	-2.95••
7. Connectivity choice							0.16	-0.04	-3.15••	0.08	-2.54••
Interaction terms											
8. Cross-product term (5 x 7)									4.50•••		
9. Cross-product term (6 x 7)											3.39••
Control variables											
10. Project duration	0.14	0.13	0.13	0.09	0.02	0.14	0.17	0.01	0.06	0.16	0.01
11. Project completion (%)	-0.05	-0.06	-0.19	-0.01	-0.03	0.02	0.01	-0.03	0.07	0.01	0.24
12. Project team size (total)	-0.30•	-0.28†	-0.28•	-0.28†	-0.16	-0.31•	-0.34†	-0.15	-0.16	-0.32•	-0.41
R^2	0.18	0.11	0.32	0.17	0.22	0.09	0.11	0.22	0.46	0.09	0.26
F-ratio	1.67†	1.00	3.57••	1.63†	2.21•	0.75	0.95	1.72†	4.13••	0.62	1.66†
F-change (sig.)	12.80••	6.32••									

† $p \leq 0.10$ • $p \leq 0.05$ •• $p \leq 0.01$

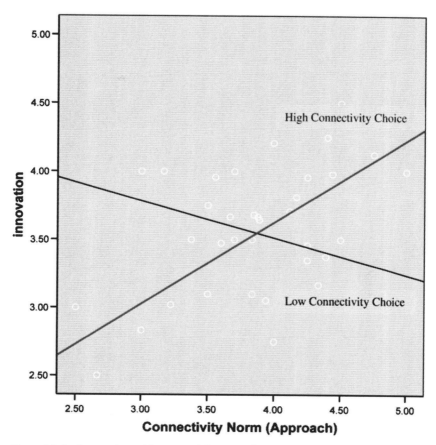

Figure 10.1 Innovation with connectivity norm by connectivity choice (approach).

coupled with low connectivity, is deadly to innovation. In fact, the level of connectivity needed for high-choice teams to realize the same level of innovation as their low-choice counterparts is more than one standard deviation above the mean. This is striking. Yet, once this high connectivity threshold is reached, the benefits of choice increase dramatically and high-choice teams significantly outperform their low choice counterparts. These findings provide substantial support to our core argument regarding the duality between connectivity and choice. We now realize that this is most true when both variables operate at the highest levels.

The same moderating relationship holds for connectivity *responsiveness* norms and choice (Figure 10.2). The more the choice, the more member responsiveness pays off for innovation. This fits the image of a highly connected team member who chooses to stay connected and whose team reaps the benefits of increased innovation. Note that high choice and low team connectivity (lower left solid blue line) results in lower innovation than

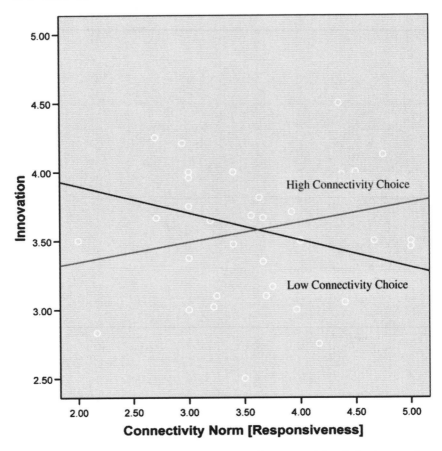

Figure 10.2 Innovation with connectivity norm by connectivity choice (responsiveness).

low choice and low connectivity (left green line). This could be a result of social loafing or the fact that low connectivity in teams suffers from the out-of-sight, out-of-mind syndrome. Taken together, we surmise that it is not simply choice that results in innovation; it is the combination of high connectivity and high choice.

IMPLICATIONS AND DISCUSSION

As technical connectivity (e.g., ICT) increases in speed, accessibility and pervasiveness (ubiquity), team members will face increasing choices as to when and how to connect with others (Baron, 2008). Such choices are especially salient when the work to be accomplished involves a creative element, something not lost on Nicholas Carr (2010), who provides a recent illustrative and ironic example of his personal need to "disconnect" from the Internet while writing a book about the Internet. He recounts,

> I know what you're thinking. The very existence of this book would seem to contradict its thesis. If I'm finding it so hard to concentrate, to stay focused on a line of thought, how in the world did I manage to write a few hundred pages of at least semi-coherent prose?
>
> It wasn't easy. When I began writing *The Shallows*, toward the end of 2007, I struggled in vain to keep my mind fixed on the task. The Net provided, as always, a bounty of useful information and research tools, but its constant interruptions scattered my thoughts and words. I tended to write in disconnected spurts, the same way I wrote when blogging. It was clear that big changes were in order. In the summer of the following year, I moved with my wife from a highly connected suburb of Boston to the mountains of Colorado. There was no cell phone service at our new home, and the Internet arrived through a relatively poky DSL connection. I cancelled my Twitter account, put my Facebook membership on hiatus, and mothballed my blog. I shut down my RSS reader and curtailed my Skyping and instant messaging. Most important, I throttled back my email application (2010, 198).

Although choice or agency has been an element of philosophical debate since the Renaissance (Emirbayer & Mische, 1998), and developed in social theory for several decades (DeSanctis & Poole, 1994; Giddens, 1984; Orlikowski, 1992), never has the amount, range and availability of choice been more acute than it is in contemporary work environments, and even more so in distributed work environments. The choice that we focus on is not *which* media to use (Daft & Lengel, 1986), but rather the *amount* of media we choose to engage with. Like Carr, our choices are less about the value or affordances of individual media (looking at his list, they all have some place in the repertoire). The question of choosing media is still important, but *type* is no longer the only media choice we have to make. We must begin to make a quantum choice, i.e., *how much* connectivity is necessary or beneficial; how much is too little or too much?

In this chapter, we have empirically explored how human agency (choice) is related to innovativeness in distributed work teams. The duality (connects and disconnects) of connectivity in the beginning of this chapter explains the complementary needs to connect and disconnect both technically and socially in order to become and remain productive. Of course, not all project teams are necessarily interested in innovation or creative solutions. Indeed, the notion of project management has control of costs, timing and other resources as its underlying premise. For many project teams, efficiency is a key driver for requisite levels of connectivity, which is to say not too little and not too much. However, for teams seeking creativity and innovation, there appears to be a need for not just a balance or midpoint between hypo- and hyperconnectivity, but for connecting and disconnecting. How conscious we need to be (or can be) about our connecting and disconnecting behavior is arguable, but making this duality or dialectic explicit means teams might begin to manage, as much as possible with other team members, their disconnects along with their attempts to "keep in touch". For example, team leaders might discuss with their teams the expectations for contact (how much, how often), the level of choice individuals have in the team context (right to be "off-line"), as well as the preferred media for different team tasks or processes.

Individual knowledge workers might also benefit from rethinking their connective practices. How much do they allow hyperconnectivity to disrupt and undermine their creative work? Do they regulate their connections and contact to include some level of "down time" for reflection, relaxation and regeneration? For some of us, the team or organization does not prescribe or make rules around connective behaviors, so it is left to the individual to establish her or his own ground rules for connectivity.

The theoretical implication of this study is that while the duality between connects and disconnects is evident (Kolb, 2008), the need for "switching off" (disconnecting) underpins the assertion that connective flow is not a mere "averaging" or balancing effect, i.e., juggling the right amount of balls in the air. It is more dynamic than that. Optimal connective states fluctuate to the extent that occasionally we put the juggling balls down, or at least that seems to be the case for creative knowledge work. It will come as no surprise to our readers that the tools we create bring challenges to integrate into social and cultural contexts, so that our quality of life is enhanced rather than eroded or disrupted. This is not to say that connective technologies and media are "bad". On the contrary, they feed and fuel our passions for communicating, for learning and for exploring the world around us. The key counterpoint, highlighted and supported in this study, is that we must each as individuals and team members, find ways to remain connected to the world *within* us.

The irony of innovation is that while there is no such thing as "stand alone" creativity. Each of us must—to greater or lesser degrees—sit alone to reflect and regenerate our creative selves. As we reach the point where the world of work is increasing hyperconnected, we must now consider the benefits of being disconnected—at least some of the time. Currently, as information is literally overflowing around and over us, we must seek connective states that allow us to gather information and process it into knowledge and meaning. Managing disconnection runs counter to believing that "more is better". As we search for requisite connectivity and/or connective flow, sometimes "less is more". To say that connectivity is both a blessing and a curse is an understatement. However, it is a good place to focus our attention as we fuel and refuel our passion for creativity and innovation.

NOTES

1. We define distributed projects teams as teams whose members are dispersed across time or space and who have common deliverables within a specified time and budget. Membership is limited to the duration of the project. Thus, unlike traditional work teams with relatively stable membership over long periods of time, distributed teams are inherently temporary in duration and limited in focus and scope. We take for granted that distributed teams can vary widely in their time and space boundaries.
2. Feldman (Feldman, 1984) argues that group norms are likely to be enforced when they: (1) enhance the groups survival; (2) increase the predictability of group member behaviors; (3) prevent interpersonal tension, including personal embarrassment; and (4) help to express the group's central values and identity.
3. Most global project teams consist of "core" members—those who are assigned full-time (75% ≥) for the duration of the project and "noncore" members—those whose involvement is temporary or limited. Our data consist of core members only.

REFERENCES

Bandura, A. 2000. Exercise of human agency through collective efficacy. *Current Directions in Psychological Science* 9(3), 75–78.

Bandura, A. 2006. Toward a psychology of human agency. *Perspectives on Psychological Science* 1(2), 164–180.

Baron, N. S. 2008. *Always on: Language in an online, and mobile world.* Oxford: Oxford University Press.

Berger, P. L. & Luckmann, T. 1967. *The social construction of reality.* New York: Anchor Books.

Bettenhausen, K. & Murnighan, J. K. 1985. The emergence of norms in competitive decision-making groups. *Administrative Science Quarterly* 30(3), 350–372.

Boudreau, M.-C., Loch, K. D., Robey, D. & Straud, D. 1998. Going global: Using information technology to advance the competitiveness of the virtual transnational organization. *The Academy of Management Executive* 12(4), 120–128.

Brown, J. S. & Duguid, P. 2000. *The social life of information.* Boston, MA: Harvard Business School Press.

Brown, S. L. & Eisenhardt, K. M. 1995. Product development: Past research, present findings, and future directions. *AMR Academy of Management Review* 20(2), 343–378.

Burns, T. & Stalker, G. M. 1961. *The management of innovation.* London: Tavistock.

Carr, N. 2010. *The shallows: How the internet is changing the way we think, read and remember.* London: Atlantic.

Clark, K. B. & Wheelwright, S. C. 1992. Organizing and leading "heavyweight " development teams. *CMR California Management Review* 34(3), 9–28.

Cousins, K. C. & Robey, D. 2005. Human agency in a wireless world: Patterns of technology use in nomadic computing environments. *Information and Organization* 15(2), 151–180.

Csikszentmihalyi, M. 1996. *Creativity : flow and the psychology of discovery and invention.* New York: HarperCollinsPublishers.

Daft, R. & Lengel. 1986. Organisational information requirements, media richness, and structural design. *Managment Science* 32(5), 554–571.

DeSanctis, G. & Poole, M. S. 1994. Capturing the complexity in advanced technology use: Adaptive structuration theory. *Organization Science* 5(2), 121–147.

Emirbayer, M. & Mische, A. 1998. What is agency? *The American Journal of Sociology* 103(4), 962–1023.

Feldman, D. C. 1984. The development and enforcement of group norms. *The Academy of Management Review* 9(1), 47–53.

Gibson, C. B. & Gibbs, J. L. 2006. Unpacking the concept of virtuality: The effects of geographic dispersion, electronic dependence, dynamic structure, and national diversity on team innovation. *Administrative Science Quarterly* 51(3), 451–495.

Giddens, A. 1984. *The constitution of society: Outline of the theory of structuration.* Oxford: Polity Press.

Hinds, P. J. & Mortensen, M. 2005. Understanding conflict in geographically distributed teams: The moderating effects of shared identity, shared context, and spontaneous communication. *Organization Science* 16(3), 290–307.

Kiesler, S., Seigel, J. & McGuire, T. W. 1984. Social psychological aspects of computer-mediated communication. *American Psychologist* 39, 1123–1134.

Kirkman, B. L., Rosen, B., Tesluk, P. E. & Gibson, C. B. 2004. The impact of empowerment on virtual team performance: The moderating effect of face-to-face interaction. *Academy of Management Journal* 47(2), 175–192.

Kolb, D. G. 2008. Exploring the connectivity metaphor: Attributes, dimensions and duality. [theory]. *Organization Studies* 29(1), 127–144.

Kolb, D. G., Collins, P. D. & Lind, E. A. 2008. Requisite connectivity: Finding flow in a not-so-flat world. *Organizational Dynamics* 37(2), 181–189.

Maznevski, M. L. & Chudoba, K. M. 2000. Bridging space over time: Global virtual team dynamics and effectiveness. *Organization Science* 11(5), 473–492.

Morgan, J. M. & Liker, J. K. 2006. *The Toyota product development system: Integrating people, process, and technology.* New York: Productivity Press.

Murphy, P. 2007. You are wasting my time: Why limits on connectivity are essential for economies of creativity. *University of Auckland Business Review* 9(2), 17–26.

Nardi, B. A. & Whittaker, S. 2002. The place of face-to-face communication in distributed work. In *Distributed work.* Eds. P. J. Hinds & S. Kiesler Cambridge, MA: MIT Press, 83–110.

Olson, G. M. & Olson, J. 2000. Distance matters. *Human-Computer Interaction* 15(2/3), 139–179.

Olson, J., Teasley, S., Covi, L. & Olson, G. 2002. The (currently) unique advantages of collocated work. In *Distributed Work.* Eds. P. Hinds & S. Kiesler . Cambridge, MA: The MIT Press, 113–135.

Orlikowski, W. J. 1992. The duality of technology: Rethinking the concept of technology in organizations. *Organization Science* 3(3), 398–427.

Pinch, T. & Bijker, W. 1984. The social construction of facts and artifacts. *Social Studies of Science* 14, 399–441.

Postmes, T., Spears, R. & Lea, M. 2000. The formation of group norms in computer-mediated communication. *Human Communication Research* 26(3), 341.

Sawyer, R. K. 2008. *Group genius : The creative power of collaboration.* New York; London: BasicBooks ; Perseus Running [distributor].

Turkle, S. 1995. *Life on the screen: Identity in the age of the Internet.* New York: Touchstone.

Woolgar, S. (Ed.). 2002. *Virtual society?: Technology, cyberbole, reality.* Oxford: Oxford University Press.

Wyatt, S., Thomas, G. & Terranova, T. 2002. They came, they surfed, they went back to the beach: Conceptualizing use and non-use of the Internet. In *Virtual Society?: Technology, cyberbole, reality.* Ed. S. Woolgar . Oxford: Oxford University Press, 23–40.

Appendix 10A   Requisite Connectivity Scales

Connectivity norms	Technical connectivity
My project team members expect me to respond to their needs within the same day. [Responsiveness]	My colleagues and I experience "anytime, anyplace" connectivity.
My project manager/team leader expects me to respond to her/his needs within the same day. [Responsiveness]	The *quality* (features, attributes) of the information and communication technologies used in this project is excellent.
We have a shared understanding of when to use various modes of communication, e.g., email vs. videoconferencing. [Approach]	The *reliability* of our information and communication technologies is high.
We have a shared understanding of the length and style of responses to each other (e.g., short vs. long, unedited messages vs. edited messages). [Approach]	Technology-wise, communicating with team members at other locations is easy.
Hypoconnectivity (too little)	My project team has all the technology it needs to work effectively across sites.
Technical communication gaps in my team (e.g., dropped connections) undermine the productivity of our work.	The use of communication technology enhances our team performance.
I feel socially disconnected ("out of the loop") from my team.	**Social connectivity**
I am unable to keep in touch with my team members in other locations.	I consider members of my team to be good friends (i.e., we share personal interests, do nonwork things together, etc.)
Ideally, my teammates and I would communicate (e.g., meet, call, email) more often.	I have known the people that I work with on this team for a long time.
There is too little connectivity in my team.	When meeting informally with teammates, our conversations include subjects, such as political or social events, leisure activities, family and friends.
	When I have a personal problem or difficulty at work, I am able to talk to someone on my team.
Hyperconnectivity (too much)	Our team has strong social ties.
The amount of email, instant messaging, etc., I receive makes it difficult to be productive in my work.	
The amount of time I spend on the phone, including conference calls, makes it difficult to be productive in my work.	**Connectivity choice** [agency]
Interruptions and impromptu meetings make it difficult to be productive in my work.	I can "turn off" any or all communication media when I want to do so.
The amount of face-to-face meetings and videoconferences makes it difficult to be productive in my work.	I can regulate the time I spend communicating with teammates.
There is too much connectivity in my team.	I can choose when and how I am in contact with others.
	I can find time to work uninterrupted when I need to do so.

11 Challenging New Ways of Working for Remote Managers in Global Collaborative Work Environments

Petra Bosch-Sijtema, Renate Fruchter, Matti Vartiainen and Virpi Ruohomäki

INTRODUCTION

Global teamwork, mobile work and telework require new ways of organizing and managing work across several locations. New information and communication technologies (ICT) facilitate work to be performed without being bound to a particular place or time (Gareis, Lilischkis & Mentrup, 2006; Vartiainen, 2008). These types of organizing work are stimulated even more by the economic climate in which companies try to reduce real estate, travel, as well as development and personnel costs, while at the same time outsourcing and off-shoring their functions. Several streams of research discuss these issues, such as telework (Sullivan, 2003; Felstead, Jewson & Walters, 2005), studying work from home and other places outside the main workplace. Others discuss distributed work (Bell & Kozlowski, 2002; Jarvenpaa & Leidner, 1999; Majchrzak, Rice, Malhotra, King & Ba, 2000) and focus on issues, such as the impact of distance (Armstrong & Cole, 1995; Hinds & Kiesler, 2001), trust (Jarvenpaa & Leidner, 1998; Zolin, Hinds, Fruchter & Levitt, 2004), conflicts (Hinds & Bailey, 2003) and cultural differences (Zakaria, Amelinckx & Wilemon, 2004). Other researchers study mobility, where work is performed in multiple locations and focus on the impact of mobility on work and productivity for both the firm and employee (Gareis et al., 2006; Hislop & Axtell, 2009; Vartiainen & Hyrkkänen, 2010). In all these studies, the challenge is how to manage these new ways of working. Large corporate teams typically engage middle managers that report to their superiors and coordinate team member activities. Managers working in global and mobile collaborative work environments often work in multiple teams (cf. Mortensen, Woolley & O'Leary, 2007) having to play a dual role, on one hand, managing global team members and, on the other hand, being team members in the management group that reports to their superior. Working in multiple teams with multiple roles is another challenge important for new ways of working. Many studies discuss either being part of a distributed team or how to manage remote employees (e.g., Kayworth & Leidner; 2000, Zigurs, 2003), but neglect the fact that these global managers fulfill multiple roles as a manager, as well as team member. New ways of working build on the core management competencies and require managers to address new challenges determined by global collaborative working environments (CWE). CWEs are a combination of infrastructures—both physical, IT-based networks, social and organization structures—supporting individual and collaborative work. Next to management competencies, critical aspects related to workplace, work practices, ICT and policies are important (e.g., MacDuffie, 2007). This chapter studies challenges that global middle managers face when engaged in global CWE driven by globalization and mobility.

The remainder of the chapter is structured as follows. First, we discuss literature within the field of new ways of working. We then present the methodology and case studies and subsequently discuss the findings. In the final section, we discuss the implications and contributions to current literature based on these findings.

CHALLENGES OF NEW WAYS OF WORKING

This study focuses on 'new ways of working' in which we build on literature from telework, mobile work and globally distributed work. For global managers in new working contexts, not only are skills important, but also workplaces, information technology, work practices and organization policy. Below, we discuss these issues in more detail building on existing literature.

Mobile, Flexible and Distributed Work

In the introduction, we discussed the different fields of telework, mobile work and distributed work research and their different research angles. We perceive the notion of new ways of work as a combination of these research fields.

Numerous studies present challenges for distributed and flexible work from communication and collaboration challenges to stress and work–life balance issues (Gajendran & Harrison, 2007; Kelliher & Anderson, 2010). Kayworth and Leidner (2002) summarize from the literature four main challenges for distributed work: (1) communication challenges such as the lack of social cues, nonverbal communication, trust and conflict issues (Hinds & Bailey, 2003; Hinds & Kiesler, 2001; Jarvenpaa & Leidner, 1999; Zolin et al., 2004); (2) cultural challenges when employees from different countries, national cultures and local organization cultures cooperate (Zakaria et al., 2004); (3) technology challenges (Townsend, DeMarie & Hendrickson, 1998); and (4) logistics (time differences and need for travel; cf. Kayworth & Leidner, 2002). Literature presenting new ways of working challenges rarely focuses on challenges faced by managers in this new CWE context.

Managers in Global Collaborative Working Environments

All these above-mentioned challenges have a large impact on both remote employees and remote management. Therefore, more and more research emphasizes the importance to study management and leadership of new ways of working (Cascio, 2000; Gronn, 2002). Researchers have studied remote management (Heckman, Crowston & Misiolek, 2007; Kayworth & Leidner, 2000; Zigurs, 2003). Many of these studies discuss either emergent leadership in remote teams (Heckman et al., 2007) or they focus on leadership effectiveness in distributed teams (Antonakiss & Atwater, 2002; Armstrong & Cole 1995; Kayworth & Leidner, 2000, 2002).

However, research neglects the fact that managers often work in multiple teams in which they play diverse roles, i.e., team member of a management team and manager of a distributed team. The new ways of working affect not only their way of managing their remote employees, but also impacts how remote management teams communicate and internally collaborate. Therefore, in our article, we focus on the context of new ways of working and its importance for managers working in global CWE. This context can include many aspects. For new ways of working the physical, virtual and social workspaces can be either an enabler or a hindrance of work practices of these global managers.

Physical, Virtual and Social Work Context

All these studies focus on specific areas like HRM, leadership roles and styles and team and individual issues. However, in the current new CWEs, not only is the organization context for individual and collaborative work important, but also the physical work context (e.g., the office), the virtual work context, i.e., the IT that supports collaboration over distance and the social work context where people can meet formally and informally (either face-to-face or online). The role of the workplace in the organization can be the emplacement of relations, of proximity, connection and perception (Faubian, 1994) that support interpersonal relations and communication. However, Cairns (2002) claims that current management literature lacks studies of the physical environment and its impact on collaboration. In our research, each collaborative working environment can be seen as an integration of embedded spaces (Harrison, Wheeler & Whitehead, 2004; Vartiainen & Hyrkkänen, 2010):

1. A physical space consisting of the all material objects and stimuli and their arrangements, e.g., an office or a customer site;

2. A virtual space in which people meet and collaborate with help of ICT, e.g., communicating through email, videoconferencing, IM, etc.;
3. A social or interaction space referring to the surrounding human social context and network existing in each physical location in which people meet formally and informally, e.g., interaction in a meeting room, coffee room, hallways and in virtual meeting places.

The physical workspace is known to affect productivity and empowerment; however, few studies focus on measuring these aspects and empirical evidence is limited (Apgar, 1998; Elsbach & Pratt, 2008; Haynes 2007; Heerwagen, Kampschroer, Powell & Loftness, 2004). The virtual and interaction space are discussed in the literature as important for remote work outcomes (Davenport, Thomas & Cantrell, 2002; Scott, 2005). Some studies show that non-job-related communication content is related to productivity and members' satisfaction of global teams and to their work climate (Hertel, Geister & Konradt, 2005). For the virtual space, Fruchter (2005) has pointed out the impact of collaboration technology on the degrees of engagement and specific interaction zones in interactive workspaces for distributed work. The intersection of the design of physical workspaces, rich electronic content such as video, audio, sketching, CAD and new ways people behave and interact in communicative events are all important in remote work. Management challenges are found in all these contexts of new ways of working and managers adjust their working practices according to contextual spaces in which they operate.

METHODOLOGY

We applied a comparative and in-depth case study analysis approach (Eisenhardt, 1989) to identify challenges of new ways of working. The research was performed in two stages, an in-depth individual case analysis and a comparative case analysis. Large corporate teams typically engage middle managers that report to their superiors and coordinate team member activities. In this study, we focus on global middle managers that engage in global CWE. As global managers, they work in multiple teams having to play a dual role, on the one hand, managing global team members and, on the other hand, being team members in the management group that reports to their superior. We studied two management teams each consisting of eight global team managers in a Fortune 100, global high-tech company. One team was located in Pan European—SERVICE—and the second team was located in the U.S.—PROTO case. We collected data using multiple methods to gain a better insight into the challenges of managing working in new ways, i.e., interviews, surveys, and observations of the workplace, meetings and managers (shadowing). We held 1–1½ hour semistructured interviews with all members in which we applied the same interview guide on both sites. Interview questions focused on team information, reporting, reward and communication structure, productivity and performance measurements and enablers and hindrances and the workplace of the team. Furthermore, the managers filled out three surveys developed for this project. Survey 1 collected descriptive data on multiple teams and roles of the managers, specific individual and collaborative work tasks, the workplace where these tasks are performed and communication tools. Survey 2 included questions on task characteristics, workload, perceived individual and team performance and satisfaction. Survey 3 focused on the workplace (i.e., reasons for coming to work, availability and suitability of workplaces for individual and collaborative work) and access to ICT for these managers to perform their work. The response rate of all surveys was very high from 80 to 100%, in both cases, because of executive level support and our direct link to the participants.

We performed observations of the workplace, management team meetings (two meetings), teleconference meetings between the PROTO case and their Asian factory (two meetings), and we shadowed (followed and observed) eight managers in total in both cases (for either a full or a half day). For the observations and shadowing, we developed clear guidelines and observation protocols, which were applied in both cases. We also collected photographs and video material during the observations. The surveys gathered exploratory data, which was used in conjunction with the interview, observation and shadowing data. Through the analysis and correlation of the multiple data sources we gained more insights related to specific findings, as well as validated these findings. All results were reported to the studied management teams through interactive workshop sessions to validate the findings.

SERVICE CASE

The SERVICE case consisted of 8 European managers in a customer relations' management team who were part of a distributed management team, as well as leading in total 332 employees all over Europe. Four managers were located in different EU countries and four managers were collocated in the Nordic European office. The managers worked, on average, in two distributed teams weekly (i.e., their management team and the team they were managing). The distributed managers traveled once a month to the Nordic office for interaction with their management team and customers.

PROTO CASE

The PROTO case consisted of 8 members of a management team leading 55 people, located mainly in the United States, engaged in prototyping, manufacturing and procurement groups of large high-tech equipment. Seven team managers were collocated and one manager was remote. The managers in the PROTO case worked in multiple project teams, on average, in 10 project teams weekly, out of which, on average, 6 teams were geographically distributed. These geographically distributed teams were located in the U.S. (mainly), Asia and Europe. The PROTO managers worked closely together with their manufacturer in Asia and held monthly videoconferences with them.

Below we discuss two main findings we identified in both case studies based on managers working in CWEs. The identified challenges are determined by the physical, virtual and interaction spaces (based on Fruchter, 2005; Vartiainen et al., 2007) of CWEs. In the context of the physical and virtual workspace, shortcomings in the organization policy were important. In studying the interaction space, we found that managers faced challenges in adapting their work practices for interactions with their team members.

CHALLENGE OF ORGANIZATION POLICY

We found that the organization policy was not always in line with the new ways of working for managers working in CWEs. Several organizational policy challenges emerged that had a negative impact on the work performed. From the interviews and surveys, managers in both cases reported their current challenges on company policies related to distributed work, such as workplace and ICT infrastructure, and lack of company support. The managers faced cost savings related to workplace, ICT and travel, which were perceived as frustrating and counterproductive. This was reflected in the following statement of SERVICE:

> One common policy across the whole company is moving more towards virtual and global teams, but the company does not give you the framework all the time to do your work . . . the company pushes you in that direction to do your work like that [virtual and global work], but it does not support you in terms of policies, in terms of giving you the freedom, in terms of giving the tools to do it.

In the following sections, we discuss two issues we found in the case studies related to company policy impacting global work: workplace and location (relating to the physical workspace) and the ICT infrastructure (relating to the virtual workspace).

Workplace and Regional Location Dependent Organization Policy

Although the office workspace differed for the two locations studied in Nordic EU (SERVICE) and the U.S. (PROTO), both cases experienced implications of the workplace policy for their work. The SERVICE case had 50% free address space, while the PROTO had only dedicated cube space.

In both cases, organization policy focused on reducing office space. The SERVICE office was transformed into open office space in order to enhance interaction and local mobility of employees. The office space offered free address desks that could not be reserved beforehand. The PROTO case office space shrunk through reducing cubicle size and lab space. These workplace policies had implications for cooperation in both cases.

The SERVICE case consisted of a distributed group of managers who came to the office once per month for face-to-face interaction. These managers tried to find desks closely located to their management team, however, they were unable to reserve this place, because of the first-come first-served free-address desk policy. Therefore, they often had desks far from their team members. This impacted their formal and informal interactions. Another organization policy was a clean desk policy on all free-address desks. This implied that remote managers who came to the office occasionally had to carry around all their paperwork, material and devices if they left the desk, for example, for a meeting. Another implication was that there was no indication where the managers were located, since they had no fixed places or any identification where they would be located as a team. As one of the managers stated:

> Certain areas for mobile workers are too small. Often one needs to move to other nonassigned areas, which basically takes away the advantage of sitting close to your colleagues. One of the most important things about being in the office is to be able to speak with my colleagues when I am here. If I am placed somewhere else, I won't have a possibility to interact with the colleagues.

The data analysis indicates that the impact of the workplace policy made it more difficult to locate the managers and had a negative impact on collaborative teamwork and team interaction.

The PROTO case managers worked in dedicated cube spaces. The organization policy imposed a reduction of laboratory and cubicle space for both managers and the engineers they managed. For the engineers, it became more difficult to perform their tasks since they had to store a large amount of equipment to develop or test prototypes in their cube (instead of the laboratory), consequently reducing the workspace in the cube even more. This is reflected in the following statement:

> The lab space has been taken away from my team for 100%. We used to be able to go to our labs, being away from the desk and concentrate on the work, being able to leave your things behind and come back to it and start working immediately in the lab. Now my team needs to share one big lab, when there is availability. As a group we had to adjust to that loss of space and it was a big hit.

For the managers it became more difficult to meet with their team members in their cube. The PROTO managers lacked private space and informal meeting space for interaction and collaboration with their own team (especially for confidential discussions).

In summary, the reduction of lab and cube space negatively impacted collaboration and productivity of the managers in their respective roles.

ICT Infrastructure Policy

A challenge global managers face is to stay connected to their people and content, anywhere, anytime. This was prevalent in both cases. In the SERVICE case, managers were able to stay connected through their company-reimbursed smartphones, while in PROTO, the managers had to provide their own mobile phones in order to stay connected. The ICT policy of the company has a big impact on how remote managers can work, especially when they are mobile and need to be in constant contact with their team. Managers in SERVICE reflected:

> Challenges are organizational . . . our IT is reducing costs and at the same time we are saving travel costs . . . Both organizational units have very strict cost reduction goals, and therefore it is counter-productive that we are not allowed to travel and not to introduce technology to replace travel.

In the surveys, the managers of SERVICE mentioned that they had little access to meeting rooms with appropriate technology for distributed collaboration—average 2.78 (on a scale of 1 = strongly disagree to 5 = strongly agree)—implying difficulties in sharing data and information with colleagues. Part of the SERVICE case was mobile and worked in different locations with their laptops and other mobile devices (i.e., home, at the customer's office, while traveling or in other offices of the firm). Mobile managers who came to the office once per month indicated:

> . . . I spotted my counterpart in the office, I saw him talking on the other side of the office, and I made a mental note to discuss things with him. So before I left the office to go back to my own country I tried to find him, but he was in a meeting somewhere. When I got to the airport, I gave him a call and we just missed each other, which we would not have done had we been seated close together.

The PROTO managers were less mobile, but they worked extensively with remote team members. Several managers mentioned the difficulties to trouble shoot, brainstorm and interact with remote members in other countries, as is reflected in the following statement:

Team members that are not within a relatively small radius (200 feet) do not have the benefit of informal brainstorming and troubleshooting. Those offsite are left out of many of the important verbal interactions and interactions around hardware or other development and test equipment.

From observations and interviews it was clear that ICT could support this interaction with help of better collaboration tools.

The ICT infrastructure of the PROTO case was not updated for new ways of working. In the PROTO case, the managers worked closely with a manufacturing site in Asia and were in need of several types of ICT to communicate remotely. However, the wireless infrastructure was disabled because of security standards and the company provided no mobile phones and webcams to share images of prototypes with their site in Asia. Furthermore, the PROTO managers had difficulties in sharing files and data with remote members because of the existing ICT infrastructure. The managers had to find new ways of working with their remote members by either taking in their own mobile phones, laptops and webcams, or by traveling to Asia to solve problems in person. One of the managers mentioned:

IT infrastructure: I feel like I'm working in a museum. Things work more poorly than they did just a year or two ago. Tools I use outside of [the firm] far exceed the capabilities I have at work.

From the PROTO survey question—"I have the appropriate technology to get teamwork done in a meeting room with remote members"—we found that particularly ICT access for remote work was not supported with an average score of 2.8 (scale was 1 = strongly disagree to 5 = strongly agree). Furthermore, access to meeting rooms with appropriate ICT for distributed collaboration to share data and information with colleagues scored, on average, 3.1 for PROTO.

One of the managers mentions the problems with ICT when communicating between U.S. and Asia:

We have sometimes communication problems, Netmeeting [IT-tool for application sharing] is challenging and we have to rely on the fact that Netmeeting is working in Asia and the U.S. for our meetings. Sometimes when this does not work, it takes a productivity hit and we have to try to work around it. Either we reschedule or work around the problem, e.g., call the Asia conference system for support or share files via email and talk them through (blindly) when Netmeeting is not working.

Consequently, the ICT policy of the organization impacted connectivity and collaboration in a negative way.

COLLABORATION AND INTERACTION CHALLENGES

From our observations, in both cases, we found that work practices were not always aligned with new ways of working.

Visibility and Awareness Lead to Interaction

In both case studies, we found that managers working remotely tried to have visibility and a certain type of awareness of their colleagues and teams. In SERVICE, the managers traveled to the office location once per month to meet their customer and to talk face-to-face to their team. During interviews they emphasized the importance of face-to-face meetings especially for complicated collaborative tasks. Important for them was to build a sense of belonging and identity within the team (71%), as well as interact informally with their colleagues (71%) and being visible to their co-workers (42%). One manager of SERVICE states:

> Face-to-face meetings are very important . . . The most effective communication is meeting persons face to face, because other media lack social context of the person . . . Meeting people is important for common understanding and therefore for our team performance.

From the survey data we found that managers mentioned visibility to their team members (80%) as an important motivation for coming to the office. In the PROTO case, the management team held 3-hour weekly staff meetings to update each other on the work. Most of the managers of PROTO are typically collocated, sit close to each other and they can see each other. However, global managers and team members are not visible to the local manager.

Although both teams used telephone conferences, intranet, instant messages for updating, they still relied heavily on the regular face-to-face contact, as well as on traditional reporting ways.

Cultural and Time Challenges for Interaction

In the SERVICE case the management team and their remote team members worked practically in the same time zone. The PROTO case worked closely with an Asian manufacturer. They had monthly teleconferences and, when available, used videoconferences. The managers had to work across cultures, different work practices and significant time zone differences. Managers need to develop work practices to work in different time zones and cultures in order to deal with coordination, rework and wait time. As one of the PROTO managers mentioned:

The biggest challenge is to find time for overall needed meetings with offsite partners.

Due to cost constraints managers have less travel budget. PROTO members mentioned:

> Cost constraints imply no travel for Asian engineers to come to the U.S. site to support building prototypes—(because of time zone differences and visibility).
>
> Probably the most difficult is to work with engineers from Asia and keep them up to date on designs without them seeing the parts.

These comments emphasize the hindrances because of lack of visibility to the U.S. team members and close understanding of the prototyping intent.

The organization policy to reduce travel and cost impacted the collaboration between the PROTO site and their Asian partner, which, in turn, made the coordination between the two sites even more difficult. The sites tried to have monthly meetings using either teleconference or high-end videoconference systems. However, from the data we found that next to cultural and language differences work practices also differed as well. This had implications for finalizing the product on time. One of the PROTO managers mentioned that engineers from his team had been to Asia to help finalize the prototypes and manufacturing process. In addition, his team had to adjust to the situation in Asia in order to train and demonstrate how a product should be manufactured:

> The employees working in the factory in Asia, all came from different regions in Asia with all their different dialects. Translators were available, but were not always present. My team had to think through how to demonstrate and train people in Asia in many different ways and they had to use very different styles for learning to demonstrate this in Asia.

Workload

In both cases it was clear that the workload of remote managers was extremely high. Managers in both cases studies worked in multiple teams and, in some cases, reported to different senior managers (Fruchter, Bosch-Sijtsema & Ruohomäki, 2010). Being able to deal with multi-teaming and different roles, working irregular hours because of time differences and working in multiple locations had an impact on efficiency and performance. This work situation leads both to hidden work and hidden costs. The SERVICE case reported working between 40–70 hours per week.

Lack of resources and a heavy workload are a problem for me and my team . . . All tasks cannot be done and we must prioritize tasks all the time. This situation in the team affects on quality of our work and it is frustrating.

Similar data in the PROTO case emphasized too little time for reflection and working 51 hours on average per week. In both cases, the workload was perceived as a big challenge. In Figure 11.1 we present the responses of the survey from both cases in which it is clear that especially slack time (reflection time on work) and enough time to perform tasks is rated "low" in both cases.

As indicated in the interviews:

> Cost reduction leaves one-person manufacturing teams with multi-disciplinary tasks which are not efficient and not satisfying. Personal influence-based leadership is less effective when all team members have overcommitted goals requiring elimination of all discretionary activities and elimination of most skill development tasks leaving only a few key critical path tasks.

On average, every manager engaged in 6 teams, going to extreme cases where a manager in PROTO worked in more than 25 different global teams in very many different areas. This manager worked with large time differences and had long and flexible work hours to work with her global teams.

WORKLOAD

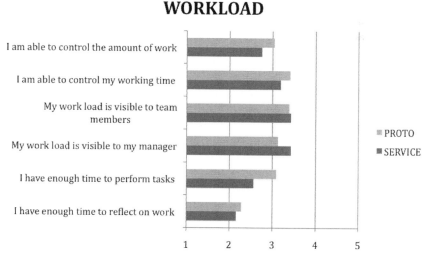

Figure 11.1 Workload scores of the SERVICE and the PROTO cases (scale 1 = strongly disagree; 5 = strongly agree).

The managers' heavy workload is a challenge as they fulfill different roles in different teams working in global CWEs.

DISCUSSION AND CONCLUSION

The study highlights a number of key challenges faced by global managers that work in multiple teams, including their own management team, and play different roles. These challenges are driven by globalization and mobility and new ways of working in global CWE. Many studies focus on managing global teams, with a strong focus on how to effectively manage these teams (Antonakis & Atwater, 2002; Armstrong & Cole, 1995; Gronn, 2002; Kayworth & Leidner, 2000, 2002; Oertig & Buergi, 2006; Zigurs, 2003). Few studies, however, discuss the challenges managers working in global CWE's face when collaborating with multiple teams in diverse roles; they often have a dual role of simultaneously being a member of a management team while working as team leaders. Multi-teaming in distributed settings imposes new challenges for managers individually, in managing a team as well as organizationally (Mortensen et al., 2007). Problems associated with multi-teaming are workload, increasing complexity and resource allocation. The global CWE consists of the physical and virtual, as well as the social interaction environments, for global teams. In our study, we found that global managers were hindered by the global CWE they were working in. From our findings we can conclude that the internal organizational policy in terms of the physical workplace, i.e., workplace policy, as well as the virtual workplace, i.e., IT infrastructure policy, had a strong impact on communication and collaboration with remote team members. The development of organizational policies and work practices is a central area in order to create consistent CWE strategies. More specifically, for global managers our data shows that it is important to provide workplaces with suitable tools, devices, infrastructure and overall company support that respond to the local needs and activities. These would enable managers to be visible to their team members and be aware of their local conditions, i.e., workload, resources and infrastructure. Furthermore, it would provide managers with the necessary space for their individual and collaborative tasks, support diverse modalities to communicate and collaborate anywhere, anytime through appropriate devices and ICT infrastructure that addresses the work–life balance challenge determined by the time zone differences and other workload factors among global locations. The findings discussed above are in line with the main challenges found in literature on remote work (Kayworth & Leidner, 2002), i.e., communication challenges, cultural challenges, technology challenges and logistics.

In all, it is a question of organization policies and managerial competencies needed to manage and organize work in global CWEs. Global managers need to develop new work practices that respond to the new ways of working and leverage the new global CWE. Organization policies including workplace, ICT and human resources infrastructures should be developed to support managers' work. In studies of remote work and management the physical work environment is often neglected (Cairns, 2002). However, in facility and building design studies the importance of the physical workplace for performance, communication and collaboration is addressed (Chan et al., 2007; Heerwagen et al., 2004; Vischer, 2005), though not always clear (Elsbach & Pratt, 2008). According to Vischer (2005), right sizing and redesign of space can lead to a better fit between workspace design and user's tasks.

The data indicate that the internal organization policy for workplace and IT infrastructure was a challenge for global managers adjusting to new ways of working. Managers perceived that their local physical and virtual work environment was not supported by the organization policy for ICT and workplace. For managers to work effectively, not only their competencies, experience and ability to display diverse behavioral repertoires (Kayworth & Leidner, 2002) are important, but also the context in which the managers work has an impact on their effectiveness to manage their multiple roles.

These findings correspond to literature stating the importance to integrate the physical (workplace management), virtual (ICT infrastructure) as well as human resource management (Joroff et al., 2003; Harrison et al., 2004; McDuffie, 2007). The above reported findings correspond to work performed in physical, virtual and social spaces (Fruchter, 2005; Vartiainen et al., 2007). Challenges related to organization policy and ICT infrastructure correspond to physical and virtual workspaces of global managers, while the interaction work practices are part of the social and interaction space. An integrated organization approach, supported by the executive level that brings together organization policy, workplace, ICT and work practices will be beneficial for managers to deal with new ways of working challenges.

Future work needs to expand and further validate these findings, as well as study cases in which new ways of working practices have been adopted and what organization policies support global managers.

ACKNOWLEDGMENTS

This study is a joint Stanford University—Aalto University School of Science and Technology research project ProWork: Workplace Management sponsored by the Finnish Funding Agency for Technology and Innovation (TEKES), ProWork project company partners, and the PBL Lab at Stanford University.

REFERENCES

Antonakiss, J. & Atwater, L. 2002. Leader distance: a review and a proposed theory. *The Leadership Quarterly* 13, 673–701.

Apgar, M. 1998. The alternative workplace: Changing where and how people work. *Harvard Business Review* 76(3), 121–136.

Armstrong, D.J. & Cole, P. 1995. Managing distances and differences in geographically distributed work groups. In *Diversity in work teams*. Eds. S. E. Jackson & M. N. Ruderman. . Washington, DC: American Psychological Association, 187–215.

Bell, B.S. & Kozlowski, S.W.J. 2002. A typology of virtual teams. Implications for effective leadership. *Group and Organization Management* 27(1), 14–49.

Cairns, G. 2002. Aesthetics, morality and power: design as espoused freedom and implicit control. *Human Relations* 55(7), 799–820.

Cascio, W.F. 2000. Managing a virtual workplace. *Academy of Management Executive*, 14(3), 81–90.

Chan, J.K., Beckman, S.L. & Lawrence P.G. 2007. Workplace design. A new managerial imperative. California Management Review, 49, Winter, 6–22.

Davenport, T.H., Thomas, R.J. & Cantrell, S. 2002. The mysterious art and science of knowledge worker productivity. *MIT Sloan Management Review* 44, 23–29.

Eisenhardt, K.M. 1989. Building theories from case study research. *Academy of Management Review* 14(4), 532–550.

Elsbach, K.D. & Pratt, M.G. 2008. The physical environment in organizations. In *The Academy of Management Annals*. Eds. J.P. Walsh & A.P. Brief. New York: Lawrence Erlbaum, Vol. 1, 181–224.

Faubian, J.D. (1994). *Aesthetics: Essential works of Foucault 1954–1984*. London: Penguin, Vol. 2.

Felstead, A., Jewson, N. & Walters, S. (2005). *Changing places of work*. New York: Palgrave Macmillan.

Fruchter, R. 2005. Degrees of engagement in interactive workspaces. *International Journal of AI and Society* 19, 8–21.

Fruchter, R., Bosch-Sijtsema, P. M. & Ruohomäki, V. 2010. Tension between perceived collocation and actual geographical distribution in project teams. *International Journal of AI & Society* 25(2), 183–192.

Gajendran, R. S. & Harrison, D. A. 2007. The good, the bad, and the unknown about telecommuting: meta-analysis of psychological mediators and individual consequences. *Journal of Applied Psychology* 92(6), 1524–1541.

Gareis, K., Lilischkis, S. & Mentrup, A. 2006. Mapping the mobile eWorkforce in Europe. In *Mobile virtual work- A new paradigm*. Eds. J. Andriessen & M. Vartiainen. . Heidelberg Germany: Springer, 45–69.

Gronn, P. 2002. Distributed Leadership as a unit of analysis. *The Leadership Quarterly,* 13(4), 423–451.

Harrison, A., Wheeler, P. & Whitehead, C. 2004. *The Distributed Workplace*. London and New York: Spon Press.

Haynes, B.P. 2007. The impact of the behavioural environment on office productivity. *Journal of Facilities Management* 5(3), 158–171.

Heckman, R., Crowston, K. & Misiolek, N. 2007. A structurational perspective on leadership in virtual teams. In *Virtuality and Virtualization*. Eds. K. Crowston and S. Sieber . . . Oregon: Springer Verlag, 151–168.

Heerwagen, J. H., Kampschroer, K., Powell, K. M. & Loftness, V. 2004. Collaborative knowledge work environments. *Building Research & Information* 32(6), 510–528.

Hertel, G., Geister, S. & Konradt, U. 2005. Managing virtual teams: A review of current empirical research. *Human Resource Management Review* 15, 69–95.

Hinds, P. J. & Bailey, D.E. 2003. Out of sight, Out of sync: Understanding conflict in distributed teams. *Organization Science* 14(6), 615–632.

Hinds, P. J. & Kiesler, S. (Eds.) 2001. *Distributed work*. Cambridge, MA: The MIT Press.

Hislop, D. & Axtell, C. 2009. To infinity and beyond? Workspace and the Multi-LocationWorker. *New Technology, Work and Employment* 24(1), 60–75.

Jarvenpaa, S. L. & Leidner, D.E. 1999. Communication and trust in global virtual teams. *Organization Science* 10(6), 791–815.

Joroff, M.L., Porter, W.L., Feinberg, B. & Kukla, C. 2003. The agile workplace. *Journal of Corporate Real Estate* 5, 293–311.

Kayworth, T.R. & Leidner, D. E. 2000. The global virtual manager: A prescription for success. *European Journal of Management* 18(2), 183–194.

Kayworth, T.R. & Leidner, D. E. 2002. Leadership effectiveness in global virtual teams. *Journal of Management Information Systems* 18(3), 7–40 (winter 2001–2002).

Kelliher, C. & Anderson, D. 2010. Doing more with less? Flexible working practices and the intensification of work. *Human Relations* 63(1), 83–106.

Majchrzak, A., Rice, R.E., Malhotra, A., King, N. & Ba, S. 2000. Technology adaptation: the case of a computer-supported inter-organizational virtual team. *MIS Quarterly* 24(4), 569–600.

MacDuffie, J. P. 2007. HRM and distributed work. *The academy of management annals*. New York: Lawrence Erlbaum, Vol. 1, 549–615.

Mortensen, M., Woolley, A.W. & O'Leary, M. 2007. Conditions enabling effective multiple team membership. In *Virtuality and virtualization*. Eds. K. Crowston, Sieber, S., Wynn, E. . BostonSpringer, Vol. 236, 215–228.

Oertig, M. & Buergi, T. 2006. The challenges of managing cross-cultural virtual project teams. *Team Performance Management* 12(1/2), 23–30.

Scott, P. B. 2005. Knowledge workers: social, task and semantic network analysis. *Corporate Communication: An International Journal* 10(3), 257–277.

Sullivan, C. 2003. What's in a name? Definitions and conceptualizations of teleworking and homeworking. *New Technology, Work and Employment* 18(3), 158–165.

Townsend, A.M., DeMarie, S.M. & Hendrickson, A.R. 1998. Virtual teams and the workplace of the future. *Academy of Management Executive* 12(3), 17–29.

Vartiainen, M. 2008. Facilitating mobile and virtual work. In *21st Century Management. A reference handbook*. Ed. C. Wangel. . Thousand Oaks, CA: Sage, Vol. II, 348–360.

Vartiainen, M., Hakonen, M., Koivisto, S., Mannonen, P., Nieminen, M.P., Ruohomäki, V. & Vartola, A. 2007. *Distributed and mobile work; Places, people and technology*. Tampere: University Press Finland.

Vartiainen, M. & Hyrkkänen, U. 2010. Changing requirements and mental workload factors in mobile multi-locational work. *New Technology, Work and Employment*, 25(2), 117–135.

Vischer, J.C. 2005. *Space meets status: Designing workplace performance*. New York: Routledge.

Zakaria, N., Amelinckx, A. & Wilemon, D. 2004. Working together apart? Building a knowledge-sharing culture for global virtual teams. *Creativity and Innovation Management* 13(1), 15–29.

Zigurs, I. 2003. Leadership in virtual teams: Oxymoron or opportunity? *Organizational Dynamics* 31(4), 339–351.

Zolin, R., Hinds, P., Fruchter, R. & Levitt, R.E. 2004. Interpersonal trust in cross-functional geographically distributed work: A longitudinal study. *Information and Organization* 14, 1–6.

12 Observations and Conclusions on New Ways of Working

Clare Kelliher and Julia Richardson

INTRODUCTION

The aim of this chapter is to organize the preceding ten chapters and identify and connect emerging themes and theories. It will take stock of the issues raised and consider the respective findings in the context of the overarching developments discussed in the introductory chapter, namely, globalization, developments in Information and Communication Technology (ICT) and organizational responses to changing demographic and social trends.

The need for complexity and dynamism in our understanding of contemporary work organization permeates this book. Yet, in addition to complexity and dynamism, a number of identifiable themes have emerged. The value of these themes is that they may be used to start to build a developmental frame of reference, which may be added to and refined as the field and our understanding of it evolves. We address and explore each of the themes below, noting, however, that they are evolving and that the boundaries between them are permeable and, in some instances, blurred rather than clearly demarcated.

THEORETICAL AND SUBSTANTIVE COMPLEXITY

The contributors to this book present empirical data reflecting a diverse range of contemporary work arrangements. Although these arrangements reflect organizational responses to more general economic, social and political developments, they take different forms with different implications for employees and managers, even where similar language has been used to describe them (see, for example, the discussion below regarding different forms of remote working). This suggests that no clear trend has emerged in terms of how organizations have responded to the combined influences of globalization, trends in ICT and changing demographics. Rather, organizations appear to respond in more composite and complex ways, according to contextual influences such as national, industry and market dynamics and/or employee skills and professional and personal requirements. Organizational processes may also influence the way work is organized, as well as familiarity with emerging work arrangements and their implications for performance. This highlights the importance of context in relation to contemporary working arrangements and experiences. It also cautions against trying to simplify or generalize.

Recognizing the complexity of new ways of organizing work has important theoretical implications. Rather than suggesting the possibility of an overarching 'grand theory' the studies reported here imply smaller 'mid-range' theories are more valuable. Thus, for example, while some theories and models may be used to explain some dimensions of a particular work arrangement, they do not explain all its dimensions. This composite approach, while important, introduces a significant amount of challenge, not least of which is the extent to which such complexity can be managed. Perhaps the more important message here, however, is not about management per se, but about communicating that complexity to relevant stakeholders (employers, employees, researchers and/or policy makers), particularly if conceptions of management conceal an underlying desire to simplify.

NEW WAYS OF WORKING WITHIN
AND ACROSS NATIONAL CONTEXTS

In addition to theoretical complexity, the contributions in this volume present evidence on various forms of new ways of organizing work in different national contexts. Studies include employees based in the UK and Ireland, continental Europe (France and the Netherlands), North America (U.S. and Canada), Asia (China, India, Indonesia, Japan, and Malaysia), Australia and New Zealand. This demonstrates that changes to the way in which work is organized are widespread, occurring both within and across countries and regions. Although the majority of the studies draw on data from one country, two chapters are concerned with distributed teams operating across continents (Collins & Kolb and Bosch-Sijtema, Fruchter, Vartiainen & Ruohomäki). This suggests the need to develop both intra- and intercultural appreciations of such practices.

Changing Work Organization Within
and Across Industries and Professions

The studies in this volume are drawn from data collected in a number of industries and from both the public and private sectors, including hospitality, financial services, information technology (both software and hardware), professional services and health/home care. The evidence and arguments presented show that changes in contemporary working arrangements are evolving in and impacting on employees and managers in a broad range of organizational and professional settings. Thus, for example, although the majority of studies in this book are concerned with some form of knowledge worker, studies of non-professional hotel housekeeping staff (Knox) and non-professional healthcare workers (Linehan) are also included. Collating the experiences in and practices of different working environments further signals the spread of these changes and sensitizes us to the increasing diversity of respective stakeholders. From a public policy or managerial perspective, it suggests that any attempts to manage or regulate such practices must acknowledge stakeholder diversity.

Complexity, Dynamism and Variation within Working Forms and Processes

The majority of the studies in this volume are concerned with some form of remote work. Broadly speaking, this includes remoteness in two principal ways. First, there are studies of where employees work away from their workplace for varying proportions of their working time (see Besseyre des Horts, Dery & MacCormick; Wilkinson & Jarvis; Richardson; Wade Clarke; Peters & Wildenbeest). Second, there are studies of work teams where co-workers are not colocated and, because of geographical distribution, are unlikely to have frequent (if any) opportunities to meet face-to-face (see Collins & Kolb; Bosch-Sijtema et al.). These categories are, of course, not mutually exclusive, since those who work in distributed teams may do so remotely from their workplace for part of their working time. Alternatively, they may not even have a designated workplace. However, even within these categories there are considerable variations in the ways in which arrangements are enacted. Even the language used varies between contributions to describe broadly similar working arrangements (remote working: Wilkinson & Jarvis; flexwork: Richardson; telework: Wade Clarke; telecommuting: Peters & Wildenbeest).

This raises the question of whether or not it is desirable for scholars or practitioners to move towards adopting consistent or at least similar terminology. While at one level this might be deemed to offer clarity to the field of study, it also runs the risk of over-simplification. Richardson (2010), for example, has suggested that rather than adopting a generic term, it is important to adopt the term used by the employer and/or employee themselves. Hence, she has used the term 'flexwork', because it is the term used by actors in the host organization (Richardson, 2010). Conversely, telecommuting was understood as something different—denoting employees who were working from home on a consistent basis, rather than the ad hoc arrangement of coming into the office on an irregular basis, as was the case for flexworkers. This approach may be valuable because it provides a more accurate reflection of the lived experiences of our subjects. Even so, we would add that it is important to acknowledge the similarities and/or differences between these categories or terminologies and those used by others in the field.

Multiple Workspaces

The studies in this book suggest considerable variation in where work is performed, with the implication that a single and definitive 'workplace' may be inappropriate and in need of re-evaluation. For example, some of the authors have described working arrangements comprising rare absence from the traditional workplace (twice a month), to instances where employees spend most of their time working at home and which, therefore, becomes their main workplace. Mostly commonly though, the employees were working both in an employer-provided space *and* in the home space.

Autonomy in Deciding Where to Work

The contributors to this volume also suggest differences in levels of autonomy for decisions about where to work. In some cases, employees were able to choose when they worked remotely and when they worked at employer premises in the office, whereas, in other cases, employers controlled where and when work was carried out. For example, some respondents in Wilkinson and Jarvis's study no longer had a designated workplace, following the closure of a local area office and as such had no choice about where to work. Conversely, in Richardson's study, flex-workers had access to a hot-desk, or temporary work cubicle at their employer's premises, which they could use according to their own prefer-ences, although they were discouraged from making use of these spaces on a permanent basis. The employees in Peters and Wildenbeest's study were also able to decide where to work. This provides evidence of further complexity, where our understanding of changing working arrangements must also acknowledge that it is not just a matter of where work is carried out, it is also about where the power resides to decide where and when and the implications of those decisions on both organizational and indi-vidual dynamics and experiences.

While autonomy and choice in deciding where and when to work is important, such decisions may be constrained by factors such as length of commute time (Wade Clarke), gender, workplace culture and norms (Gregory & Milner, 2009; Lewis, Gambles & Rapoport, 2007). Although not dealt with in this volume, it is acknowledged, that 'choice' over where to work depends on a number of personal and professional factors and, as such, the extent to which choice is really available may be questionable. For example, the availability of space in the home or elsewhere (Tietze & Musson, 2002) may influence where the individual 'decides' to work. Alternatively, employees who have access to a designated workspace at home (or other remote location) with few other distractions may be more likely to elect to work there, than those living with extended family mem-bers, or with young children and where home space is less conducive to work activities. In such circumstances, their 'choice' about where to work is impacted by whether they are able to carve out a workspace and/or where there are others present in the home who may have competing claims on space and resources.

Workspace as Every Space

In Chapter 2, Besseyre des Horts et al. draw our attention to the idea of workspace and work time as ubiquitous. They suggest that wireless technologies have created a situation where, for some employees, workspace is everywhere rather than 'somewhere' and all times rather than some times. In this respect, we observe how technological advancements have taken remoteness one step further, since employees do not need to be present in any particular workspace or at any particular time to undertake work activity. While, at one level, this may suggest increased individual freedom and flexibility, Besseyre des Horts et al. also suggest that it may create feelings of obligation to be available outside of normal time and place conventions. Clearly, the specter of wireless technology as having a 'dark-side' looms large here.

Diversity in Organizational Responses

Chapters 10 and 11 (Collins & Kolb and Bosch-Sijtema, Fruchter, Vartiainen & Ruohomäki, respectively) provide some insight into the differences in how organizations might respond to the pressures created by globalization. Of particular note is how work teams are reconfigured across different regional and national contexts according to organizational markets and economic demand. In Chapter 3, Knox also provides an example of where organizations have responded to increased competitive pressure by seeking to reduce labor costs. Here hospitality employers in Australia have reduced costs by matching the supply of and demand for labor more closely by using a combination of permanent and temporary agency staff.

Knox's study also shows how new ways of organizing work can be used to reduce recruitment and training costs, in addition to the costs of overtime payments to permanent staff. Interestingly, in this context, many temporary employees were migrant workers, mostly overseas students on working visas. Cost savings were also a driver for the redefinition of work in Linehan's study, Chapter 5, where budgetary cuts in the public sector required a redefinition of the services provided and, as a result, had implications for the work carried out by the care assistants.

Social Construction of Work and Work Organization

The social construction of work and what is seen as acceptable and desirable work has emerged as an important theme in how contemporary working arrangements evolve. The importance of individual experiences of work and the extent to which those experiences impact on how work is understood and ascribed meaning emerges in several chapters (notably Chapters 5–9 in the second empirical section of the book). In Chapter 4, however, Eikhof and Summers add a more critical dimension to our understanding of work and specifically work opportunities for women as socially constructed. The value of this contribution is that it extends our understanding of emerging working arrangements, not simply as a response to organizational needs, but also as a reflection of societal norms and expectations. Moreover, it is not simply what 'is' that is socially constructed, but also what can be and what should be. Extending this theme further, Eikhof and Summers also raise important questions by juxtaposing the lived experience of contemporary work forms versus public (i.e., media) representations of the same.

The 'Darker Side' of New Ways of Organizing Work

Several of the studies in this book draw our attention to what might be seen as the 'darker side' to new ways of organizing work. This addresses Tietze, Musson and Scurry's (2009) call to expose both the positive and negative dimensions of such arrangements and their impact on individual well-being. It also echoes the work of other authors who have been more guarded about the extent to which employees and employers are likely to use such practices (Rasmussen and Corbett, 2008)

In contrast to much of the practitioner literature, which espouses positive outcomes for individuals and for organizations, many of our contributors are more circumspect. For example in Chapter 3, Knox reports on temporary workers who were not only employed under inferior arrangements and without the employment security of their permanent counterparts, but who also felt that they were treated differently by other staff. Also in the context of cost pressures, in Chapter 5, Linehan reports how managers may struggle to cope with the competing priorities of maintaining the services provided and budgetary pressures and the consequent breakdown of trust relations with both senior management and front-line staff. Similarly, in Chapter 7, Richardson reports the pressures and potentially negative impact of juggling the responsibilities to the work and home domains experienced by flexworkers.

The four chapters concerned with employees who work remotely for some or all of their working time revealed a number of negative consequences. In Chapter 6, Wilkinson and Jarvis document emotional outcomes, such as the isolation, frustration and guilt experienced by remote workers and the wider impact on their identity. In Chapter 7, Richardson examines how remote workers negotiate the boundaries between work and nonwork activity. Alongside positive experiences of being able to customize work–home boundaries, she also reports evidence of stressors, particularly in the early stages of working remotely, caused my multiple demands and the need to manage both the 'home' and 'work selves'. Likewise, in Chapter 8, Wade Clarke examines resistance to remote working and explores this in the context of notions of place, aspiration and identity, which may be challenged by the absence of physical presence. Finally, and adding further to the 'darker side' analogy, in Chapter 9, Peters and Wildenbeest report countervailing outcomes for remote workers. While certain conditions facilitated flow, factors such as work–home interference and work overload contributed to exhaustion among those studied.

Focusing specifically on the 'darker side' of wireless technology, in Chapter 2, Besseyre de Horts et al. draw our attention to how it provides the freedom to exercise greater control over work, on the one hand, but also feelings of obligation to be available, on the other. More specifically, they suggest that increased job demands, brought about by extended working hours and intensity of work, resulted in increased job strain for many respondents. Yet they also point to the value of flexibility and the potential advantages of such technologies.

The two contributions that examine distributed teams, Chapters 10 and 11, also explore some of the difficulties encountered by team members working under this type of arrangement. In Chapter 10, Collins and Kolb suggest that connectivity can be both a blessing and a curse and draw our attention to the need for choice in order to reap the benefits of regeneration from disconnecting. In Chapter 11, Bosch-Sijtema et al. also explore the demands placed on managers who work in multiple teams, both as managers of global team members, but also being a team member in their management group. In particular, they highlight the implications of increased workload, complexity and resource allocation.

Knowledge Workers and New Ways of Organizing Work

Many of the studies in this book are concerned with knowledge workers. Although it has been observed that knowledge can have a significant, positive impact on the bargaining power of employees where their intellectual capital is in short supply (Storey, 2001; DeFillippi, Arthur and Lindsay, 2006), these studies draw our attention to the negative consequences of new ways of organizing work for knowledge workers. They suggest that a number of these new working arrangements have explicitly moved away from prescribing ways of working for employees, giving the employee greater discretion over how they organize themselves. While on the face of it this move may appear positive, some of the studies in this volume suggest that knowledge workers, imbued with notions of professional behavior, regulate themselves more harshly than would an organization's control procedures.

The flexibility to exercise discretion over their place of work may encourage knowledge workers to reciprocate with extended effort. This suggests that the intangible assets of intellectual capital that reside in the heads of this type of employee should be managed very carefully. One way to retain and preserve their well-being would be for employers to organize work in ways which are acceptable to both parties, but which also prevents knowledge workers from working in ways which may be harmful to themselves.

METHODOLOGIES

The studies in this volume reflect the principles of both positivist and interpretive approaches. In accordance with their respective ontological assumptions, they have used a range of methods to investigate issues concerned with the implementation of new ways of organizing work. Several studies, particularly those located in an interpretive paradigm (Richardson, Wade Clarke, Eikhof & Summers, Linehan and Wilkinson & Jarvis) have used qualitative methods, with some form of semi-structured interview being most common. These interviews ranged in number and depth from 1 (Lineham) to 76 (Richardson). The volume also includes an ethnographic study carried over an 8-month period (Wade Clarke). Two chapters, located within a positivist paradigm, draw on either a survey or a structured interview instrument (Collins & Kolb, Peters & Wildenbeest). One chapter has employed a multi-method approach, based an in-depth case study with data collected by interviews, questionnaires and observation (Bosch-Sijtema et al.). Taken together, these chapters represent both statistically significant associations between new ways of working and outcomes, such as exhaustion and innovation, alongside richer, more detailed data, which allows explanations for some of these associations to be constructed. We observe how several of the studies afford an 'emic' understanding of individual experiences of new or emerging work forms, as well as opportunities for subjects to explicate those experiences in their own words (Marshall & Rossman, 2011).

IMPLICATIONS

The collection of studies presented in this book assist in developing our understanding of how changes to the nature and organization of work are experienced by employees. The implications of those experiences for employers and managers have also been addressed. In some cases, these have not been what were expected and there have been some unforeseen and negative outcomes for employees. These findings raise issues for organizations, both in terms of how such arrangements may impact on, for example, employee motivation, commitment, retention and performance, as well as how they might impact on employee well-being more generally.

The doctrine of New Public Management has been pervasive across the administration of public sector services across many countries (Mathiason, 2005) and there has been much focus on the benefits that can be realized by importing principles more commonly found in the private sector. However, the chapter by Linehan shows that the resulting effect of cost reduction can have a negative impact on employees, which may ultimately reduce the quality of service provided in at least two ways: by cutting service levels in order to reduce costs and by impacting on the morale of staff and, hence, their commitment to customer service.

Several of the contributions in this book have significance for organizations that are globalizing, thus extending our understanding of the 'in here' consequences of globalization observed by Giddens (2002). Some of these contributions also signal the potential implications, both positive and negative, of taking advantage of developments in ICT to organize work and conduct business. Remoteness, whether periodic remoteness from the workplace or permanent remoteness from team members, who are located in other parts of the globe, raises a series of questions for organizations. Where increased use of technology is concerned, allowing the boundaries of where and when work is conducted to be eroded and enabling work to be done almost any time and any place has been shown to have both negative and positive outcomes. This suggests that while there are positive outcomes for organizations and for individuals, there are also potential dangers from using technology in this way.

Regulating bodies such as the European Union have attempted to contain working hours by placing an upper limit on the amount of time an employee may be asked to work by their employer. However, based on some of the findings reported in this volume, it is difficult to see how work of this nature (taking a telephone call, or responding to an email out of working hours) can be controlled by this type of regulation. Furthermore, as has been reported here, some employees may be willing, or feel obliged to collude in the ubiquity of workspace and time by not, either physically and/or psychologically, disconnecting from it. Technology which enables remote working may, therefore, need to be carefully managed by both employers and employees.

When organizations become both placeless and spaceless (Lawrence, 2002), their relationships with their members become increasingly complex. Several of the studies reported here offer evidence of a number of both intended and unintended consequences of the 'placelessness' and 'spacelessness' created by remote working arrangements. Those which reveal more of a dark side are potentially corrosive for both organizations and individuals. While having employees who are ever available, or who experience 'flow' may initially be appealing for employers because of what they might achieve (at least in the short term) in terms of performance, there is also a need to be aware of the longer term consequences of work intensification (Burchell, 2002; Fairris & Brenner, 2001; Warr, 1987). It may be that, in the long run, some of the benefits of different ways of organizing work are eroded by the negative outcomes for individuals and organizations.

Consequently, organizations would be well-advised to take account of the findings presented in this volume and ensure that their practices and policies are not only formally in place, but also become part of the organization's culture. In other words, the ability to 'switch-off' and disconnect from work needs to be embedded in the organization's culture, as well as its more formal work practices. Nevertheless, we acknowledge that this is a difficult area for policy and regulation more generally. In spite of some of the negative outcomes discussed here, these activities by their very nature take place away from the workplace and, therefore, out of view, thus making them hard to monitor and regulate. Furthermore, where these activities cross national borders, there may be differences in legal regulation, cultural attitudes to work and employee expectations. For example, if remote teams operate in different parts of the world, is there a case for equalization upward, or the commonly referred to 'race to the bottom' in the extant globalization and employment literature.

While the findings presented in this volume suggest that some new ways of organizing work need to be treated with caution, there is also room for some optimism. The idea of such arrangements having a 'darker side' has permeated much of the discussion in this final chapter. Drawing on the evidence presented here, we suggest that rather than rejecting such practices because of potential negative outcomes, the challenge may be to build on the strengths of these arrangements, while attempting to minimize their weaknesses.

The differences these contributions have highlighted between the activities under broad labels, such as remote working or teleworking, suggest that in future work there is a need for the types of arrangement to be clearly defined, so that conclusions drawn can be specifically related to the character of that working arrangement. Given that many of our studies have revealed a 'darker side' to new work arrangements, there is a concomitant need to consider the long-term implications in more depth.

REFERENCES

Burchell, B. 2002. The prevalence and redistribution of job insecurity and work intensification. In *Job insecurity and work intensification.* Eds. B. Burchell, D. Ladipo and F. Wilkinson. . London: Routledge, 61–76.

DeFillippi, R., Arthur, M.B. & Lindsay, V. 2006. *Knowledge at work.* Blackwell, MA.

Fairris, D. & Brenner, M. 2001. Workplace transformation and the rise in cumulative trauma disorders: Is there a connection? *Journal of Labour Research* XXII (1), 15–28.

Giddens, A. 2002. *Runaway world: How globalization is reshaping our lives.* London: Profile Books.

Gregory, A. & Milner, S. 2009. Work-life balance a matter of choice? *Gender, Work and Organization* 16, 1–13.

Lawrence, P. 2002. *The change game: How today's global trends are shaping tomorrow's companies.* London: Kogan Page.

Lewis, S., Gambles, R. & Rapoport, R. 2007. The constraints of a 'work-life balance' approach: An international perspective. *International Journal of Human Resource Management* 18, 360–373.

Marshall, C. & Rossman, G. B. 2011. *Designing qualitative research*, 5th Ed. Thousand Oaks, CA: Sage.

Mathiason, D. (2005) International public management. In *Oxford handbook of public management*. Eds. Ferlie, E., Lynn, L. & Pollitt, C. , Oxford: Oxford University Press, 643–670.

Rasmussen, E. & Corbett, C. 2008. 'Why isn't teleworking working?' *New Zealand Journal of Employment Relations* 33(2), 20–32.

Richardson, J. 2010. Managing flexworkers: Holding on and letting go, *Journal of Management Development* 29(2), 137–147.

Storey. J. 2001. Looking to the future. In *Human Resource Management: A critical text*. Ed. Storey, J. London: Thompson Learning, 364–367.

Tietze, S. & Musson, G. 2002. When "work" meets "home" temporal flexibility as lived experience. *Time and Society* 11(2/3), 315–334.

Tietze, S., Musson, G., & Scurry, T. 2009. Homebased work: A review of research into themes, directions and implications, *Personnel Review*, 38(6) 585–604.

Warr, P. 1987. *Work, unemployment and mental health*. Oxford: Oxford University Press.

Contributors

Dr. Charles-Henri Besseyre des Horts is Associate Professor of Human Resources Management and Organizational Behavior at HEC Paris. He has earned two doctorates: in France (University of Aix-Marseilles) and USA (University of California, Los Angeles). He is actively involved in a number of international training, research and consulting activities in Europe, Middle-East, Russia, Africa, Americas and Asia. His research interests focus on (1) the impact of mobile technologies on organizational structures and processes and (2) the relationships between human resources management and business strategy, the international HR strategies in multinational companies. He has published a number of articles (primarily in French) and several books. His most recent book was published in 2008: "L'Entreprise mobile" ("*The mobile enterprise*"), Pearson Education.

Dr. Petra Bosch-Sijtsema is an associate professor at Chalmers University of Technology, Construction Management, Sweden and performs research on new ways of working, distributed work, knowledge work, innovation and knowledge creation and sharing, and collaboration within and between firms.

Dr. Paul D. Collins (Ph.D., Sociology, Rutgers University) is Associate Professor of Management, Business Administration Program, University of Washington-Bothell, USA. He previously served on the faculty of University of Washington-Seattle and Purdue University. Paul is a recipient of several prestigious research awards, including the Academy of Management's Best Paper Award (OMT Division). Paul's current research on sociotechnical connectivity in distributed project teams is a natural extension of his long-standing research emphasis on the dynamics of organizations, technology and innovation.

Dr. Kristine Dery is a Senior Lecturer in Work and Organizational Studies at the University of Sydney Business School in Australia. Her research focusses on the impact of technology on work, with a particular interest in mobile connectivity. Additionally, her work on the impact of ERP systems and, more recently, Human Resource Information Systems, has been widely published in both academic and industry publications.

Dr. Doris Ruth Eikhof is Lecturer in Work and Organization Studies at Stirling Management School, University of Stirling. Her research focuses on creative work and enterprise, social theories in Organization studies, work life-boundaries and women's work. Dr Eikhof has published in international books and journals. She is co-editor of *Creating Balance? International Perspectives on the Work-Life Integration of Professionals* (Springer 2011), *Work less, live more? Critical Analyses of the Work-Life Relationship* (Palgrave 2008) and of an *Employee Relations* special issue on work-life balance (2007, Vol. 29:4).

Dr. Renate Fruchter is director of the Project-Based Learning Lab at Stanford University, USA, and studies cross-disciplinary, geographically distributed teamwork, new ways of working, knowledge work, innovative ICT, work places and spaces and their impact on team dynamics and emergent work practices and processes.

Dr. Carol Jarvis is Associate Head of Department for Organization Studies at Bristol Business School, University of the West of England, UK. Her research focuses on the experience of complex organizational change, with a specific interest in emotional responses to complex change and its implications for unwritten contracts.

Dr. Clare Kelliher is Reader in Work and Organization at Cranfield School of Management, Cranfield University, UK. She has a longstanding interest in flexible working including both flexibility of and for employees and has published widely in this field. Dr. Kelliher is currently co-chair of the International Labour and Employment Relations Association (ILERA) Study Group on flexible work practices.

Dr. Angela Knox is a Senior Lecturer in Work and Organizational Studies at University of Sydney Business School, University of Sydney, Australia. She focuses on researching flexible work forms within the service sector, examining issues related to the regulation, management and implications of such work. Dr. Knox has published in *Work, Employment and Society, the International Journal of Human Resource Management, the Human Resource Management Journal* and *Gender, Work and Organization*, for example.

Dr. Darl G. Kolb is Associate Professor of Management and International Business at the University of Auckland, New Zealand. For the past decade his research has been focused on technical and social 'connectivity,' that is how we are increasingly able to be connected to more and more people around the world and around the clock, and the opportunities and challenges that presents in contemporary work contexts. With Paul Collins (University of Washington), he has conducted a large-scale international survey of distributed work teams within large multinational firms.

Dr. Carol Linehan lectures in the Department of Management and Marketing, University College Cork. Her key interests relate to the impacts of organizational flexibility and work practices on employees' identities and experiences of work.

Dr. Judith MacCormick is a Post-Doctoral Research Fellow at the Australian School of Business, University of New South Wales, Sydney. Judi's research and executive teaching focus is around optimizing outcomes for firms and individuals. Studying the work practices and perceptions of employees globally, and having written widely in this field, Judi's particular interest is on understanding what organizational ambidexterity means in practice for leaders and employees.

Dr. Pascale Peters is Assistant Professor of Business Administration, Strategic HRM at the Radboud University Nijmegen, Netherlands. Her research interests include (gendered) labour market participation, work-life balance, employability, and the contemporary and sustainable organization of work, in particular, home-based telework, 'New Ways to Work,' and Working Carer Support in organizations. These topics are studied in the contexts of globalization and individualization, cultural variety and welfare-state regimes, labour-market and household developments, innovation, institutionalization and organizational change. Peters publishes in outlets such as Human Relations, Human Resource Management Journal, Information & Management, Community, Work and Family Journal, Work, Employment & Society (forthcoming), Journal of Manpower, International Journal of HRM, Leisure and Society, Time and Society, The journal of E-working, and in several Dutch journals. She has also written chapters in national and international books, for example on Telework. She co-edited a book on labour-market and work-life issues, entitled *Competing Claims in Work and Family Life* which was published by Edward Elgar in 2007.

Dr. Julia Richardson is Associate Professor of Organizational Behavior at York University, Toronto. Her research interests include flexible work practices and particularly the impact of such practices on career development and job performance. Dr. Richardson has a long standing interest in the study of careers and is currently Associate Editor for Career Development International and Program Chair for the Careers Division of the Academic of Management. She has worked in both the private and public sector in a number of countries, including New Zealand, Japan, Singapore and Indonesia.

Dr.Juliette Summers is a lecturer in HRM at the Institute for Socio-Management, Stirling University, Scotland. Her research uses social identity theory to examine the role of social and professional identity transitions. She is currently involved in three key areas of research; social identity theory; work/life balance and gendered identities; worker participation and voice.

Dr. Matti Vartiainen is Professor of Learning Organization at the Laboratory of Work Psychology and Leadership at Aalto University School of Science, Finland and studies organizational innovations, mobile distributed work, reward systems, knowledge work, collaboration, and new working environments.

Dr. Virpi Ruohomäki is a senior researcher at the Finnish Institute of Occupational Health in Finland. Her research focuses on knowledge work, distributed teamwork, mobile work, new work environments and workplaces.

Marijn Wildenbeest MSc LLM is a former student at University of Nijmegen, the Netherlands. Her education included Business Administration and Dutch law. She contributed to the book as a master student in Business Administration. Marijn Wildenbeest is currently working as attorney-at-law at Van Doorne N.V. in Amsterdam, the Netherlands. She advises on various legal issues in the fields of arbitration, liability law, insurance law and procedural law.

Dr. Daniel Wade Clarke lectures in Marketing and Qualitative Research Methods at the Business School, Liverpool Hope University, UK. His research to date has used visual research methods to study place making processes and outcomes. He is also interested in the general area of design research and the built environment.

Dr. Jennifer Wilkinson is a Senior Lecturer in Organization Studies at Bristol Business School, University of the West of England, UK. Her research focuses on organizational change, with specific interest in remote working, and how employees' experience identity, trust, and emotions, in such contexts.

Index